POOR TOM

POOR TOM

Living *King Lear*

❧

SIMON PALFREY

The University of Chicago Press
Chicago and London

Simon Palfrey is professor of English literature at Brasenose College, University of Oxford.

The University of Chicago Press, Chicago 60637
The University of Chicago Press, Ltd., London
© 2014 by The University of Chicago
All rights reserved. Published 2014.
Printed in the United States of America

23 22 21 20 19 18 17 16 15 14   1 2 3 4 5

ISBN-13: 978-0-226-15064-2 (cloth)
ISBN-13: 978-0-226-15078-9 (e-book)

DOI: 10.7208/chicago/9780226150789.001.0001

Library of Congress Cataloging-in-Publication Data

Palfrey, Simon, author.
    Poor Tom : living King Lear / Simon Palfrey.
        pages cm
    Includes bibliographical references and index.
    ISBN 978-0-226-15064-2 (cloth : alk. paper) — ISBN 978-0-226-15078-9 (e-book) 1. Shakespeare, William, 1564–1616. King Lear.   2. Edgar (Fictitious character : Shakespeare)   I. Title.
    PR2819.P35 2014
    822.3′3—dc23
                                                                        2013043062

♾ This paper meets the requirements of ANSI/NISO Z39.48-1992 (Permanence of Paper).

To Dad

For he who lives more lives than one
More deaths than one must die.
   —OSCAR WILDE, *Ballad of Reading Gaol*

Contents

On Texts   ix

1. Prelude: The Hanging Man   1
2. Introduction   5
3. Interlude: The Stranger   25
4. Scene 1: Into the Hollow   26
5. Interlude: Job Redux   34
6. Scene 2: Enter Tom   45
7. Interlude: Tom Is . . . ?   61
8. Scene 3: Tom's Voices   67
9. Interlude: To Be Allegory   78
10. Scene 4: Tom's Places   83
11. Interlude: History Man   91
12. Scene 5: Lurk, Lurk   118
13. Interlude: Living *King Lear*   130
14. Scene 6: Shuttered Genealogy   132
15. Interlude: Decreated   142
16. Scene 7: Fool to Sorrow   151

17.	Interlude: Humanist and Posthumanist: A Dialogue	162
18.	Scene 8: To the Edge of the Cliff	167
19.	Interlude: The Binding	180
20.	Scene 9: Fallen, or Not?	183
21.	Interlude: Everyman	193
22.	Scene 10: Alive, or Dead?	195
23.	Interlude: The Pending World	212
24.	Scene 11: Dark Places	216
25.	Interlude: Jacob and Esau	225
26.	Scene 12: Departures	228
27.	Conclusion: Shakespeare's Radical	250
28.	Afterword	257

Bibliography 261
Index 267

On Texts

Quotations from *King Lear* are taken either from *The First Folio of Shakespeare: The Norton Facsimile*, prepared by Charlton Hinman, 2nd ed. (New York: W. W. Norton, 1996) or from *King Lear, 1608 (Pied Bull Quarto)* (London: The Shakespeare Association and Sidgwick and Jackson, 1939). Unless otherwise noted, line references are to the through-line-number (TLN) of the Folio edition.

PRELUDE

The Hanging Man

In a corner of one of El Greco's pictures, lost in the folds of sky or curtain, floats a strange mustard-colored sufferer. The figure is naked, arms aloft, lacking a parachute but somehow resisting gravity—unless he isn't, and he is falling like a stone through yellow space. He is invisible to the casual eye. El Greco painted him, and then pretended that he hadn't. Perhaps no one else has ever seen him, this barely palpable ghost, wrapped away beneath the picture's nominal theme. Because if we don't magnify the details, he disappears into the yellow drapery wash. But once we have seen him, whether we see him or not when we look once more at the entire picture, he is there. Unborn or deceased or waiting, the homunculus is. The picture is never the same again.

What to do with this image? Perhaps hurry to accommodate him to men or myths that we already know. Maybe it is Christ: witness the thin bent knee, the emaciated cheek and shadow of a beard, the vague suggestion of a loin cloth. And the arms are almost certainly there—unfinished, lost in yellow, but begun at sixty degrees, the painful angle rendered by the slumped head. It must be Christ, suffering and almost forgotten. He is in the last days, perhaps the already-dead days. It is the deposed saviour, strung out in an eternal Easter Saturday, between death and return, denied even a hell to harrow. He is in-between: perhaps once a Christ, perhaps one day once more, but for now, for this world's visible duration, the hanging man.

But then it isn't Christ at all. It isn't anyone that has ever had a name. No: it is a vision of what Gottfried Leibniz calls the incompossible: things that do have existence, because imagined by the creator, but not in this world. Here, in the given dispensation, they are not possible.[1]

When I think of Shakespeare, there is one figure above all that El Greco's hanging man suggests. It is Poor Tom in *King Lear*. Tom too is called forth from forgotten deeps; he demands attention in his isolation and ongoing excruciation; and then, the gaze of witnesses once upon other things, he disappears.

Did he ever exist? If he did, where did he come from? And if he did, where does he go?

Really, the homunculus is a wash of paint, nothing more. Or a painter's joke, a secret to keep from the patron. Like the repetition of some compulsive cartoonist unable to resist doodling, again and again, his woebegone everyman. Let the whimsy be.

Yet the image remains.

The body's verticality does not work in the usual way of late El Greco, when his saints, madonnas, and martyrs are given impossibly long torsos or limbs, suggesting that some sort of extra-mundane, denaturing stretching is already at work in the heaven-headed body. Instead the verticality is found in the tiny body's hanging suspension, which might be falling, or might be ascending, but either way the feet do not touch ground. The body merges into and out of surrounding space, such that it can seem a smear of the elements, a brief mirage shaped by the slurry of cosmic matter, rather than a distinct constitution of its own. It is paint and color, or a coalescence of strokes that may at any moment separate into formless matter.

Of course there is no such thing as empty space. The figure is in fact

---

1. Incompossibility is an idea expressed at many points in Leibniz's writing. A characteristic instance: "I have reasons for believing that not all possible species are compossible in the same universe, great as it is; not only with regard to things existing at the same time, but also with regard to the whole succession of things. My view . . . is that there must be species which never did and never will exist, since they are not compatible with that succession of creatures which God has chosen. . . . The *Law of Continuity* states that nature leaves no gaps in the orderings which she follows, but not every form or species belongs to each ordering." *New Essays on Human Understanding*, trans. and ed. Peter Remnant and Jonathan Bennett (Cambridge, U.K.: Cambridge University Press, 1996), 307.

flushed through with stuff. I see bruised streaks of light, an invisibly teeming void. To one side are globed shapes, indeterminate whether maternal or vegetable or rock, and below are curves, like swans' wings or breaking waves or the crest of a waterfall. It is impossible to say whether the figure has issued from the wash, or resists its sucking pull, or is simply bearing up as the wash tumbles upon and around him. Or perhaps there are no fluids at all, and he is fathoms deep in gas. Who knows what element is his?[2]

The here and now, the visible and quotidian, hardly defines possibility. Mundane apprehensions of space and time cannot reach to this vision at all. Seen and not-seen, it is neither inside nor outside, living nor dead, human nor inhuman. Is it in space at all, if its thingness isn't certain, or if it doesn't coincide with others? Is it in time, if it isn't assuredly an event? It is at one glance pure cuspal potentiality; at another glance, silently screaming prevention. It looks like a whirl of nothing, but perhaps this smeared patch is in fact memory's incipience: the nothing awaits; it foreshadows. It is incompossible with the present dispensation—but there are more things in the world than can be measured by the daily senses. Perhaps it promises, however distantly, to resolve the crippling antinomies of our temporal half-life. This floating spiritualized being is here. It is possible.

Unless it isn't. Unless he is flatly impossible, doomed to be strung out in incommensurable solitude.

Surely the price of this kind of presence, a shuttered presence, is awesome and awful loneliness, rarely spoken, even more rarely heard. Does the yellow man exist? Or is he dead? Or waiting?

---

2. I am not alone in finding El Greco's smallest details expressive of tragic pathos. The Soviet filmmaker Grigori Kozintsev reports that in one of the unfinished books of his great contemporary Sergei Eisenstein, *Nature Is Not Indifferent*, Eisenstein "studied the structure of pathos, going beyond its limits to the uttermost degree of influence. Eisenstein understood perfectly both the laws of pathetic composition and the price which has to be paid for it. Choosing a detail from an El Greco painting (only a detail), a stormy landscape in Toledo, he wrote: the colours 'shimmer . . . with no less animation of holy excitement than as if the blood-stained artist had been alive, crucified on one of the crosses.'" Kozintsev wryly comments, in words that speak profoundly to Shakespeare's Tom (and to Shakespeare): "I don't think that the demon in the innermost recesses of his blood ever managed to get enough sleep." *King Lear, the Space of Tragedy: The Diary of a Film Director*, trans. Mary Mackintosh (London: Heinemann Educational Publishers, 1977), 215.

In more than one way, El Greco's homunculus is lost. I cannot find him. I cannot find where he came from, I cannot place him in his home, he has retreated only god knows where. He came out of my printer, quite unexpectedly. I hadn't called for him at all. I wanted to print the full picture and instead I got a tiny fragment of it, some arbitrary zoom. It kept happening. Instead of neat framed miniatures I got faceless white beards, and tearful eyes glistening like moons in night-ponds, and this sole falling sufferer. And now I don't know which picture or mural it was, and because the yellow man is so small, and El Greco's jaundiced mustard color so ubiquitous, he has retreated back into nonbeing. And so here he is, falling through mustard space, through the casing air and the viewless winds, this single image the only trace of his possibility. All there is of him is my creased printout, taped to a board, curling and perilous. The image gathers a curious twinned pathos, partly of unwonted survival, partly of accident. Or rather, of an accident that has somehow stolen the gift of duration. Perhaps better to call it a life.

Tom's a cold.

❋ 2 ❋

INTRODUCTION

This book begins with a single supposition. That deep in the secret recesses of Shakespeare is the figure of *King Lear*'s Edgar-Tom: passionate subject of, and passionately subject to, Shakespearean history and futurity and theatrical poetics. It is a figure without conventional limits, a limitlessness that corresponds to the unhoused, barely imaginable ambitions of Shakespeare for his art.

The Edgar of my book is not so much a character as a nest of possibilities: at every moment intensely centered, and in this centering stretched and shattered and shared; at every moment mutating into other forms, human and nonhuman. Consequently, this plaything is burdened more than any other with the experience of suffering and the difficulty of release.

In this savage immersion, the Edgar-part embodies a kind of *living political*, and the fact that lives happen in networks of dependence. It takes on historical possibility, past and coming, as its own ever-mutating burden. And yet, uniquely and uncannily, fundamental aspects of the part evade all historical or socially continuous categories. It is not so much unreal (let alone fantastical), as a negative version of what Husserl called the irreal: omnitemporal; unbound by the horizons of an objective world; without spatial extension or motion.[1] Clearly, a figure like

---

1. See Edmund Husserl, *Experience and Judgment*, trans. J. S. Churchill and K. Ameriks (Evanston, Ill.: Northwestern University Press, 1973), 250ff. "A determination is irreal if it is

that cannot simply die: it will lurk before or beyond customary states of reality, occupying the shadowlands past sense. Putative ends can be existed in; nothingness trembles with possibility. In this way, Edgar/Tom becomes Shakespeare's most intimate sensor of what cannot be known, and yet may exist; or what cannot exist, and yet may be known. But then the Edgar-part, almost as its calling card, also repeatedly suffers the opposite of such supertemporal ideality: tortured by an immovable object-world, captive in tiny spaces, running for his life, combustible with too much of everything, and yet forever forbidden to burst.

More simply, this book is also a sustained reading of *King Lear*. Think of the play as an electrical circuit, with the Edgar-part connecting the network, a kind of multiwired semihuman synapse. It is plugged into everything: volatilized by others, startled in its hiding places, and darkly casting light, willfully or otherwise. The part's transmissions are often very swift, and often subvisible. But my methods in adducing them are very simple. I try to look and to listen very closely, and still more closely when there seems to be nothing there. I trust to voices. Above all I try to pay attention, and attend to the fluctuations of attendance, my own as much as anyone's in the playworld.

To the extent that moral or political or spiritual questions are at stake, they are discovered by—indeed often discovered as—such attendance. Correspondingly, the book is structured in two interweaving forms. First, I move moment by moment through the relevant events in the play, trying to draw out what might be happening: these sections I call Scenes, and they should in the first instance be read in page order. Second, I meditate on possibilities—philosophical, theological, political—generated by the play action: these sections I call Interludes, and they can be read in any order.

❦

I say *King Lear*, but what this denotes is no longer self-evident. There are two *Lear* texts—some would say two *Lear* plays: the Quarto of 1608,

---

founded in spatiotemporal reality but can nonetheless appear in different realities." J. N. Mohanty, *Edmund Husserl's Freiburg Years: 1916–1938* (New Haven, Conn.: Yale University Press, 2011), 240.

and the Folio of 1623. I should clarify from the start how I see this vexed question. The Folio probably succeeds the Quarto, both as a publication and a composition. But to my mind this endows neither text with authority over the other. Instead I take this bibliographic fact as serendipitous—whether through luck, happenstance, or arch intent, a happy clue to the polyploid world we have entered.

So, I think of *King Lear* not as two distinct works, but as a single playworld enterable via two phantom versions. These two versions are at once separate, superimposed, simultaneous, successive (each behind and ahead of the other), and mutually re-visioning. I take them as coincident takes upon, or alternative snapshots of, the same series of moments. The action moves in and out of evident focus, sometimes close and palpable, sometimes receding into apparent nothingness.

Each playtext, then, is an imperfect witness, an imperfect rememberer, an imperfect predictor of action that is at once in the past and unfinished, and therefore both here and yet to come. Neither text is quite in possession of the scenes it reaches for. There is often more than meets the eye: and occasionally less. At times a scene may only resemble—or perhaps re-assemble—possibilities that the given technology, of word or body, struggles to harness. Both texts have scenes that the other does not, counterfactual what-ifs that exist in one take and not the other, that are at once in the world and gone from it. But they are no less real for that. Because in this playworld, history and ontology are essentially subjunctive. More than that, things *do* happen in more than one way at once. Actions *are* fractured and fractal, whether a spoken word or extemporary gesture or plotted event-point; they are shuttered and cut-up; they are instantaneously recessive with self-superimpositions; they are endlessly occurring differently, both in the moment of utterance and in the ongoing history of the play through ages and places.

In all of this, the fact of two texts is not a bibliographical accident, or the sediment of performance revisions, or the supersession of one sequence over another. It is the merest necessity of the playworld, of its take upon time, event, and identity. And the same can be said for the duplex ontology of Edgar, as the figure who most faithfully iterates, almost incarnates, the split-and-spliced, here-not-here morphology of both playtext and playworld.

The titles alone tell us much about this multivalent constitution. In the Folio, it is *The Tragedie of King Lear*. The Quarto is usually referred to as the *Historie*. But in fact the Quarto title is as follows:

> M. William Shak-speare:
> HIS
> True Chronicle Historie of the life and death of King LEAR and his three Daughters.
>
> *With the unfortunate life of* Edgar, *sonne* and heire to the Earle of Gloster, and his sullen and assumed humor of TOM of Bedlam.

The stories are symmetrically advertised, as though they are modular blocs of narrative interest. This twinned presentation immediately suggests a puzzling modal plurality: this play is at once a history, a tragedy, a picaresque ("unfortunate life"), a prince-and-pauper tale of noble privation, and something else besides—some tantalizing phantom quality bound up in the nonfigure who closes the title. And this is part of a more profound elusiveness. The play's hetero-generic mode implies a refusal to choose between living and dying. For this world, the advertisement tells us, is defined by a foundational existential impasse: a tale ending in death, and a tale remaining in life. It implies a kind of split telos in which both annihilation and survival are the predestined end, at equal odds, each apparently untouched by the other. It is, I think, unique. Of course, other tragedies keep someone alive at the end to clean things up or to limp into futures. But what other play announces, as its plot and purpose, such an equipoise of catastrophe and continuance? And if the two stories are coordinate, if they shadow and interpret each other—which surely they must, by all the rules of double plots—then what can it mean to at once die and live?

It is a strange and audacious thing to assay. But one thing seems clear enough from the title page. Whatever the mechanics of this exploded-and-unexploded dispensation, the figure who concludes the description must be in some way decisive: Tom of Bedlam.

I will have much to say of Tom; he strikes me as one of the most expressive figures Shakespeare ever created. He irrupts in the middle of the Edgar-role, somehow its totem, in some obscure way almost the role's cause, at once a patchwork of the already lived and previously spoken, and an image of pure potentiality. Stephen Booth calls Poor Tom "perhaps the most thoroughly documented briefly assumed identity in literature." Booth's wryness is recognition that the attention garnered by this strictly nonexistent figure is somehow of the play's essence: the "sense that we lack a hold on categories and that categories lack the power to hold reality results from the unexpectedly literal truth of 'Edgar I nothing am.'"[2] Poor Tom is the issue of such category mistakes. There can be no home for such a being, no place for abidance or forgetfulness. This makes Tom an enormous problem for Edgar. At times Edgar can seem to sit on Tom, like some jealous prefect, or as though Tom really is his to dispose of, his very own jointed doll, to be folded into his case when opportunity ceases to knock. But as we shall see, this is impossible.

Something of this difficulty is evident even in the Quarto title. After all, what can it mean to be a "humor" of someone else, and yet in the shape of a man? Clearly there is potential for a humor to be a character—witness many of Ben Jonson's characters, monomaniacal carriers of a single defining affect (jealousy, intemperance, vanity). But is Tom a character? If not, what is he? The humor isn't Edgar; it is *of* Tom. It perhaps suggests some sort of emanation from an original body, but it remains ambiguous whether it is temperamentally compelled, capriciously entertained, or even demonically automatized.

The chosen modifiers of this humor compound the enigma: *sullen* and *assumed*. It is sullen, meaning silent, unyielding, deep dwelling. A sullen humor, we might feel sure, is not to be lifted quickly; this figure

---

2. Stephen Booth, *King Lear, Macbeth, Indefinition, and Tragedy* (New Haven, Conn.: Yale University Press, 1983), 46.

somehow remains, as his position at the close of the title may seem to attest. *Assumed* is similarly pregnant. We might think it indicates simply Edgar's improvised simulation. But this was not the principal meaning of the word in 1608. Far more forcibly, *assumed* meant taken on or taken into some service, particularly an official or vocational obligation. What is more, a prime meaning of the word was spiritual: received into heaven. Now I doubt that any such implication is at work here (as apt as it may be to the part's pioneering eschatology). But the repeated and clearly salient implication is unfreedom: a taking-on that is a kind of sacrifice or indenture, even as it is a false pretence. After all, who said that the act of playing is free, or is anything other than an exigent and recurrent enthrallment? Insofar as Tom is assumed, this humor may epitomize the sleepless dependence of Shakespeare's foundational existential contract: an actor with a part, one that isn't him, perhaps isn't even his, but which cannot be off-loaded.

※

As much as I think the Edgar-figure is deeply inward with Shakespeare's imagination, I am not going to claim any strict autobiographical correlation. Even so there are hints—little more than hints—of congruent intimacy in the two lives, if the scratchy attestation of biography and sonnets is to be believed. Both are players, sturdy vagabonds and itinerant guests, shifting shape as occasion or exigency demand. Both can seem somehow vaporized, insubstantial, without the parts they suffer to create. Both are intermittently disgusted by their arts—"Alas, 'tis true, I have gone here and there / And made myself a motley to the view" (Sonnet 110)—and raddled with ambivalent motive. Both seek to change hearts through fictions and are brought short by the treacherousness of moral summary. Both harp obsessively on sexual slavery and degradation; both are exiles from family; both can be imagined at the edge of court life, haunting the feast, unrecognized.

Intriguingly, the name Edgar might be thought to interpret and even redeem that of his maker: Ed-gar means a *blessed spear*. Of course, the coincidence of names may be accidental; it may be the self-castigating author's ironical private joke. Equally, it may suggest that Shakespeare designed this character to shake the spear—of injustice, at injustice, secular and divine—so as to test the possibilities of blessedness. This in turn may imply—contrary to assumptions of Shakespeare's religious diffidence or disinterestedness—a work fired by spiritual purpose and eschatological risk: not orthodox, perhaps only erratically or residually Christian, but pushing as hard as thought and theater can at life's ultimate passage: moving between life and death, countenancing coexistence, and asking what the fact of one condition means for the other. But this is no ethereal mysticism, teasing with the extra-mundane, toying with metaphysical puzzles. *King Lear* lives on the fault line between being and not-being, and knows at every moment that this place is violence—made by it, chock-full with it—whether it takes the form of passion, privation, or terror. What else to expect from a spear? Shaken or shaking or blessed, the spear makes a wound, and the wound must be entered.

※

A traditional search for sources will not get terribly far in accounting for Shakespeare's Edgar. Nonetheless there are suggestive traces on the wind. It is well known that in plotting the Gloucester story Shakespeare draws on a brief inset narrative from Philip Sidney's *Arcadia*, detailing the sorry plight of a sinful king with two sons.[3] He favors the bad son and realizes his mistake too late. The bad son blinds him and boots him out. The old man asks the neglected good son to lead him to a rock from which he might jump to guilty death. The good son virtuously disobeys, and so now they spend their time moralizing the tale, the old man contrite and self-rebuking, the good son earnest in ameliorating his father's misery, sick of life himself, but enduring for love of his parent. The bad son hunts the good, is foiled by Sidney's heroes, and the good son eventually ascends to his father's throne. The father dies, stretched unsustainably between affliction and "excess of comfort" (he bursts smilingly). The good son forgives his apparently ashamed and despairing brother. Clearly there is a core dynamic here, which Shakespeare folds and twists and fissions with typical ingeniousness.

---

3. Sir Philip Sidney, *The Countess of Pembroke's Arcadia* (London: William Ponsonbie, 1590), book 2, chapter 10 (pp. 142–47).

More uncertainly influential is Holinshed's account of England's King Edgar, crowned in 959, around the same time as *Macbeth*'s Malcolm of Scotland (a King Edgar of Scotland soon followed, but Holinshed spares little time in dismissing his significance).[4] England's Edgar is a suggestive case. A small, neatly made man; a lover of peace, protective of his people, sleeplessly warding off invaders; a stickler for rules, fiercely punitive to robbers and malefactors; a favorer of monks and establisher of abbeys. His reputation survived to Tudor times and beyond. So the humanist diplomat Thomas Elyot praised "the noble kynge Edgar" for returning "the monarch to his pristinate astate and figure: whiche brought to passe, reason was reuiued, and people came to conformitie, and the realme began to take comforte and to shewe some visage of a publike weale: and so (lauded be god) haue continued."[5]

Edgar here is the hinge-point and model of something very like civic modernity, a model for Elyot's dedicatee, Henry VIII, to imitate. Queen Elizabeth's "philosopher," John Dee, reminded her that her sovereignty over "British ocean sea" was due to King Edgar's vigilance; Lord Chancellor Francis Bacon three times invoked Edgar as a precedent for James I.[6] All in all a suitable model, it might seem, for Shakespeare's King Edgar-to-come. But then Holinshed spends much of his brief portrait detailing Edgar's compulsive womanizing. He was a slave to female beauty; a notorious deflowerer of virgins, whom he demanded like ale for his stomach; a pitiless ravisher of nuns, who was aroused more than deterred if they hid from him in terror; a man who claimed a second wife, of irresistible physical perfection, by secretly murdering her husband. Evidently good King Edgar is painfully divided, piloting between extremes, his piety and good works a compensatory ricochet from the daily spoil of appetite. This ambivalence is crystallized in Holinshed's report of his end. He has a dream vision of being smote on the breast

---

4. Raphael Holinshed, *The firste volume of the Chronicles of England, Scotlande, and Irelande* (London: John Harrison, 1577), 231–35.
5. Thomas Elyot, *The Boke Named the Governour*, vol. 1 (London: J. M. Dent, n.d), 2.
6. See F. T. Flahiff, "Edgar: Once and Future King," in *Some Facets of "King Lear": Essays in Prismatic Criticism*, ed. Rosalie Colie and F. T. Flahiff (London: University of Toronto Press, 1974), 229–30, 236–37.

with a spear. Nine days later he was dead. Holinshed claims not to know if the tale is apocryphal. He half apologizes for the serendipitous allegory of a prince delivered from life by his own prophetic spear, symbol of a nature as sharp as it was blessed—or blessed by too much privileged license.

The two sources, Sidney and Holinshed, combine to present a tantalizing invitation to drama: the good son, intimate with vice and betrayal, desperate to attain the high ground; the good prince, vigilant about law, yet churning with semisecret transgression and guilt. At the very least, they suggest that rectitude exacts its price; that moral precision, inextricable from allegory, might in itself tempt its paragon to apostasy.

These are Edgar's sources. But what of Tom? Poor Toms—also called "Abraham-men"—thronged the countryside, announcing themselves by their whoop and holler and alarming stare, a byword for reviled fraudulence.[7] But Tom o' Bedlam was also the subject and speaker of a widely circulating popular ballad, whose eerie, haunted measures evoke something much less demographically placed, and far less easily dismissed, than a common or garden vagabond. The earliest surviving version of the song was collected by one Giles Earle, in a book of lyrics dated 1615-1626. It is impossible to know whether the ballad or any parts of it were circulating before Shakespeare wrote *King Lear*.[8] It seems

---

7. Thomas Dekker: "He calls himself by the name of *Poore Tom*, and coming neere any body *cries* out *poore Tom* is a colde." *Belman of London; Bringing to Light the Most Notorious Villanies* (London: N. Butter, 1608), fol. D3r. Tom takes his place in a cavalcade of rogues and wayfarers: "Next are *Wilde Rogues*, then *Prigges*: Then *Palliards*: then *Fraters*: then *Tom* of *Bedlama* band of madcaps, otherwise called *Poore Toms Flocke of Wilde-geese* (whome thou seest by his black and blew naked armes to be a man beaten to the world) . . . or *Hayre-braynes* as called *Abraham-men*"; "Of all the mad rascals . . . the *Abraham-man* is the most phantastick . . . you see pinnes stuck in sundry places of his naked flesh, especially in his armes . . . some be exceeding merry, and doe nothing but sing songs, fashioned out of their owne braines, some will dance, others will doe nothing but either laugh or weepe, others are dogged & so sullen both in looke and speech." Thomas Dekker, *The Guls Hornbook and the Belman of London in Two Parts* (London: J. M. Dent, 1905), 85, 98-99.

8. Giles Earle, *Giles Earle His Booke*, ed. Peter Warlock (London: Houghton, 1932), 97-100. See Stanley Wells, "Tom O'Bedlam's Song and *King Lear*," *Shakespeare Quarterly* 12, no. 3 (1961): 311-15, for a transcript of Archbishop Sancroft's version from (probably) slightly later in the century. Also see Robert Graves, "Loving Mad Tom," in *The Common Asphodel: Collected Essays on Poetry, 1922-1949* (New York: Haskell House, 1949), 197-212.

likely that the ballad draws on the time-grafted community lore from which Shakespeare drew; less likely, but not at all improbable, that the lyric is directly influenced by Shakespeare's Tom. But either way, as influence or appropriation, the ballad powerfully opens the uncanny worlds of *Lear's* Poor Tom:

> From the hag and hungry goblin
> That into rags would rend ye,
> And the spirit that stands by the naked man
> In the book of moons, defend ye
> That of your five sound senses,
> You never be forsaken,
> Nor wander from yourselves with Tom.
> Abroad to beg your bacon.[9] (TLN 1-8)

He is chased by demons, cursed into indigence, bereaved of his good senses. But still more suggestive is Tom's plea to his hearers not to "wander from your selves with Tom": the warning is partly not to do as he has done, and lose possession of self; equally, it is not to join with Tom. His exiled body, then, compacts a kind of beleaguered collective, half the hag and goblin ripping at his skin, half the other lost souls, compounding with Tom in self-evacuation. Tom is more than a single life; his experience defies chronology and arithmetic. It is instead sustained on a principle of multiplying suffering, definitively in excess of individual forbearance:

> Of thirty bare years have I
> Twice twenty been enraged,
> And of forty been three times fifteen
> In durance soundly caged. (TLN 13-16)

Coterminously, Tom has existed for untold generations, back to before the recording of history or the establishment of a modern pol-

---

9. All quotations are from the version of "Tom a Bedlam" quoted in Earle, *Giles Earle His Booke*, 97-100.

ity. Still worse, his experience is either deathlike sleep or unremitting insomnia:

> I slept not since the Conquest,
> Till then I never waked. (TLN 26-27)

He abides in secrets, gestates with long historical evolution, and then he is awoken and cursed with the imperative to suffer history, as though Merlin's hate-child or a diabolic version of some promised patriotic chevalier. Exile, itinerance, sleeplessness, all become metonyms of each other. Living is torment, enduring every moment without remission, his eyes bleeding, each instant like the sting of a whip:

> Brave bracelets strong, sweet whips, ding dong,
> With wholesome hunger plenty. (TLN 19-20)

But suffer as he does, this Tom is also beyond human. He travels in the lands beyond sight—not after this world, not before, but uncannily parallel:

> And when benighted
> I walk in Powles with waking souls,
> Yet never am affrighted . . .
> I know more than Apollo,
> For oft when he lies sleeping
> I see the stars at bloody wars
> In the wounded welkin weeping (TLN 45-52)

This transversal inhabiting—Tom the ghostly night-walker, stepping between metaphysical realms—makes of his life an audacious rehearsal of apocalypse:

> With an host of furious fancies.
> Whereof I am commander,
> With a burning spear and a horse of air
> To the wilderness I wander. (TLN 67-70)

All of which ends in a strange summons from a revenant knight to take up arms in a duel of the last days, in a place far beyond the here and now, yet where this spectral Tom already is:

> By a knight of ghosts and shadows
> I summoned am to tourney
> Ten leagues beyond the wide world's end
> Methinks it is no journey. (TLN 71–74)

If we dreamt-up a source to concentrate the environment and progress of Shakespeare's Tom, we could hardly have come upon something more suggestive than this lyric. All the same it should remind us just how violent, how simply unexpected, Shakespeare's conception for Edgar really is.[10] Each of the sources is already riven in itself, generating an uncertain assemblage of saintly leader, brother in sin, casuistic moralist, secret lecher, menacing vagrant, whipped innocent, time-traveling revenant, agent of Armageddon, diabolic messiah. But once they are yoked together, we can begin to intuit a figure who is at once a boundary haunter at life's extremities, wired for alarming advents, and directly at the cultural center, suffering the world's necessities.

※

Perhaps the murky ambivalence of these sources, a whiff of bad faith in correctness, has hung around Shakespeare's Edgar, because centuries of readers and spectators have left him alone, ignored or unloved or obscurely resented.[11] There are reasons for this—assuming that we can think of Edgar as an individual, more or less human. No one else in the play attempts philosophical distance, and to do so can feel an outrage

---

10. I discuss Tom's well-known debts to Samuel Harsnett's *A Declaration of Egregious Popish Impostures* (London: James Roberts, 1603) in the Interlude following Scene 4: Tom's Places.

11. D. J. Enright speaks for many when he writes of Edgar: "Such a dreary and heartless moraliser, with a pronounced inclination to priggishness." *Shakespeare and the Students* (Chatto and Windus, 1970). Even A. C. Bradley, in the midst of a sympathetic appreciation of Edgar's buoyancy and resourcefulness, admits that there "remain in him touches . . . which a little chill one's feeling for him": *Shakespearean Tragedy: Lectures on Hamlet, Othello, King Lear, Macbeth* (1904; reprint, Basingstoke, U.K.: Macmillan, 1985), 254.

against raw experience. No one else in the play clings so to religious categories ("he interprets everything religiously," avers A. C. Bradley[12]), with an occasional whiff of primitive vindictiveness. This can again seem a kind of scandal, perhaps against the sufferers, perhaps against the gods.

This links to other suspicions of unpleasantness: Edgar the moralizer, the time-server, the sex-hater; Edgar the insufficiently candid revenger. No one else in the play is so difficult to pin down morally. Others are cruel, we know it and know why; others are good, whatever their mistakes. But Edgar? His actions are often fathomless, his motives murky, such that often it is hard to be sure that he has any motives at all, or whether he is substantially absent from much that the Edgar-part does. His thoughts often come downloaded from past authority, as though from the old world of feudality and service, and yet he is radically new, pushing into numerous possible dispensations. He endures enough for scores of lives, is somehow older than anyone, and yet he is dropped like a calf in a field, and forced again and again to suffer strangely contingent or inadequate births, as though forever cued and never quite arriving.

He at once endures, inflicts, and comforts suffering; indeed, the very plenty of the Edgar-part is a suffering, a deprivation. For in this most emotional of plays, a work that beggars our empathies dry (as August Wilhelm von Schlegel put it, "the science of compassion is exhausted"[13]), Edgar is left behind, a parched paragon of virtue and vice. G. Wilson Knight's summary is killing: Edgar is "faultless but without virility."[14] He never truly receives our love, just as the actor never gets to play his character's love. No wonder Nahum Tate did what he did in his Restoration revision, remaking Edgar as a sturdy romantic hero and building his entire confection on the fact that Edgar's intentions and worth are never in doubt: he loves Cordelia, he deserves her love, he knows what he deserves, and he acts in faithful consistency to this unwaver-

---

12. Bradley, *Shakespearean Tragedy*, 254.
13. August Wilhelm von Schlegel, *A Course of Lectures on Dramatic Art and Literature*, vol. 2, trans. J. Black (London: Baldwin, Cradock, and Joy, 1815), 204.
14. G. Wilson Knight, *The Wheel of Fire* (1930; reprint, London: Routledge, 2001), 201.

ing knowledge. Tate's revision is more than a kindness: it is sane, and transparent, and speaks to the model of a man worth imitating.[15]

Shakespeare's Edgar, by contrast, is opaque and inchoate. He is half a lurker, half a kind of principle of suddenness, a horrible irruptiveness he both suffers and commits. But if this suggests a stuttering, shivering, shuddering, shuttered mode of existing—which surely his is—and so a life that is physically volatized and agitated, made of raw skin and shredded nerves and epileptic convulsions, then his is also the most spectral life in the play, the most metaphysically prone, its presence often more virtual than physical, and his bodily movements only obscurely or asymmetrically related to his mind. Often it can seem that he finds his home not in any individuated self, but in the role's specular or echoing relations to others, many of them quite beyond Edgar's awareness. He exists in (or as) suprasubjective matrices, in tight connection, as mirror or metonym, to every one of the play's sufferers.[16] He throws out or is thrown upon all kinds of simultaneous lifelines, like attenuated, criss-crossing arcs of possible becoming. And yet he never, at any moment, moves at the same pace or in the same place as another character—not even when he, if indeed it is he, leads his eyeless father arm-in-arm to the nonexistent cliff.

Time and again Edgar is either shooed away or somehow forgotten

---

15. See Nahum Tate, *The History of King Lear*, ed. James Black (London: Edward Arnold Press, 1976). Peter Womack, "Secularizing *King Lear*: Shakespeare, Tate, and the Sacred," *Shakespeare Survey* 55 (2002): 98-104, remarks how it "is really surprising how many incoherences are resolved" when Edgar and Cordelia's love is made the play's cohering motive-force. The play becomes "newly purposeful," making Shakespeare's play "appear as a structure disabled by passivity," engendering "small, irritating enigmas" (98-99). As it happens, these words are almost a perfect gloss on the figure of Edgar, as are the things that Tate's revision expertly writes out: in Womack's neat summary, "silence, opacity, disjunction," and "transcendence" (101). Norman Rabkin likewise recognizes Tate's "brilliant" job of eliminating "the terrifying convolutions and perplexities" of Shakespeare's tragedy, not least by rationalizing the otherwise "inexplicable cruelty" and "gratuitously wounding behaviour" of Edgar toward his blind father. *Shakespeare and the Problem of Meaning* (London: University of Chicago Press, 1982), 82-83.

16. Booth gives a pithy list of Edgar's doubles: Cordelia (wronged innocents); Edmund (brothers with interchangeable names who play upon the father's gullibility); Gloucester (credulous victims); Goneril and Regan (elder siblings with a fairy tale curse); Fool (loyalty and pretend folly); Lear (naked wandering); Oswald (proud servant), Albany (contemptible virtue). *King Lear, Macbeth, Indefinition*, 21-22. I might add France (loyal noble, and probably played by the same actor as Edgar); and—I think necessarily, to complete the circle—Cornwall (gratuitous cruelty).

by the other characters, or he is left to pick up the pieces, if there are any to pick up. In almost everything he is excessive, and very often he seems to speak bizarrely or damagingly more than the immediate context demands: consider the entire storm-Tom, the cliff-Tom, the postcliff exorcist, the Mummerset peasant, even the dilatory tale-teller extending his story as Cordelia gets wiped out off-stage. Perhaps only Mercutio rivals Edgar in the production of discourse for which conventional speech act theory, or indeed Ludwig Wittgenstein's theory of language games, is so inadequate; his words perform things, certainly, but always far in excess of definable social illocutions.

How to make sense of the mixture in the role of absence and surplus? Of course there are practical reasons for it. As the plots multiply, it is Edgar who unites them, as the accidental figure who is the medium between worlds (meeting his father, leading him to "Dover"), or as the intervening figure who interrupts and redirects story lines (killing Oswald, reading Goneril's letter). Edgar is a convenience at such moments, but this hardly makes his difficulty disappear. For he is at once transparent (we can see what he does and where his actions lead) and opaque (we cannot see through these actions to *him*). Furthermore, at the same time as Edgar has the job of relaying basic information, he is given no real intimacy with an audience, because he has no comic or ironic perspective.[17]

Edgar's role has various things in common with chivalrous heroes, with the exiled prince or falsely reviled true-bred who garners both populist and aristocratic credit from slumming it without boasting or complaining. And yet he isn't this romantic figure at all. He really does lose self-possession; he really does suffer the fall; he isn't in anything ascendant. Likewise, he has some of an old-fashioned clown's function— think of intermediaries from earlier Elizabethan romances, like Mouse in *Mucedorus*, or Strumbo in *Locrine*—but little of a clown's contingent

---

17. Michael E. Mooney claims that it is "Edgar whose experience we emulate in viewing the play. We are, in fact, even closer to Edgar than to Lear. . . . [Lear's] tragedy is the one we must learn about, but it is Edgar who teaches us the way we should react. Because we share so much of Edgar's perspective, however, we . . . often find him wanting. We will not forgive him for being a less than perfect *raisonneur*, forgetting to realize that he is himself learning and growing in the play, and that his choric speeches are only provisional judgements." "'Edgar I Nothing Am': Figurenposition in *King Lear*," *Shakespeare Survey* 38 (1986): 164.

permission to be foolish, skeptical, or irresponsible. Increasingly Edgar becomes metaphorical in a curiously mechanistic, literal way as he carries across news from one place to another, the vehicle of combative tenors, some of his own constructing, some not, and none quite possessing the moment.

Bradley says this of *Lear*:

We seem to trace ... the tendency of imagination to analyse and abstract, to decompose human nature into its constituent factors, and then to construct beings in whom one or more of these factors is absent or atrophied or only incipient.[18]

Maynard Mack links Bradley's observation to the play's deep indebtedness to medieval Moralities, to psychomachias and the Summons of Death, in which every character that is met, vicious or virtuous, is an extension of one's own possibilities.[19] Mack refers to the king, but Edgar is a more absolute incarnation of this compositional principle—and capable of coherence, one might conclude, only as some kind of quanta on the rack, with each incarnation of this decomposed and recomposed "human nature" like a sinew popping as it strains to connect to its brother.

The part certainly challenges any assumptions we might have about the singleness of a life. Any memories it speaks move uncertainly between individual and collective. Indeed the role virtually incarnates the strange subjective misprision of theatrical ontology, in which any thought is instantly shared, and indeed cannot exist without becoming the memory of untold numbers of auditors and witnesses. What is more, Edgar's continual hiddenness, in tree and hovel, rags and armor, adumbrates a life in the shade, whose substance is a kind of ontological negativity, as though his face is another's, and his words, without which he is nothing, truly as fleeting as voice. Again, the theatrical contract is uncannily in tune with whatever he is.

18. Bradley, *Shakespearean Tragedy*, 212.
19. Maynard Mack, *King Lear in Our Time* (London: Methuen and Company, 1966), 56–57. On Edgar's resemblance to Morality figures, see pp. 61–62.

Repeatedly the part recalls a non- or posthuman form of living: not machinic, because there is mind and suffering in it, but not returnable to or resolvable in any recognizably humanist contract. Instead there is something like a manifestation, as human life, of a play or character's compositional materials. The part is at once the distillation and explosion of Shakespearean form: its opacity and plenitude, fathomless reaches, tentacular networks of implication. This implies more than some generalized notion that the Edgar-part is mediated by the forms and materials of theater. For the specific suffering of this part is almost to *be* the instruments of Shakespeare's craft: a part, severed from the whole, spoken in disconnected fragments; a metaphor made real; a disguise so spare and complete that it *is* the body; a suspension in the cue-space, waiting for reentrance, or in the dark rent between scenes; living as an aside, unheard by anyone in the same world; a functional shift, a breathing polysemy, the abysses that lurk in metalepsis. Such conditions are the part's moment-by-moment reality, both where it comes from and where it goes.

❧

Edgar can seem as colorless as any of Shakespeare's unprepossessing worthies, those noble weaklings who at play's end inherit the earth, having been upstaged or outwitted from go to woe by more mercurial creatures, usually women. But he has to be accounted for. Perhaps no part is more used by Shakespeare than this one, as he loads the play's instrumental requirements onto Edgar; perhaps no part can seem more superfluous to the things we truly care about, or its motions more in excess of psychological or circumstantial expedience. It can seem the most strictly unnecessary assemblage that Shakespeare ever conceived. But on the principle that Shakespeare is never more serious than when his art appears superfluous, this doubled excessiveness suggests to me the profoundest compulsion. Surely Edgar must be more than a water carrier for the storms and tears all around. "Reason not the need," says the king at one point; but of course we must try:[20]

---

20. Emmanuel Levinas: "To contain more than one's capacity is to shatter at every moment the framework of a content that is thought, to cross the barriers of immanence. . . .

The Art of our Necessities is strange,
And can make vilde things precious. (TLN 1725-26; italics mine)

It is easy to resent Edgar, as insipid and inadequate next to the mesmerizing Tom or charismatic Edmund or pitiful Lear. The temptation is real, but it needs to be countered. It is easy to be dulled to goodness, easy to downplay loyalty to the idea of it, even in the teeth of collusion and ugliness and rage. This is not to say that Edgar is saintly, or even sees virtue clear and straight. I doubt Shakespeare believed in saints. But he knew the strain of tortured moral absolutism, and how it curdles into cruelty and loathing, if not of others then of self.[21] Hamlet is his greatest such figure. Edgar is cut from the same cloth: but not from the start, like Hamlet or Angelo or Coriolanus (or maybe, counterintuitively, even Edmund).

Edgar, by contrast, arrives as the nothing, the semiskeptical semimodern semihumanist semiman. And then he comes upon moral absolutes, and they act in him as though his origin, or his birthright. It is a strange entrance, belated and torturous, into a predicative purpose: as though grafted for, and grafted to, an allegory, the violence of which he is never quite inured to. The part suffers and commits much violence; and yet, for all its exposure, it can never quite find its place in the world, because its time has either gone or has not yet arrived. This strikes me as an authentic kind of tragedy—not competing with Lear's, indeed barely noticed by it, but surviving in and beyond the play as the slow lightning of true suffering.

And the stage, like history, is still to catch up with this role, yet really to see or hear it. It is no surprise that the history of acting the part has generally been so dismal and compromised. Tate's Edgar was a ro-

---

What, in action, breaks forth as essential violence is the surplus of being over the thought that claims to contain it, the marvel of the idea of infinity." *Totality and Infinity: An Essay on Exteriority*, trans. Alphonso Lingis (Pittsburgh, Penn.: Duquesne University Press, 1999), 27.

21. Marvin D. Rosenberg says of Edgar that he "hates well": *The Masks of King Lear* (Berkeley: University of California Press, 1972), 245; Stanley Cavell sees "Edgar's capacity for cruelty" as "the *same* cruelty as that of the evil characters": *Must We Mean What We Say?* (New York: Scribner's, 1969), 283. Compare this to Harley Granville-Barker: "a man of character indeed, modest, of a deserving mind, and, in this pagan play, a very Christian gentleman, . . . he is, I think, as true a gentleman as the plays give us": *Preface to Shakespeare*, Vol. 1 (London: B. T. Batsford Ltd., 1930), 321.

mantic hero, easily enough played. But since Shakespeare's text was restored in the nineteenth century, it has been evident that the part grotesquely exceeds the modes or styles expected for a subsidiary "noble" character—one that, for all its changes and explosiveness, must remain in the shadow of the Lear-tale. Every acting choice—comic relief, moral avenger, choric guide, and so on—has meant the sacrifice of numerous incompatible (or simply unnoticed) alternatives, and often, inevitably, the sacrifice of many of the part's lines.[22] Perhaps only once in stage history has Edgar stolen the stage (and perhaps the play): in Ian McKellen's virtuoso 1974 performance for the Actor's Company. But even here he seems to have done so out of actorly desperation at the impossible role:

> In preparing my disguise as Mad Tom, I flung off all my clothes and stood briefly on stage as the bare fork'd man. This was a simple image to counterpoint the impenetrable obscurity of Edgar's language.[23]

McKellen did much the same thing thirty-three years later when he came to play Lear, stripping himself naked in a full-frontal display of man in the raw. Such gestures are in their own way apt and heroic. But still the suspicion is that Shakespeare's words are being waylaid in the longing for quicker, more sensational effects. Germaine Greer for one was scathing, conflating McKellen's two shows of nudity into one act of dismayingly exemplary avoidance:

> Edgar's language is our language, our most valuable inheritance. There is no point in our massively subsidised cultural institutions if they

---

22. See J. S. Bratton, ed., *Plays in Performance: King Lear* (Bristol, U.K.: Bristol Classical Press, 1987).

23. From the program for McKellen's one-man show, *Acting Shakespeare*: http://www.mckellen.com/stage/lear74/index.htm. Theater critic Michael Coveney is quoted on the same website: "Ian McKellen is an inexpressive Edgar until he busts upon the stage as Tom. Here is a creature brilliantly created by the avenging Edgar, a tousle-haired wood demon who has not stopped at anything to muster his effect: on leaving the court, Mr McKellen ceremoniously removes his clothes, improvising a loin-cloth and following with alarming accuracy the precedent of those Bedlam beggars. His left arm is bloodily savaged by a huge thorn, his movements studiously contorted, his mouth agape and his body grimed with mud and gore. This throbbing image of distraction and anguish is the strongest visual element in the production."

devalue our greatest asset by blandly assuming that Shakespeare's language is impenetrable. Edgar does talk fake visionary nonsense but it has a point, one that Nunn and his minions ignored. No wonder we sat unmoved in the Courtyard Theatre as Edgar/Tom, in a crude version of quack aversion therapy, tricked his blind father into jumping from a precipice that wasn't there. There's no way an audience can get the point if the actors are persuaded that there isn't one.[24]

There has never been a sufficient Edgar. The part truly is "unaccommodated," but in ways that neither visual shorthand nor familiar sentimentalisms about outcasts can do justice.[25] Perhaps one body isn't enough for this sort of being; perhaps one voice is not enough either. Be that as it may: we must attend to the part's movements, of mind and word and flesh and digits, as unflinchingly and compassionately as its maker surely did. Or at least let us try.

24. Germaine Greer, "So Ian McKellen Drops His Trousers to Play King Lear. That Sums Up the RSC's Whole Approach," *The Guardian*, May 6, 2007, www.guardian.co.uk/stage/2007/may/07/rsc.theatre.
25. Compare Cavell, *Must We Mean*.

3

INTERLUDE

The Stranger

Let's imagine a single idea; an idea in the form of an image; an image that composes a character.

The idea is something like this: look once, and see nothing. It doesn't exist; it is a white sheet, a cipher without a figure: nothing. And then the nothing moves. Its body is moved through or into places. It mutates. The nothing becomes radically open to possibility. The it becomes a he. But then we look again, and he has moved again, and that thing he was is once again nothing.

Now imagine the same figure rendered by brushstrokes. Each brushstroke composes just this tension. The whole part is this brushstroke, and each gesture or scene or feeling in it: each is this brushstroke, variously magnified, more or less smeared or grainy, revealing more or less of the actions that make the brushstroke. Always the brushstroke is anguish, of being nothing and anything, one then the other, unpredictably.

And now imagine that this brushstroke is sounded. The sound is at once silence and a scream. The sound, in turn, is a feeling body, shivering or palpitating or suddenly arrested, as though into a statue or numbed icon—and always, again, all at once. And this in turn is what is seen: a movement without clear articulated lines, a ghost of some once-known figure, from dream or myth, who is yet, here and now, the stranger.

4

SCENE 1

Into the Hollow

The initial negativity of Edgar is remarkable.[1] It is an exercise in penumbral characterization, a figure whose substance is shade. The Folio text cuts the only line in the Quarto that hints at personality ("How long have you been a sectary Astronomicall," I. ii. 165), and the virtue we are happy to concede him is characterized by little more than absentminded gullibility: "a brother Noble, / Whose nature is so farre from doing harmes, / That he suspects none" (TLN 499–501).

His younger brother declares that his father wants him dead, and Edgar believes it. This alone, we might think, signifies the need for the elder brother's immediate sacrifice. It is hard to dissent from what Granville-Barker calls Edmund's "proper contempt," or from his judgment of his brother as a kind of woebegone Dulcinea, good for little but the knackers-yard, "on whose foolish honestie / My practices ride easie"

---

1. Harley Granville-Barker: "Edgar himself is indeed dismissed from the second scene upon no more allowance of speech than 'I'm sure on't, not a word'—with which the best of actors may find it hard to make his presence felt; and at our one view of him before he had been left negative enough." A later footnote of Granville-Barker's is astute: "it follows that upon these lines [Edmund's false allegations] we cannot be brought to a very close knowledge of Edgar too. Give him the same scope, and he must either get on the track of the truth or prove himself as great a fool as his father. So Shakespeare, now and at his next appearance, does as little with him as possible. This delays—and dangerously—our gaining interest in him. But a play survives sins of omission when the smallest sin of commission may damn it." *Prefaces to Shakespeare*, Vol. 1 (London: B. T. Batsford Ltd., 1930), 273, 314.

(TLN 501–502).[2] Hence Edmund's opening cue for his brother: "Pat: he comes like the Catastrophe of the old Comedie" (TLN 463). Edgar is the belated harbinger of mock-tragic closure: hostage to an outmoded world, missing the joke, trundling his automaton path to doom. And at the same time as Edmund is mocking his brother as a man out of time, he is preparing to make Edgar a puppet in his own up-to-the-minute fairground motion.

All of this is true. But Shakespeare doesn't allow us a full share in Edmund's ascendant contempt. The primary thing about Edgar is that he is released, with as little harm as possible, into future trials. He arrives to depart. But of course he hasn't truly arrived at all. Shakespeare always takes great care with his introductions; they are always predicative, if not predictive. Edgar's predicate, then, is this oddly manufactured mix: an emptiness which is somehow open to experiment, and therein abuse. Existentially he can start from nothing, be flung into nothing, be nothing, and from that condition take on any number of burdens and losses and traumas. In the most basic sense, the Edgar-role can relive mortal peril from nakedness to the grave and back.

At the same time, this absence, this cipher, is a man of substance. Lest we forget, Edgar is an elder brother, the inheritor-in-wait to a dukedom. Timon apart, there is no starker case in Shakespeare of a fall from fullness. It is important, however, that Shakespeare never lets us witness Edgar in his comfort and pomp, or even in his active decency. We cannot rest, as we might in a comedy, in the assumption that he is on a temporary exile from fullness and possession. He is never anything but nothing. What he has been, as much as what he may or would or should be, must be discovered in what he finds. It is precisely this catalytic emptiness that warrants us identifying memory and recapitulation in his subsequent masks and personae. The compositional principle of the part is diffidence and lacunae, and therefore inferential temptation. But it is also nothingness, nonbeing as the condition of persisting: a condition in some basic sense not to be outgrown.

He arrives to depart; or we might say he departs so as to arrive. The second coming of Edgar is his first soliloquy:

---

2. Ibid., 319.

> I heard my selfe proclaim'd,
> And by the happy hollow of a Tree,
> Escap'd the hunt. No Port is free, no place
> That guard, and most unusall vigilance
> Do's not attend my taking. Whiles I may scape
> I will preserue myselfe: and am bethought
> To take the basest, and most poorest shape
> That euer penury in contempt of man,
> Brought neere to beast; my face Ile grime with filth,
> Blanket my loines, elfe all my haires in knots,
> And with presented nakedness out-face
> The Windes, and persecutions of the skie.
> The Country giues me proofe, and president
> Of Bedlam beggars, who with roaring voices,
> Strike in their num'd and mortified [Quarto: bare] Armes,
> Pins, Wodden-prickes, nayles, Sprigs of Rosemarie:
> And with this horrible object, from low Farmes,
> Poore pelting Villages, Sheeps-Coates, and Milles,
> Sometimes with Lunaticke bans, sometime with Praiers
> Inforce their charitie: poore *Turlygod* poore *Tom*,
> That's something yet: *Edgar* I nothing am.
>
> (TLN 1252-72; italics in original)

The speech is helpfully detailed, explaining what has happened and what he will now do. Only one thing is missing. Why *this* disguise? The pragmatic explanation is that he is trapped on the island. No port is free; exile here will be internal; he will go to ground and emerge only from there. But this hardly accounts for the disguise's excessiveness, or for Edgar's move from secret pain to this baroque performance of suffering.[3]

---

3. Elaine Scarry notes that torture is often accompanied by the "false motive syndrome": "it prevents the mind from ever getting to the place where it would have to make such comparisons" between causing or witnessing pain and suffering it. "Power is cautious. It covers itself. It bases itself in another's pain and prevents all recognition that there is 'another' by looped circles that ensure its own solipsism." *The Body in Pain: The Making and Unmaking of the World* (Oxford: Oxford University Press, 1985), 58-59. Perhaps to think of Edgar in this

Edgar is being taken by purposes far beyond the immediacies of plot and strategy. Correspondingly, the noun phrases shimmer with abstracting, allegorical susceptibility. So it is clear that the shape he is forming will show contempt for humankind, but it is unclear whether he is expressing or suffering this contempt. His simulation might be an epic act of sympathy, a taking on of the worst in the name of suffering humanity.[4] Equally, Edgar may be unraveling from comfortable association with his own supposed species: "man" has become cruel and alien. There is a suggestion of pickling or salting in "preserue," as the pins and pricks immerse him in elements that will transform his very chemistry, rendering a quite new microbiological constitution. The sum effect is an ontological question mark: something in between human, animal, spirit, man-god, even vegetable—and yet still something other. This is not just a figural thing. Edgar really is opening up to possibilities outside inherited categories.

At a glance, Edgar's move into exile may seem to resemble Agamben's account of the state of exception:

> He who has been banned is not, in fact, simply set outside the law and made indifferent to it but rather *abandoned* by it, that is, exposed and threatened on the threshold in which life and law, outside and inside, become indistinguishable. It is literally not possible to say whether the one who has been banned is outside or inside the juridical order.[5]

In this paradoxical model, the condition of banishment becomes paradigmatic of "the structure of sovereignty": there is nothing outside

---

way is strange; it makes of Tom's torture something like a recapitulated expression of Edgar's complicity—as a silent partaker in and inheritor of unjust institutions—in the same systems of cruelty that send him running for his life. But does he ever allow himself to recognize Tom's pain or to explain his own creating of it? See the discussion of Simone Weil and decreation in the Interlude following Scene 6.

4. Paul Ricoeur: "The suffering, or rather the act of suffering, is revealed as that liminal action which is already setting itself up in opposition to fate. It is as a response, a counterthrust, a defiance, that suffering begins to be tragic and not only lyric." *The Symbolism of Evil*, trans. Emerson Buchanan (Boston: Beacon, 1969), 221.

5. Giorgio Agamben, *Homo Sacer: Sovereign Power and Bare Life*, trans. Daniel Heller-Roazen (Stanford, Calif.: Stanford University Press, 1998), 28–29; italics in original.

the law. Sovereignty is never more sovereign than when it establishes realms of surveillance beyond jurisdictional and geographical boundaries; the banished man becomes a roving instantiation of limitless state power. But Edgar has not been banished. He has been sentenced to death.

Whereas banishment grants the fact of exile a curious legal status, gives to homelessness and itinerance a certain supracitizenship, Edgar is simply running. His continued existing is not sanctioned by law; nor does it reconstitute sovereignty in some liminal zone, or even in the hounded and hiding form of his body. His condition eludes such totalizing paradoxes. Perhaps a version of sovereign power (partly Gloucester's diktat, partly Edgar as structural partner to the king-kicked Cordelia) produces his internal exile. But it doesn't define his abjection, which is far more than some diffused or saturating center.[6] Edgar suffers an absorption, in his own body, of an almost panoramic countryside, his body engrossing a mill, a sheepcote, a "pelting" village. But his "new" body also engrosses the figures excluded from these humble sites of work and community. It is no composed microcosm, with the nation snug and secure inside his motions. If he is composing a body, it is anything but classical. Bits stick out—the pins and pricks are like a visual metaphor of this inassimilable remainder. The disguise is one and many, inclusive and excluded, but its tension comes from the fact that the many is defined in apposition to the one, and that inclusion is premised on excluding certain particulars.[7]

But if all this is preparing meticulously for Tom, the soliloquy also works to preserve Edgar: with it he protects himself, but also remains himself. His intention is camouflage rather than simple hiding—perhaps an obscuring that will allow him to pounce; perhaps a shoring up,

---

6. Eric L. Santner: "What I am calling creaturely life is the life that is, so to speak, called into being, *ex-cited*, by exposure to the peculiar 'creativity' associated with this threshold of law and nonlaw; it is the life that has been delivered over to the space of the sovereign's 'ecstasy-belonging,' or what we might simply call 'sovereign jouissance.'" *On Creaturely Life: Rilke, Benjamin, Sebald* (Chicago: University of Chicago Press, 2006), 15.

7. Grigori Kozintsev: "With Edgar's transformation into a beggar the whole expanse of grief is introduced into the poetry in all its breadth, revealing the geography of the country of poverty." *King Lear, the Space of Tragedy: The Diary of a Film Director*, trans. Mary Mackintosh (London, Heinemann Educational Publishers, 1977), 117.

a regathering and honing of energy. The phrases express bedrock defiance, but also toy with charade and contingency. So, "presented" partly withdraws the ultimacy of "nakedness": it is in part a show, a pantomime of self-reduction. Likewise, "out-face" is both a verb (to defy, rebuke, outlast) and a noun (the countenance outside in the elements). The pun suggests a man watching himself debase himself, mordant about life's strange turns; he will indeed be subject to unusual vigilance. And in a curious sense the "happy hollow" remains throughout the play the place of Edgar's secret abiding. Tom moves out; Edgar moves in. We can imagine its stillness and darkness as the dogs and sheriffs roar by, a cocoon of intense and silent concentration. This is the gift of transgression, of criminal audacity. Edgar's is a channel, albeit framed by beleaguered captivity, into a kind of anxious apperception, more alive than ever before, seeing everything as if brand new.

Perhaps something can indeed come from nothing; or perhaps Edgar simply hibernates, comatose in the scenic cleft, as his doppelganger goes and does the business. Like a tiny sac of endangered potential, he tucks part of himself away, a coiled honing, and spools out his virtual self-figurations. For the "happy hollow of a Tree" is more than a convenient fiction to explain Edgar's escape. It is part of the landscape and—as a fabulous enclosing—a gap or fold within this landscape, a pocket in space-time where abeyance is. But like Ariel's knotty pine, the "happy hollow" simultaneously inaugurates a protean futurity. It thus resembles an Ovidian magic place: suspension outside time, but equally a place of hushed and furious gestation. It is one of the role's true self-correspondent spaces.

And one more thing: it is obvious that Edgar's dressing down apes the notorious habits of roving indigents. But partly because of this imitation, it opens seriously onto the scriptural precedents that Edgar consciously pillages. He evokes Christ on the Calvary path, with Edgar himself performing the service of jeering soldiers, dressing the martyr in the paraphernalia of humiliation. This is not to say that he renders himself a simple Christ-figure.[8] It is a pastiche as much of pathetic sim-

---

8. Jonathan Miller's BBC production makes much of this, focusing in later scenes on stigmata on Edgar-Tom's hands and a crown of thorns on his head.

ulators as of Christ's original model. The deepest intensity finds expression in layered fraudulence.

This makes it difficult to judge intent. In some ways Edgar's self-mortification suggests what Erwin Panofsky has called a pseudomorphosis, whereby images take on meanings that are not present in the precursor (Christ), a precursor that nevertheless still informs them. Different times and places, different morphologies intersect, irreducible to any single unity. We might get an illegitimate effigy of a long past truth, or a painful recollection of the same; we might get some new cultural hybrid, sketching as-yet undefined possibilities.[9] And yet this same pleonastic overdetermination—copying countrywide frauds, who copy other frauds, who copy Christ, who was mocked and scourged precisely as a fraud—gives Edgar's imposture something of the deliberative composure of an artwork: one that in full recognition of precedents, knowing form to be synthetic and meaning hostage to mediation, nevertheless touches the scandal, the raw beauty, of the idea. Here, the idea of a suffering, the most enormous commitment to self-abatement, that with willed, ablative fierceness takes on *everything*.[10]

The crucial word is "mortified"—the body is humiliated, ashamed, suffering; the body is also dead, a slab to be studied. Edgar's reducing of self to a "horrible object" really does rehearse self-erasure, and so a

---

9. Erwin Panofsky, *Studies in Iconology: Humanistic Themes in the Art of the Renaissance* (New York: Harper and Row, 1972), 71. Likewise suggestive for the layered iconography in Tom is the theory of substitution developed by Alexander Nagel and Christopher S. Wood in *Anachronic Renaissance* (New York: Zone Books, 2010), 29–50 *passim*. Also see Peter Mason, *Infelicities: Representations of the Exotic* (Baltimore: Johns Hopkins University Press, 1998), 13–14.

10. Scarry: "It is the absolute intention of all human making to distribute the facts of sentience outward onto the created realm of artifice, and it is only by doing so that men and women are relieved of the privacy and problems of that sentience." *Body in Pain*, 288. Also compare Nietzsche's fable of the movement into Apollonian form in his *The Birth of Tragedy*, in which artistic form is recovered from the furnace of self-undoing torture. Jane Goodall gives specific theatrical application to similar ideas: "The dimension of performance lifts the phenomenon of agony from its status as an expression of disempowerment and defeat to a new status as a mode of action and signification which in itself constitutes a potent challenge to mechanisms of power and control. If suffering represents the occulted trace of a recalcitrant will, the theatricalization of suffering is its reinstatement as a force belonging to will and consciousness." "To make theatre is to generate a force field; to be an actor is to 'brutalise' forms: . . . but behind these forms, and through their destruction, he joins with something that survives forms and produces their continuation." *Artaud and the Gnostic Drama* (Oxford: Oxford University Press, 1994), 102–103, 105.

passing into nonbeing.[11] Perhaps it is only rehearsed death or rehearsed dying: but the experience is at the very edge of existential permission, of what the body or the mind can bear, of the possibilities that life can survive to. And unlike Christ—but perhaps like Job—Edgar is condemned to survive.

---

11. Compare here the Calvinist notion that the subject should internalize death as a prerequisite of selfhood: "We also die in ourselves, that we may live in him": John Calvin, *Commentary on Romans*, Vol. 38, 6:5, trans. John King (1847–1850), www.sacred-texts.com/chr/calvin/cc38/cc38009.htm. See also Adrian Streete, *Protestantism and Drama in Early Modern England* (Cambridge, U.K.: Cambridge University Press, 2009), ch. 5, on Calvinist exegesis, mimesis, and *Doctor Faustus*.

5

INTERLUDE

Job Redux

> We have *Iobs* Anatomy, *Iobs* Sceleton, the ruins to which he was reduced.... Now, let me ask in *Iobs* behalfe Gods question to Ezekiel.... *Doest thou believe that these bones can live?* Can this Anatomy, this Sceleton, these ruines, this rubbidge of *Iob* speake?[1]

Both thematically and technically, the Edgar-role engages with sudden bereavement. It asks whether this violence can be borne or understood, and whether anything can return from the wreckage. It is clear that in plotting this passage Shakespeare had Job in his mind. Both Edgar and Job are emptied not only of possessions, but of all publicly endorsed personality and reputation. Whereas Job, as Primo Levi has it, is rendered the guinea pig in God's frightful laboratory, Edgar makes of himself a laboratory of both "selfe" and world.[2] If this suggests Job's rebirth out of his devastated epidermis, then it might also suggest Job's secret wish to be hidden in a grave, as though in contingent death: "O that thou woldest hide me in the grave, and keepe me secret, until thy wrath were past, and woldest give me term, and remember me" (Job 14:13).[3]

---

1. John Donne, *The Sermons of John Donne*, Vol. 9, ed. Evelyn M. Simpson and George R. Potter (Berkeley: University of California Press, 1958), 214, 217; italics in original.
2. Primo Levi, *The Search for Roots: A Personal Anthology*, trans. Peter Forbes (Chicago: Ivan R. Dee, 2002), 3–17.
3. Quotations from Job in this chapter are from the 1560 Geneva translation.

This subjective evacuation can also be understood as a temporal interruption and reconstitution. Job is taken by way of multiplying calamities beyond the lifespan of anyone he has ever known; he is a thousand years old, despairingly infinite, because he has witnessed the deaths of everything he has ever given life. Equally, in having had everything taken from him, he is divested into radical incipience: no longer a father, lost from God, suddenly orphaned. But he endures, and so he is also in a state of about-to-be, or of could-possibly-be: a radical susceptibility we might call negative capability. This devastation—surviving death, and in that somehow unkillable—is given memorable form in Job's potsherd and dunghill. There he sits, scratching himself in a mocking objectification of thinking, upon a mound made up of the ashes of his children, the dust of his belongings, and the filaments of his ravaged skin.

And just so might Edgar be imagined, between his "happy hollow" soliloquy and Tom's first appearance. What does he do in this gap? The actor, we might suppose, spends the time sticking pins in his arm, stripping down to a towel, rubbing mud into his wrinkles. But what does the character do? What does he think? Does he experience anything at all in the scenic break? One response to such questions is that he experiences "subterranean synapses" with the world of Job, as anyone might who survives the loss of all possessions, relations, and identity.[4] Edgar's passage into the *blanc* between scenes finds its correlate in Job's plunge into seven days' silence. In both cases, the interim is at once bereft of content and chock-full with pasts and possibilities: a hiatal plenum.

Consider the first return of Job into speech, after God has murdered his children and his servants, razed all else to the ground, and left Job with nothing but a foully afflicted body. And at the same time consider Edgar: as he is cast out; as he stows himself in a tree and then in a hovel; as he emerges, with dizzying procreative wildness, to figure forth degradations and temptations, spent worlds and future dispensations; as he moves between demon and revenger and comforter, life-hater and life-rescuer; and then how all the time, in every single moment, he re-

---

4. Julia Reinhard Lupton, *Thinking with Shakespeare: Essays on Politics and Life* (Chicago: University of Chicago Press, 2011), 147.

mains a figure of faith, religiously trembling, wishing that obedience were easier.

Job's great complaint emerges out of three linked conditions: first, his seven days of silence and self-enclosing; second, the friends who watch him in his grief; and third, the fact that he cannot die. (We might surmise that it isn't the admonition to "curse God" that his wife gets wrong [2:9], but the assumption that having done so he might creep away "and die."[5]) These are the predicates of Job's condition, and the key to his intimacy with Edgar. For in a sense he forever dwells in this long seven days' silence.[6] His subsequent torrents speak of this dwelling, a backward unfolding of the narrative that broods in his week of silence. It is the text of his meditation, and more specifically the thumping, obsessive repetitiveness of grief and grievance:

> Let the day perish wherein I was borne, and the night when it was said, There is a manchilde conceived.
> Let that day be darknes; let not God regarde it from above, nether let the light shine upon it.
> But let darknes, & the shadowe of death staine it: let a cloud remaine upon it, & let them make it feareful as a bitter day.
> Let darknes possesse that night; let it not be joined unto the days of the year, nor let it come into the count of the moneths.
> Yea, desolate be that night, & let no joye be in it.
> Let them that curse the day, (being ready to renue their mourning) curse it.

---

5. Richard Clerke in his *Sermons* (London: T. Cotes, 1637) calls the wife's "corrupt and rotten" words "a monsters speech"; she is, says Clerke, "but the devils *Eccho*," speaking "the devilles *Dialect*" (300). Calvin, similarly, calls her "a Sheedeuill, or . . . a feend of hell." *Sermons of Master Iohn Calvin Vpon the Booke of IOB*, trans. Arthur Golding (London: Lucas Harison and George Byshop, 1574), 40. The introduction to Job in the Geneva Bible talks of the "sharpe tentations" of Job's wife; "tentation" means temptation, but also "probing," as in a wound (tent). The wife's presence in *Lear* is spectral and diffused: partly into the women who enslave Tom in irreligious bondage; partly into the devil-take-the-hindmost dominatrix, Goneril.

6. Bruce Zuckerman sees Job as a covert parody of the traditional religious sufferer as patient or silent. *Job The Silent: A Study in Historical Counterpoint* (Oxford: Oxford University Press, 1991).

> Let the starres of that twilight be dim through darknes of it; let it look for light, but have none; nether let it se[e] the dawning of the daye:
> Because it shut not up the dores of my mother's womb: nor hid sorowe from mine eyes. (3:3-10)

Calvin's response to the speech is fascinating—at once appalled, censorious, beguiled, and ameliorating:

> Wee see here as it were a tempest or storme that maketh Iob both deafe and blinded . . . and wee shrinke our selues inwarde in suche wyse, as wee dare not once put out our heads. Euen so stoode the case with Iob.[7]

Such is Job's blasphemy that Calvin is forced to think that he "did lette slippe such woordes at random."[8] But the words are deeply cogitated, and strike at the heart of Job's dilemma. Certainly he is cursing God, offering an almost theomorphic challenge.[9] But still more foundationally, Job is cursing life and calling for what he knows is for him impossible: death. The speech thus manufactures a kind of proxy death-cell—Job's version of a world-excluding "happy hollow." Just like Edgar on the cusp of becoming-Tom, Job's curses seek a separate channel, a black-magic space into which—and inside which—he can send *and* suffer his malediction. Job is asking that a particular fragment of the creation—the miserable day of his birth—be granted to him as his correspondent space of eclipse. He wants it to be severed as he has been severed; he wants it to become an echo-chamber of mourning, as he has become; he wants it to be inconsolably "solitary," as he is now; and he wants it to be dark, beyond all dawning, and dead, as he to all intents feels himself to be. It is as rebellious a statement as can be imagined.

Job's entire life now appeals to him as a preparation for suffering.

---

7. Calvin, *Sermons*, 56.
8. Ibid., 54.
9. Calvin: "But now it seemeth that he turneth all topsi terviw, and that he is angrie with God. . . . Iob then is here as it were in a mamering. . . . Wordes escape him which are euill, and proceede from a faultie minde, and can not be iustified." *Sermons*, 47.

Everything was built to be lost, in one day of Armageddon. His curse insists upon exactly this predestined misery. Correspondingly, the cosmic damnation he seeks is at once torturously gradual and shockingly sudden. He pleads for a blanket eclipse, as though ineradicably switching off a light. But the sheer scope of the agents, all of those slowly suffocating clouds, and voices joined in mourning, and endlessly repeated solitude, has the effect of a huge armoring of the cosmic arsenal, an epic militarization specifically to mark, to mourn, and to eternalize one man's devastation. It is an aesthetic frieze, suspending Job in an eternal pathetic fallacy, as he travels far out of himself and transforms a slice of space-time into an allegory precisely of *him*.[10]

But it is a simulacrum of annihilation that Job—as both poet and subject—must survive. Hence Job's strange posthumousness, his status as self-mortician. He witnesses it all, like some cursed revenant at a beyond-tragic theater, unable to depart the scene of the undead. Because survival, not death, is the ultimate punishment. This is why the final thing returned to Job is not livestock or slaves or even children, but precisely death: "So Job dyed, being olde, and ful of dayes" (42:17). Edgar at play's end perhaps looks ahead to some such comfort ("We that are young / Shall never see so much, nor live so long")—but still it is refused him. In *King Lear*, Shakespeare takes inspiration less from the Book of Job's horizontal narrative arc (loss, protest, restitution) than from the radical verticality of a single moment—that of absolute abandonment and privation—and how this moment can instantly extend as a life sentence.

It has long been recognized that Lear echoes Job.[11] The King too prays

---

10. Calvin: "But here Iob passeth somewhat further. For he woulde plucke the stares out of the skie, he would set the whole worlde on fire to burne vp the earth, and he would haue the cloudes, and the windes, and all things els too mingle themselues together at this desire." *Sermons*, 50-51. Calvin elsewhere notes Job's love of "fine Rhetoricke": "He coulde not holde himselfe from this kinde of Rhetorike which is totoo flowing. For whereto serveth his setting downe of so many fashions of speache, which ehe heapeth up as it were into a little pyle" (*Sermons*, 57).

11. See, for example, John Holloway, "King Lear," in *Shakespeare: King Lear, a Casebook*, rev. ed., ed. Frank Kermode (London: Macmillan, 1992), 185-88; Rosalie Colie, "The Energies of Endurance: Biblical Echo in *King Lear*," in *Some Facets of* King Lear: *Essays in Prismatic Criticism*, ed. Rosalie Colie and F. T. Flahiff (London: University of Toronto Press, 1974), 117-41; Harold Bloom, *William Shakespeare's* King Lear (New Haven: Yale University Press, 1987); Steven Marx,

for a small part of the creation to witness his specific suffering; he seeks to universalize his own discursive circumstances; he seeks partners in crying; he would turn the entire world into his own echo. But if much of Lear's protest echoes the overreaching, optative impotence of Job's cries, it is Edgar who is truly taken by this cry, rendered the somatic and pneumatic echo of a world in pain and fury. His "strange mutations" make Job come true again:

> I shal say to corruption, Thou art my father, and to the worm, Thou art my mother and my sister. (17:14)

> And hast made me ful of wrinkles which is a witness thereof, and my leanness riseth up in me, testifying *the same* in my face. (16:8)

In Job and Edgar both, the human subject's most intimate words—I, me, my—become weirdly alien. The blank pronominal impasse—so plaintive and baffled, almost mute in wonder and protest—suggests how a vestige of "old" Job watches this new specter rising up to claim him, indeed almost to name and shame him ("a witness against *me*," as the King James Version has it [italics in original]). And yet this foul body becomes the thing in which he most surely sees what he is, what he must accept and recognize as himself: "*my* leanness rising up in *me*" (italics in original). The image is scandalously kinetic, the "rising" provoking the kick of recoil, the gorge of disgust, as Job's body turns before his very eyes into an acting of undoing. Hence the terrifying near-oxymoron of "leanness rising": it invokes a burgeoning of emaciation,

---

Shakespeare and the Bible (Oxford: Oxford University Press, 2000). Edgar is rarely mentioned in these accounts, which concentrate on the king, the storm, and structuring patterns of suffering and endurance, loss and return. Booth sees correlations in the "comfort provided by pattern" in both tales. *King Lear, Macbeth, Indefinition, and Tragedy* (New Haven: Yale University Press, 1983), 27–28. The exception is Harold Fisch: "Naked, helpless, and demanding our pity, and at the same time innocent of any wrongdoing, Edgar as the bedlam beggar is the most obviously Job-like figure in the play.... He is essentially Job on his dunghill.... In the figure of Edgar Shakespeare's play thus provides a Joban contrast to the Promethean model." *The Biblical Presence in Shakespeare, Milton, and Blake: A Comparative Study* (Oxford: Oxford University Press, 1999), 127.

an enveloping vacancy, as though he is mutating into wrinkle, or the nightmare accordion coils of a worm.

And yet Job is also the potential vessel of a new creation tale—an audacious, even scandalous pertinacity. For there is a passion in Job that will not wait for God, will not submit to his brutal kneading and bolting. In Calvin's reading, the very thought of self-collection betrays Job's susceptibility to temptation. Thus he identifies in 14:4 ("Who can bring foorth a cleane thing out of uncleannesse?") an errant nostalgia, as Job longs for "*some starting hole*, to abate the damnation that lieth upon all men."[12]

The lesson here can seem chilling for human agency: it is God's province alone to give and to take away; his alone to rebuild or restore, in his own good time. The key question pertains to God's withdrawal. Has he gone? Or is he just watching, waiting for his moment?[13] The answer in Job is always the latter—sadistically enough, it can often seem. But Shakespeare, I think, takes the subjunction seriously.[14] This is the moment he recovers as the immanent environment of his playworld. *What if God truly has gone?*[15] In *Lear* the satanic wager that God makes at Job's expense is no aberration, no jesting hypothetical. Divinity truly is indistinguishable from capricious fortune and captive-making passion. And this is where Edgar-Tom's experiences join with Job's: not in his intermittent clinging to faith and hope, but in the terror of the interim that has become the reality, when the bare facts of living are

---

12. *Sermons*, 250; italics in original.

13. Job: "Beholde, if I go to the East, he is not there: if to the West, yet I can not perceive him: If to the North where he worketh, yet I can not se him: he wil hide him self in the South, and I can not beholde him." 23:8–9.

14. Jan Kott: "It is Job's stage that constitutes the main scene. On it the ironic, clownish morality play on human fate will be performed. But before that happens, all the characters must be uprooted from their social positions and pulled down, to final degradation . . . repeated at least four times." But whereas the biblical book of Job is a "theatre of the priests," in *Lear* (and in Samuel Beckett's *Endgame*) "the *Book of Job* is performed by clowns": *Shakespeare Our Contemporary*, trans. Boleslaw Taborski (London: Methuen, 1964), 124, 128.

15. Julia Reinhard Lupton: "Shakespeare draws on Job, in all of its proto-secular literary ambivalence, in order to create a religious zone in his texts that is not strictly theological, in which God enters as an afterthought, a late addition, and thus can be imagined as not entering at all." *Thinking with Shakespeare: Essays on Politics and Life* (Chicago: University of Chicago Press, 2011), 158

withdrawal and pain, Job stuck in his hole with nothing but a stripped body and a voice.

And the result: these figures have to substitute for themselves, become their own hostages, weave fantastical para-worlds in the face of shutdown. But there is far more than abjection in this. Calvin's condemnation speaks eloquently of the radical potency of such speaking: the possibility of voice to coin forgotten or alternative lives; for criminal pretense or blasphemous imagination or merely suffering protest, in the face of government's withdrawal or tyranny, to claim historical or even prophetic authority. Where Edgar channels misery into a sequence of disguises, Job imagines his words printed in a book—a text to monumentalize his lacerated voice, a stone to hold the stray dribbles and shattered corpus of the body.

> Why do ye persecute me, as God? and are not satisfied with my flesh?
> Oh that my wordes were now writen! Oh that they were written even in a boke!
> And graven with an yron pen in lede, or in stone for ever.
> (19:22–24)[16]

Job projects into the condition of his own death, longing to exchange the mutable flesh for cast stone and the wailing voice for the "graven" inscription. It is the necessary price for the audience he longs for, and also a template for the redemption that he trusts will then come

---

16. Jonathan Lamb identifies these lines, along with the ones that follow—"For I know that my redeemer liveth" (19:25)—as a "textual-redemptive event": Job is "presenting himself as an issue capable of recurring by means of the interaction of two substitutes or delegates: the text in the rock, and the redeemer who will release its message and vindicate its author.... This writing will act as a bandage to soothe, or as a garment to hide, the pain of the other writing, whose message he will never understand, which is inscribed in his boils and ulcers.... Only if the temptation to narrativize the advent of the redeemer is resisted will the sequence of substitutions—mark for flesh, book for mark, engraved rock for book, redeemer for rock, Job for redeemer—reconcile the various agencies mentioned and the times in which they are supposed to operate." *The Rhetoric of Suffering: Reading the Book of Job in the Eighteenth Century* (Oxford: Oxford University Press, 1995), 45–46, 48. Much the same analysis can be applied to Edgar's "delegation" to (or of) Tom.

("For I am sure, that my Redeemer liveth," 19:25). Job's wish is impossibly whimsical, but of course it has also already come true. His speaking is contingent on a prior act of writing. Job's is a brief moment of metagraphic awareness, predicting how his despair has become a text and therein cashed in—and as the Wisdom Book's typological logic implies, implicitly redeemed.

But there are strange cruelties inside all of this. Job is in his pain, howling in degradation and powerlessness. He projects into the eternalizing power of God, as though to say, *Write me*, or *Write upon me; turn me into an example*. But he is simultaneously beyond the event, safely exemplary, a wise patriarch and loved child of God. Consequently, he is made complicit in the desperate pact that makes the book possible. Job is split. He is the man abandoned to his pain, a true radical of unaccommodated possibility; and he is the prototype of faith, seeing what is needed to make the suffering worthwhile. The ironies are deep and troubling. Does Job repeat the scandalous bogusness of God and Satan's catalytic wager, visiting horrors upon "Job" for the sake of a lesson? And what then of Edgar's Tom? Is he also a fake experiment? A disguise that isn't truly a crystal of possibility, but is instead always superintended by the scripter who survives it? A thing that, whatever its pretensions to personhood, is finally an object, defined by teleological dialectic, created for the purpose of testing and affirming the triumphant subject?

Hegel is the great thinker of such processes—not so much in his *Lectures on Aesthetics* (a defining influence on A. C. Bradley's understanding of Shakespearean tragedy) as in his *The Phenomenology of Spirit*. In particular, we might recall his celebrated account of lordship and bondage, a stunning parable of the becoming of self-consciousness. Briefly: subjectivity requires some reflecting other, the mirror that confirms one's coherence as a subject. But according to Hegel's parable, the consequent recognition is murderous, and produces a fight to the death. The mirror is a rival and a threat, to be sublated into one's serviceable object: subjectivity is predicated on the other's subjection. But then in Hegel's next twist, the "slave" finds dignity through "work" (here is the Hegel that Marx fed upon). He may be tortured, the affliction might seem unending, but there is greater nourishment for evolving self-consciousness in productive abjection than in a power beyond account or challenge:

> Work . . . is desire held in check, fleetingness staved off; in other words, work forms and shapes the thing. The negative relation to the object becomes its *form* and something permanent, because it is precisely for the worker that the object has independence. . . . This *negative* middle term or the formative *activity* is at the same time the individuality or pure being-for-self which now, in the work outside of it, acquires an element of permanence. . . . The shape [the external thing made by the bondsman] does not become something other than himself through being made external to him; for it is precisely this shape that is his pure being-for-self, which in this externality is seen by him to be the truth. . . . If consciousness fashions the thing without that initial absolute fear, it is only an empty self-centred attitude. . . . If it has not experienced absolute fear but only some lesser dread, the negative being has remained for it something external, its substance has not been infected by it through and through.[17]

So the slave works and produces self-correspondent artifacts, external translations of both misery and dignity; these at once acknowledge unfreedom and project beyond it, into the instinct for freedom that motivates the resistance and its arts. We might see this as an antinomian accommodation to suffering and cruelty, both legitimated by teleology. Or we might see it (as Marx did) as a testament to something unkillable about the human spirit, however much it is reduced to what Edgar calls a "horrible *object*" (italics in original). In this reading, objecthood is the truly necessary condition. And it is this that explains and justifies Tom: a piece of "work," a "shape" fashioned from "absolute fear," "infected by it through and through," whose very "externality" can be recognized as Edgar's "pure being-for-self," and thus garner prophetic pathos. Work makes you free.

Perhaps this will do for Edgar. Perhaps it is his terrible sentimental education, a serious version of the future prince slumming it, immersing himself in alien conditions the better to "feel" them when he is king. Perhaps the play ends with the barely-spoken promise, presaged

---

17. G. W. F. Hegel, *The Phenomenology of Spirit*, trans. A. V. Miller (Oxford: Oxford University Press, 1977), 118–19; italics in original.

in Hegel, that dread and loss are purposive, that suffering, in the scale of things, is for the best.

But life must protest: on behalf of life, named or not. Tom lives, Cordelia lives, just as Job's slaves and children and animals lived. They lived, and were swept away, before finally being tabulated in the arithmetic of genre. I want to insist on their lives, and on the grief felt at their going. Perhaps something returns at the work's end: but not them. Some substitutions are not ethical. And by the same logic, I want to insist upon Tom.

6

SCENE 2

Enter Tom

The first thing to recognize about the storm scenes is that this is no longer a normative social world. These scenes ensue from absolute expulsion—expulsion from visible life, nameable life, family life, legal life. But as exceptional as their conditions are, it is not quite right to understand the situation as the notorious "state of exception"—a state-controlled precinct beyond legalistic niceties. Certainly the terrifying castles of Regan and Cornwall suggest just such a state, in which the body of the subject is at the mercy of the lawless, law-enforcing sovereign. Indeed the whole of this playworld is a kind of exploded state of exception, in which there is at once no sovereign at all and too many of them; each is in some irreducible way illegitimate, even the "good" ones: Lear because he is a tyrant or has abdicated, Albany because he is an impotent consort, Cordelia because she is the queen of France.

There is no point worrying here about constitutional niceties, as we might rightly do in the English history plays; such niceties do not exist. But the storm scenes propose something still more radical: history, its time and place and all its institutions, is foundationally unwritten, perhaps de-written. Whether we conceive of this terrain as pre- or posthistorical, the eye of sovereignty, legitimate or not, cannot quite spy into it. Edgar has "escap'd the hunt," and Lear admits no rival authorities other than the gods. Shakespeare thus cracks open the "egg," or slides through the earth's "fault," and enters a place that in vital ways is not compossible with the built world.

To say this is not to deny other possible worlds in these scenes—for example, the world of the miserable and poor. But it also isn't such a world. It is violently unprecedented. The action leaves all the castles behind, and tears the curtain into the torn world. From the moment action is cued by *"Storm still"*—notated in the Folio no less than six times—it is clear that a new principle of matter and motion is in play. The opening exchange of the storm scenes tells us as much:

> *Storme still. Enter Kent, and a Gentleman, severally.*
> *Kent*. Who's there besides foule weather?
> *Gen*. One minded like the weather, most unquietly. (TLN 1615-17)

The Quarto text is perhaps better: *"What's* here?" Kent asks, as though unsure whether personal pronouns still apply. It is no accident that the same species-straddling questions surround Tom's delivery: *"Who's* there?" *"What* art thou that dost grumble there ith' straw?" asks Kent, as though fearing some demonic talking piglet (my italics). Elementary distinctions are under threat. It isn't enough to speak of pathetic fallacies or the like—dark and stormy weather, dark and stormy minds—as much as this is pertinent. Things are literally porous, permeable, mutating from the swamp.[1]

This liquid creativity finds particular expression in Lear. Often he speaks in petulant rage, wishing for the impossible, or so it will seem to those of a more secular bent. But Lear, I think, always speaks with absolute simplicity and literalness, and as a primitive king expects his words to come true. Nothing is abstract for the old king—everything

---

1. Timothy Morton: "The ecological thought consists in intimacy with the strange stranger. We can't ever predict exactly who or what strange strangers are, whether they are a 'who' or a 'what.' If we can, then we are still clinging to a reified concept of Nature . . . Since the strange stranger is not my mirror, there is no way of knowing whether she, or he, or it is a person. So before we get to mutual recognition, we must have radical openness. . . . The encounter is loving, risky, perverse. Because the strange stranger is uncanny and uncertain, she, he, or it must give us pause. . . . The idea of species is far too rigid and arbitrary to account for the mutagenic, liquid strange stranger." *The Ecological Thought* (Cambridge, Mass.: Harvard University Press, 2010), 46, 80-81, 85.

is peopled, charactered, personified. Even his insults and hyperbole are, in his scale of things, oddly domestic. He presumes the intimacy of gods, who are as titanic and as childlike as he is. (Lear's speech often anticipates the "salvage beast" Caliban in *The Tempest*, judging things very elementally, according to understood gradations of value—high, low, more, less.) Albeit channeled as an old man's strained or superannuated prejudices, his speech is everywhere faithful to Shakespeare's modal realism, as each thought produces a corresponding body. Before analogy, before simile, Lear implicates all natural things in his emotions. Just as he is genuinely submerged in the watery element, Lear hardly speaks in metaphor at all. What he says *is*.

> His *tears temper* the *clay* (TLN 823)[2]
>
> He knows *the sea-monster* (TLN 773)
>
> The gods' *bellies* are *full* and *rumbling* (TLN 1669)
>
> The cocks are *drowned* (TLN 1658)
>
> Nature is an individuated *goddess* (TLN 789)
>
> The *germaines spill* (TLN 1663)

Each image is an inspirited animation of substance.[3] A world is in motion as he calls these things into being:

> Cracke Natures moulds, all germaines spill at once
> That makes ingratefull Man. (TLN 1663-64)

---

2. These statements are not direct quotes. The italicized words do appear in the text.

3. Valère Novarina: "We must henceforth think by thunderclap, think more quickly, more compactly, in proportion to the world which will thus be precipitated." *The Theater of the Ears*, trans. and ed. Allen S. Weiss (Los Angeles: Sun and Moon Press, 1996), 99. This suggests how the intensified ecology of the storm scene is also an intensification of theater's potential for "precipitating" (a crucial word at the cliff scene) new possibilities, and a summons to our intensified attention.

> Tremble thou Wretch,
> That hast within thee undivulged Crimes
> Unwhipt of Iustice (TLN 1704-706)
>
> Caytiffe, to peeces shakes
> That under covert, and convenient seeming
> Ha's practis'd on mans life. Close pent-up guilts,
> Rive your concealing Continents, and cry
> These dreadfull Summoners grace. I am a man,
> More sinn'd against, then sinning. (TLN 1708-13)

The first-time audience may not yet know it, but everything here prepares for what it literally speaks to: Edgar/Tom, hidden center stage beneath the trapdoor, waiting to emerge as the animation of Lear's apostrophes. And not only Lear's. Repeatedly the dialogue between Lear, Kent, and Fool seems to picture some unknown shiverer, punished beyond his sins, at once frozen stiff and secreted in the dark:

> *Kent.* The wrathfull Skies
> Gallow the very wanderers of the darke
> And make them keepe their caves
>   ... Mans nature cannot carry
> Th'affliction, nor the feare. (TLN 1695-701)

Accordingly, the scene moves relentlessly toward the hovel in which this figure hibernates or incubates:

> Gracious my Lord, hard by here is a Hovell (TLN 1715)
>
> Where is this straw, my Fellow? (TLN 1724)
>
> Come, your Hovel (TLN 1726)
>
> Come bring us to this Hovel (TLN 1733)
>
> Here is the place my Lord (TLN 1778)

good my Lord enter (TLN 1778)

Good my Lord enter here (TLN 1782)

Good my Lord enter (TLN 1785)

Good my Lord enter here (TLN 1803)

The hovel is *the* place—the place of nature, the place to endure, the place to fall, the place, unavoidably, to enter.

And yet Lear resists. Instead he insists that the Fool enter before him, and decides to speak a little "prayer." There is an enormous narrative depth charge in Lear's speech. It is the moment the play has been waiting for: hopes and visions tremble on the speech's strings. Concomitantly, it heralds the decisive passage of Tom's gestation. Shakespeare has long been preparing Tom's appearance. Edmund's cue of Tom o' Bedlam (TLN 464) and Edgar's "happy hollow" soliloquy are merely the most obvious of premonitions. But this genetic compounding briskly intensifies in the storm scenes, as the "germens spill" and novel life forms threaten to mushroom and mutate. But it is Lear's prayer that delivers the birth:

> You houselesse povertie,
> Nay get thee in; Ile pray, and then Ile sleepe.
> Poore naked wretches, where so ere you are
> That bide the pelting of this pittilesse storme,
> How shall your House-lesse heads, and unfed sides.
> Your lop'd, and window'd raggednesse, defend you
> From seasons such as these? O I have tane
> Too little care of this: Take Physicke, Pompe,
> Expose thy selfe to feele what wretches feele,
> That thou maist shake the superflux to them,
> And shew the Heavens more iust. (TLN 1807-17)

The speech discharges a kind of tender lightning, a spirit of companionship between ideas and bodies and places, such that all things are at once monadic nodes of feeling and latently kin. Each thing in the speech is cherishably separate, and exactly in this separateness subject to violence. It is important that for all its clarity of focus, nothing in the speech is tagged, nothing ticked off. These things are not quite seen before us; nor are they simply described. Instead we get metonyms of suffering, small mute consequential ruins, whereby the pain is displaced onto objects that attend it: humanity has become a loop, a rag, a window, a floating head or evacuated side, the merest shank of meat. Such objects, then, are at once unmade subjects and possible citizens. Might such things add up to a person? Might a person abide inside them, or resolve into view if we focus on the patches? Pay more attention and find out.

But if the prayer generates imperative thoughts, it does so less through preaching than through confession, and thereby an indirect invitation to share in the self-accusation. The plea is to reach beyond jealous enclosures, a possibility to which Lear's present exposure gives powerful credence. Perhaps we are warm and housed as we hear, but so too was Lear when he took so little care. And so as much as the suffering of which he speaks is actual enough—primarily the misery of the naked wretches, but also his own as their sudden partner in dispossession—the mood is more pertinently of the possible: and of possibilities that can as easily be cataclysmic as redeeming.

Before names and stations—or after them—this is what we are: a brittle enduring, liable to be severed, viable to be put back together, and either way not to be blithely assumed, safe and whole before the fire.[4] What is more, part of the suffering is precisely continuance. These things are far from view and perhaps far from mind: but they are not extinct. Suffering survives; life, in Lear's perfectly apt verb, *bides*. It endures, and in doing so waits for things to change. The change might be in the weather, in the times—or in our mindfulness. The barely animate fragments of Lear's sympathy, then, are like pieces of dolls, awaiting the revivifying stitch; they are objects, pending the notice that a subject deserves.

---

4. S. L. Goldberg: "The world is metaphysically determined.... Men can only pray for deliverance.... The world is essentially unalterable by human action.... Men must endure.... They are essentially acted *upon*." *An Essay on King Lear* (Cambridge, U.K.: Cambridge University Press, 1974), 119–20; italics in original.

In this way the speech repairs the super-indicative imperatives of Lear's opening gambit: "Which of you shall we say doth love us most?" (TLN 56). Lear's love test brings garishly to light the infantilism of parental love: its lonely desire for affirmation and praise; its residual conviction that it deserves things, that it has been undervalued; its silly wish to bore others with its boasting ("Which of you shall *we say*"). Lear always knows that love is the cue and the answer. What he doesn't realize, among many points of ignorance, is that love is also always interpersonal, existing in the spaces between souls; that it comes as suffering, if not now then necessarily, in due course, when the loved one goes.

This falling short in Lear's understanding finds a correlate in the opening scene's dramaturgy—choreographed, of course, by the king. So there he addresses all that are present, indiscriminately; he tees up his daughters to speak; everyone waits to hear; and in due course each daughter says her piece. It is a parody of bad drama, a "theatrical pageant," with its punctual doling out of function, no surprises admitted, wait your turn and pronounce.[5] The meaning of this first scene, then, is generated from the gap between the king's and Shakespeare's orchestrations. We can see what Lear will not: all of his subjects on stage, smiling through their grimaces. The tragedy comes from the abyssal distance inside and between visible spaces. The fact of this is exactly what—with devastating irony—is effected by Lear's dramaturgy, which pretends that states of soul can be open to shared and unanimous witness. It is a calamitous insult to truth, not least the truths of theater and of love. Cordelia's asides are the necessary mark of Lear's category error, as well as a presage of her passing into the scenic *blanc*. In a world and a theater such as Lear dispenses, a Cordelia can only exist intervallically, between speeches, or in the long break between her scenes.

Now compare the "poor naked wretches" speech. In many ways, of course, it is the same Lear: "Your old kind Father, whose franke heart gave all," he says the moment before preparing to pray (TLN 1800). But the staging is crucially different. Once again Lear addresses all who are

---

5. Stephen Booth, *King Lear, Macbeth, Indefinition, and Tragedy*. (New Haven, Conn.: Yale University Press, 1983), 56.

present; once again the tragedy subsists in the chasms between parties. But now he is speaking feelingly: and by this I mean speaking for ears, not for sight. His eyes are closed. Even if he opens them, he sees nobody. Lear's speech is not a direct address; it is a loving apostrophe to absence. Here is where the speech repairs the love test: this, the play seems to say, is the truth of love, a kind of lodged ache that can never quite find physical surcease or correspondence. It is something like this that the dramaturgy here—so different from the pseudo-frankness of the love test—delicately stages.

Lear isn't assured of any hearing. He doesn't quite know his addressee, whether absent God or unknown wretches, and indeed in a sense is reaching for just such attendance, to warm and be warmed. But the plaintiveness of the appeal, its tantalizing promise, is also that it is heard. Each present auditor can lean into Lear's words and feel an exquisite privilege in doing so. Theater is here the model of political and moral chance. Lear cannot reach the wretches, but the Lear-actor can reach us: the vowelly appeal, *where-so-ere-you-are*, touches and blesses every listening ear, even as it reverberates beyond the auditorium to other places and future times.

But this is not all. These two groups of addressees—absent subjects and present audience—are both manifested in the speech's other secret addressees: the Edgar-actor, hidden and waiting for his cue, and the Tom-figure, who in every sense answers the prayer. Imagine the Tom-actor, hunkered out of sight (unless the spectators can see him—not impossible—lessening the surprise but intensifying the expectation), hearing these words, which he must know uncannily describe his altered part (houseless heads, unfed sides, looped and windowed raggedness). Imagine him listening for his cue, knowing it imminent but perhaps not knowing quite when it will come. Imagine him sweating or shivering, hidden in his box, suspended in the deathlike scenic cleft, lurking in the interstices of stage, part, and plot. He can see no more than he can be seen. But he can hear everything: voice is the life-bringing agent.

So the words speak directly to what he is about to enact. But Tom will not directly answer. His part does not permit it. This technique—what might be called a staggered entrance—is perfected in *The Tempest*, which is scripted such that all of the young parts (Miranda, Ferdinand, Ariel, Caliban) enter in stages: heard but not seen, or seen but not heard, or seen by the audience but not by others on stage, or present but not awake, or awake but not active. The purposes in *The Tempest* are principally three: to dramatize minds at secret or semirevealed cross-purposes; to evoke the fringes of consciousness or minds on the cusp of volition; and to suggest the copresence of different metaphysical realms and the uncertain shifting between them.[6] All of these purposes are active here, as Lear's prayer both apostrophizes and cues the presence of Tom, a presence at once now and not yet. The actor-fact of contingent presence and the character-fact of imminently morphing identities together suggest how the action is moving between present and absent characters, between material and spiritual worlds, between a world that is more or less known and named and one that is not.

Crucial here are the different subject-positions taken by Lear. He is himself the battered exile, the homeless wretch, the penitent king, the emerging human, and the painfully wistful parent. So, the speech is in part addressed to a missing child, at once a generalized subject of care and the particular girl, now in the wilderness of exile, of whom he has taken too little care. But these children, far away as in some sense they are, are also to be found nestling inside the speech's cherishing, almost maternal touch. This is partly the spell of the verse—its generous prosody, imaginative precision, and the voice that billows its protective net—and partly the facts of dramaturgy: the child really is present, nested in his box as the speech releases its blessing. Lear's prayer thus mourns a separation that has also not yet occurred, and that is also, in this very act of speaking, revoked. The child is here, she or he has returned. The loved one—figured in the Tom-actor—hears it all, or would were it not split between an agent and an essence. But here is the plaintive point, indeed the tragedy nascent in the action: only the agent hears, in the form of the actor, and he cannot communicate the knowledge into performance.

A similar impasse defines Lear. He seems able, at last, to speak the

6. Simon Palfrey and Tiffany Stern, "The Cue-Space in *The Tempest*," *Shakespeare in Parts* (Oxford: Oxford University Press, 2007), 275–310.

truth to love. But he is unaware that love is here, right now. As so often in this play, love belies touch. Poor Tom is at once addressed and present and absent. To borrow from the physicists, Tom is here both an exploded and unexploded state, a principle of doubled ontology—a condition permitted and compounded by the fact of impenetrable disguise, which spontaneously produces identity as allegory. He can be any subject, any son, any daughter. Already, then, Tom's purposes and identities are multiple. He figures the abandoned child; the houseless wretches; the absent Cordelia; the audience, needing a surrogate to prick the king into the unchartered world that beckons; and the king himself, whose exposure morphs into Tom's, with whom his discourse now echoes and ricochets. But equally Tom's role is nowhere limited to strictly human mirroring. Tom issues from the wash, literally born from it. This is palpably true of the prayer's first half, with Lear's call upon "houseless povertie." But listen also to the prayer's final few lines:

> Take Physicke, Pompe,
> Expose they selfe to feele what wretches feele,
> That thou mayst shake the superflux to them,
> And shew the heavens more iust. (TLN 1814-17)

These lines are usually understood as a simple plea for redistribution: the rich should share what they don't need. This is certainly part of the meaning. But it is also an approximating paraphrase, insufficiently alert to the language's physical specificity. *Take physic; expose thyself; shake the superflux*: the sentiments are quite radically, somatically curative. Lear is imagining a violent bodily process. Swallowing medicine, provoking a purge, vomiting out whatever lies within. This is Shakespearean catharsis, a dynamic capsule of tragic possibility.

The *shaking* speaks partly of self-induced distemper, partly of retributive rage. It is anything but a calmly possessed political science or detached advocacy of a more equitable social contract. Lear imagines a single body taking it all on, genuinely suffering the purge: pomp takes the physic and shakes with the consequences; it takes itself by the throat and exemplifies new justice. The sentiment exactly requires pomp made wretched: an Earl degraded to a Tom.

But it goes still further. *Superflux* isn't just a funny way of spelling superfluity. It is Shakespeare's coinage: *flux* is the truly active form. The word was current around 1605, attested by new coinages such as "fluxive" and "fluxion," its principal meanings all having to do with liquids and flow. Shakespeare isn't positing some abstract notion of unnecessary wealth or possessions. He means a superflow. The sentiment is one with the deluge and with the porous connectivity between one element or party and the next. This confirms the humoral basis of the metaphor, which posits a body disgorging waste matter. Equally, to apply a flux meant a medicinal purge. But the most common applications of *flux* at the time referred less to water than to blood and excrement and miscarriage (called "effluxion").[7]

Lear's great cry here thus joins with his earlier calls for the wind to blow and crack its cheeks (the weather gods farting) and to smite flat the world's rotundity and spill the seeds of life (the earth pregnant, its load aborted, its ejaculate wasted). His prayer is similarly grotesque: to "shake the superflux" might be to shit on creation, a carnivalesque call for rebellion. Equally, the superflux is gynecological, poised characteristically between disgust (the flux of menstrual discharge—a common application) and rehabilitation (the flux as the waters break and new life floods into being). And there is further salience in the fact that the superflux emits from both above and below: speech and vomit from the mouth; feces, blood, and babies from the nether-holes. It was seen at the time as a sure sign of demonic possession and exorcism:

> It is speech or voice that constitutes this ideal emanation; the ideal form of speech being prayer, or upwards-directed voice. In possession, there is a disturbance of this ideal arrangement, in that some unclean substance or agency refuses to be evacuated from below, but presses to be released from the upper orifices (where typically it is also believed to have entered).[8]

---

7. David Cressy, *Birth, Marriage, and Death: Ritual, Religion, and the Life-Cycle in Tudor and Stuart England* (Oxford: Oxford University Press, 1997), 48.
8. Steven Connor, *Dumbstruck: A Cultural History of Ventriloquism* (Oxford: Oxford University Press, 2000), 155–56.

These specifically imagined connotations precede the word's metaphorical sense: *flux* connoting change, alteration, the constant flow and counterflow of time. As ever in Shakespeare, time is no abstract flow or container: it is heavy with the surge and countersurge of events.

The superflux, then, is not something that can be subtracted from, as though a pile of coins or potatoes. It isn't subject to the same quantifying logic that confounded Lear earlier in the story. The superflux continues: it is the flow of experience, of agitation and suffering and pressure to change. Still more particularly, the superflux is the world that the speech heralds, that physically breaks forth. This "wretch," pretty much literally, is a retch, vomited into commission. The figure that arrives, and the scene that follows, *are* the shaken superflux; they are the superflux shaking, localized in Tom's epileptic convulsions.[9] It is hardly enough to describe such an overdetermined moment as the king taking shelter from the storm or the king and his party stumbling upon the disguised Edgar. This speech truly is the play's cathartic event.[10]

But Shakespeare has not yet finished with Tom's graduated arrival. For even after being cued, he does not quite appear. That Shakespeare wants the moment to mean things, that he worries at it, is evident from the fact that the Folio adds a single line to the part, heard invisibly from the depths, at an irregular angle to the king's summons:

> Fathom, and halfe, fathom and halfe; poore *Tom*. (TLN 1819; italics in original)

It is an oblique self-annunciation, defying clear purpose or referent. The "spirit" is heard before it is seen, just as it is here before it is noticed (true in both texts but made more explicit in the Folio). In this

---

9. Quoting Paul Celan, Eric L. Santner writes: "Nature becomes divided from itself, becomes 'written asunder,' through exposure to the violence of human history." *On Creaturely Life: Rilke, Benjamin, Sebald* (Chicago: University of Chicago Press, 2006), 19.

10. Compare Lear's "hysteria passio," his "climbing sorrow," with its palpable terror at being overcome from the ground up. Richard Halperin: "*Historica passio* [is] the bearing or enduring or manifestation of historical force through one's person and one's body ... which constitutes him [Lear] as a dramatic character and invests his every gesture with a richness of historical signification": *The Poetics of Primitive Accumulation* (Ithaca, N.Y.: Cornell University Press, 1991), 218.

world, common knowledge is not the imprimatur of life. That the voice precedes his visible appearance suggests mystery or ghostliness. Disconnected from body, it is also disconnected from source. Perhaps the exiles have stumbled upon some spring of nature's secrets; perhaps it speaks demonic automatism.[11] Either way, it is not bound to a singular verifiable consciousness.

Indeed, we might understand this floating voice as speaking semi-known place. Accordingly, the most obvious sense relates to the weather: the poor man is drowning, calling from a place of frantic submersion. A fathom is a measure of six feet, derived from the supposed length of two spread arms; it is also the proverbial depth of a grave. The "half" may suggest that he is rising from buried depths, the first half three feet, the second half the next three feet—so he reaches dry land or air. Equally, it may imply that he is plummeting deeper and deeper, into subterranean channels of privation or possibility. Or is he perhaps sinking in a swamp, or buried to his head in a bog, some kind of Lindow Man, sacrificed millennia past and kept miraculously intact by the peat? Or perhaps the geography is still more fiercely inward, true to a storm in which micro and macro shudder and bleed into one another. Perhaps here we find the place's brain or its pulse or even its predestined issue, bursting the amniotic sac and discharged, wailing and premature, from the filthy birth canal.[12] Certainly it promises something—but quite what remains enigmatic.

Steven Mentz has written suggestively of the "false floor effect" in the latter half of *Lear*, whereby it seems that experience has reached rock bottom, only to reveal still further levels of loss, degradation and misery.[13] But it is important to see how this effect is underscored, even inaugurated, by scenography. That the Tom-actor is hidden beneath a trapdoor (or perhaps in the discovery place) shows how disguise begins with place, with the nooks and crannies of the stage. This alone is in-

---

11. Connor sees in Protestantism an anxiety that voice should be decorporealized, "making it the expressive trace of the self, rather than a bodily action performed upon the self." *Dumbstruck*, 163.

12. A gentleman at a talk I gave in Stratford-upon-Avon told me that "fathom and half" is the call of a sea pilot entering narrow straits. I haven't been able to confirm this, but it is a beautiful idea, and well suited to the idea of Tom's still-perilous emergence from a journey.

13. Steven Mentz, *At the Bottom of Shakespeare's Ocean* (London: Continuum, 2009), 17–18.

dicative of Shakespeare's purposes. He is moving away from individuation, its dignities and superintendence, as the moving locus of passion. Instead, place itself is alive. Humans are as much a part of such place as anything else, but no more than a rat or the scum on a pond. The voice we hear is thus a kind of ecological dreaming.[14]

It may be that this kind of apprehension was more easily felt in Shakespeare's day. Humoral thinking assumes an interconnection between world and body, such that the individual is always a concentration, biased this way or that, of materials found likewise in soil, geese, weeds. Contemporaries like Donne and Browne come to mind, over-curiously or neurotically feeling the loam in each body, its vermicular porosity, its elemental interpenetration with all matter. But *Lear* takes such thoughts far beyond intellectually refined morbidity. And it is Tom, above all, who ensures this autochthonous democratizing. For it is crucial to cede to Tom his authority: his scenic authority, and a kind of authority that attaches to the weird decorum of his presence. He is the storm scene's resident spirit.

In profound ways, the other exiles are Tom's guests. Partly it is right that a homeless beggar should be in such a place. They have left the fireplaces behind and entered the pelting elements. But there is far more to Tom's decorum than his poverty. This is a world, remember, where men presume to sit in the same place as gods, to address and rebuke them: and Tom has *been there*. This, perhaps, is what the mad old king recognizes—some golem, still wet or glistening from the god-birth or the god-bath, from the parental whipping or judgment. This figure—call him the thing itself, a magician, an Athenian, a demoniac—has been close to the sources of creation, or carries them immanently, as though the lightning itself, messenger of the thunder he is asked to explain.

---

14. Alfred North Whitehead: "Our bodies lie beyond our own individual existence. And yet they are part of it.... The body is part of the external world, continuous with it.... If we are fussily exact, we cannot define where a body begins and where external nature ends. Consider one definite molecule. It is part of nature. It has moved about for millions of years. Perhaps it stared from a distant nebula. It enters the body; it may be as a factor in some edible vegetable; or it passes into the lungs as part of the air. At what exact point as it enters the mouth, or as it is absorbed through the skin, is it part of the body? At what exact moment, later on, does it cease to be part of the body? Exactness is out of the question. It can only be obtained by some trivial convention." *Modes of Thought* (New York: Free Press, 1938), 21.

Tom is the key that retunes the playworld, stretches its pitch far beyond daily concourse. His irruption from the straw tantalizes with possibility, occupying a series of temporal stations.[15] It is a coming-true of the king's passion; it is an interruption, a stump in the dark to trip on, forcing assumptions to stumble and rebalance; it is an antic annunciation, a new host to spiritual possibility. This is not to say that Tom is a Christ-figure; it is nothing quite so determined or hypostatic. But it has long been acknowledged how *Lear*, pre-Christian or not, taps into millenarian excitements. And so Tom is, in the eyes of Lear at least, hedged by a spiritual corona, as of prophet or seer, the obverse of the more immediate judgment that he is a demoniac, or a fraudulent simulator of the same. For let's not forget that Lear's speech is a prayer. He doesn't address the gods or heavens or even the elements, as he does elsewhere, but certainly he is reaching for some kind of agency beyond the normative cloister. Of course, he is doing so at the very edge of sanity: yet this alone permits Shakespeare to push at scandalous possibilities.[16]

---

15. Henry S. Turner writes of Lear's entrance into the storm: "If an actor were to enter the stage as a character recognizable from the play and fail to designate a new location; as a character, moreover, who has been excluded first from one fictional place and then from another; if this actor were to occupy the stage and gesticulate wildly, gratuitously, even to run about the playing area, as other characters entered to him from the world of the play and urged him to depart with them to other places in that world; and if, despite their entreaties, this actor were to remain stubbornly on stage and refuse to recognize the presence of these characters or the locations they spoke of: 'where' exactly would this actor be? And how would a superstitious world describe such a character, except as mad? In such a moment the places of the theatre and of the fiction would coincide with equal vividness—and if this 'moment' was one of any duration, it might even qualify as a 'scene'. The resolute *negation* of place by one character, surrounded by the equally persistent affirmations of place by others, would result in a glimpse of the stage's potential to produce these places, and thus of its space." *The English Renaissance Stage: Geometry, Poetics, and the Practical Spatial Arts, 1580–1630* (Oxford: Oxford University Press, 2006), 175–76; italics in original. Turner's analysis is as strikingly pertinent to Tom as to Lear, but with two caveats: in the *Lear*-world, extended temporal duration is not needed to make a scene, and in its relish for geometrics, Turner's final move somewhat reifies stage space as the ultimate revelation, even as he identifies the attributes of this space as a "heterogeneous" and "unfamiliar" "point of articulation for a radical critique" of early modern conventions (185). I think Shakespeare (and Tom) is better elucidated by the Leibnizian principle: space is the place of events, a derived abstraction rather than substantial origin.

16. James Kearney compares Tom to the Odyssean "abject stranger," the "figure of abjection" who "can always be the king or the god," identifying this in turn with Levinasian ethics: "Lear's failure to recognize Edgar within poor Tom dramatizes for the audience the excess or alterity of the other that eludes Lear in this moment. In other words, the dramatic irony of the audience's knowledge of the identity of the figure in disguise renders visible the secret

Tom is the coming-true of a world in which the lines of individual things—people, words, conjunctions, relationships—are blurred or multiple, such that individuation is in part a convention rather than a truth. Each thing has other things nesting inside it, or adumbrating it, or merging with it. Hence the way characters in *Lear* exist either in sets—brothers, sisters, fathers, servants, daughters, disguises, in which the "species" is every bit as powerful as the individual instance—or as multiplicities. Each proper name houses many changes. This is true even of Cordelia, in her transmogrification from silent youngest child to warlike foreign princess.

In this context, the miserable machinations of Edmund, which briefly interrupt the storm scenes, are a tiny and pitiable egoism, almost wistful in their busy devotion to social measurements of success (land, power, sexual allure). The discrete human subject is still there, but dwarfed by far stronger and more aboriginal elements, such that a self-determining, self-possessing citizen, far from some prediction of an emergent bourgeois individuality, begins to be revealed as a nostalgic fiction. Shakespeare is generating a completely different ontology from anything social. Whatever elements make us, of earth or air or liquid or fire, their collection in the named human body is the briefest formalized recess in an unspeakably enduring anonymity. This is the matter that has here been joined. And Tom is its genius.

---

interiority, the unknowable excess of the other." Kearney sees the same thing in Gloucester's failure to see how Tom "is pregnant with a surplus," which is not a king or god but his lost son: "'This Is Above All Strangeness': *King Lear*, Ethics, and the Phenomenology of Recognition," *Criticism* 54, no. 3 (2012), 456–57, 459.

7

INTERLUDE

Tom Is . . . ?

1. Tom is as Lear says: "Thou art the thing it selfe" (TLN 1886).
2. Tom is the distillation and generalization of life: the true human abstract.
3. Tom is the constituents of the statement, each word a discrete capture of his essence.
4. Thou: familiar as a friend//distant as a god
5. Art: to be//to be made
6. The: definite article//modifying adverb
7. Thing: before names//creature
8. It: raw object//nonhuman
9. Selfe: raw subject//human
10. Tom exists between human and not, object and subject, name and anonymity, specific and general, noun and verb, being and making. He is the thing itself: creaturely and transcendent, phenomenal and noumenal, and the antinomy of the two.
11. If indeed Lear's sentence is true.
12. Tom is a disguise. Edgar makes him up. Tom is nothing but a name for a part of his play act.
13. Tom has no more substance than a shirt flapping on a line. He falls short of the full life contract. He is disguise, depending on a borrowed rag and simulated manner, which can be left in a box at the appropriate time. His truth speaking, such as it is, is

delegated by the role player. It is scripted by him, it returns to him, it is on his behalf.
14. Tom is Edgar's repressions, bursting into life. Behind the glaze of strangeness, a boy's familiar neuroses.
15. Tom is his maker's guilt, a political guilt. Edgar must have done something wrong to be punished and hated as he is. Tom is the one that the Earl's son took too little care of, the one he would never look in the eye, begging at the castle gate. There is gain even in loss.
16. Tom is a good man's projection, a demo-symbol, mediating between a violent past and a future that can arrive only through healing, a future that present violence prevents from coming, a coming that would mean Tom going, or changing: and Tom cannot change.
17. Tom is the agitation of being-Edgar. It never felt right. When no one was looking, he would touch his thin neck inside his heavy garments. On his pillow at night, he would shut his eyes tight, thankful the meal was over, with all of those other eyes watching him, the expectation to talk and to attend. Tom is the itch of dis-integrity, secretly scratched until it bleeds without remission. Blank conformity is never at peace.
18. Tom is the fact that Edgar did nothing wrong. Tom is the proof of innocence.
19. Tom is a facelike refuge, with Edgar hidden and clean beneath the mask.
20. Tom is the necessary scapegoat. It is Toms who get punished, they always have, they will again now. His father has robbed Edgar of power. It would be decimating, were it not for the fact of Tom. Tom gives Edgar his power back, the power of being able to hurt another, feel pity for another, allow and control and end another.
21. Tom is Edgar's spectacle, not to be allowed a single moment alone, a single unwitnessed act.
22. Tom is a remnant who assures Edgar of his wholeness, a doll to stick pins into, a wound-up gesture machine to purge the unquiet mind.

23. Tom is Edgar's theatre of cruelty.[1]
24. Tom is the actor inside Edgar, bursting from every hole.[2]
25. Tom is theatre, a manufactured object, nonliving, designed to take away pain. Or to give pain its necessary scream.
26. Tom is the scream made real; Tom is the scream in motion.
27. Tom is the doll come to life.
28. Edgar lapses, and the projection takes over. Something that is not is here.
29. Tom is here. He has as much body as any other character, speaks more of a past, owns to more fears, more desires, more places, more dread.
30. Tom demands and receives recognition. No one else's life is so vouched for, the fact of it, as life. No other character is so predicted, so anticipated, subject to so graduated an arrival. His provenance is forever on probation, revealed in action, and yet never quite granted and understood.
31. Tom is what it would be to never quite make it to the status of a life.
32. Tom touches the possibility of life more than any other character, precisely because its achievement is in doubt.
33. Tom is multiply conceived, over and over again.
34. Tom knows the original sin. All those spermatozoa going off the cliff, and yet not dying. All those possibles, hanging there, waiting to be gathered like samphire. All those spilled

---

1. Antonin Artaud: "Practising cruelty involves a higher determination to which the executioner-tormentor is also subject and which he must be *resolved* to endure when the time comes. Above all, cruelty is very lucid, a kind of strict control and submission to necessity. There is no cruelty without consciousness . . . since it is understood that being alive always means the death of someone else. . . . Rising from his repose and straining himself towards being, Brahma suffered, and this may perhaps convey joyful melodies, but at the limits of the curve it is only expressed as an awful crushing." *The Theatre and Its Double*, trans. Victor Corti (Richmond, U.K.: Oneworld Classics, 2010), 72–74; italics in original.

2. Valère Novarina: "There exists in each actor something like a new body, desiring to speak. Another economy of the body which comes forth, which thrusts aside the old prescriptions." *The Theater of the Ears*, trans. and ed. Allen S. Weiss (Los Angeles: Sun and Moon Press, 1996), 61. "This man was like all the others. He wanted to risk being something other than his visible body, to reinvent another man in his place. It is quite unbearable for us to have but one head, feet down below, and only two arms." *Theater of the Ears*, 119–20.

seeds, spilled but still multiplying, like spores of ambitious milk.

35. Tom is suffering this original sin—the dirty washed world, where the cocks are drowned and the seeds are spilled and there is an almighty battle to make or hold onto life. He is battered in the birth canal, not knowing which way he is going, upward or outward, seeking conception or thrashing to stay in the happy dark or pushing violently into presence.
36. There are multiple conceptive events, and multiple Toms.
37. One Tom can replace another Tom.
38. No single Tom quite is.
39. Tom is survival, yet without the full gift of life, a creature under erasure, a figure of existential disappointment and ontological default.
40. Tom shudders with the difficulty of being, the uncanny weirdness and contingency of life.
41. Tom is the logical impossibility of conceiving life. How can a life issue from that chaotic gunk? How can the odds against coming true ever be overcome?
42. Tom is that humiliation: to be so at the mercy of chance; to be taken like that; and yet to be given this abundance of spirit, of mind and emotion and memory, and all of the suffering that is the necessary price for the plenty.
43. Tom is the fact that once life is here, it could never have been otherwise.
44. Tom is the single life, in itself a miracle.
45. Tom is the singular being whose life implies the prevention of countless others.
46. Tom is all of these others, alive in Tom's motions, adumbrated or potentiated in his barely actable multiplicity, thrumming in his loneliness.
47. Tom is the tragedy of substitution, the tragedy of survival. One gets to live rather than another; both cannot. One life means the annihilation of others; survival is holocaust.
48. Tom is dancing on the graves of millions.
49. Tom is the infinite brothers who cannot share.

50. Tom is the fact that we only know a fraction of those we might.
51. Tom is the risk and the cruelty of presence.
52. Tom is the incompossible—the things exiled beyond visible community and recorded history; the possibilities that are deemed not possible, or that have been forgotten, or whose time has not yet come.
53. Tom is the buried world, the drowned world, the prevented world—the lives unlived.
54. Tom is the lives that already are, cursed with appetite and perception, and yet still not allowed fully to be, floating in the mantle of ponds, unnameable monads in an infinity of frog spawn.
55. Tom is the fact that life kills, over and over, but life cannot in the end be killed.
56. Tom is tragedy renewed: not the fall of a great man through an excess of some failing, but prevented being, a nonbeing that yet is.
57. Tom might mean: look over your shoulder, sublate your sibling, attempt the prevention of those that would prevent you.
58. Tom might mean: beware the fiend, pray for a blessing, hope to get out alive.
59. Tom might mean: I have taken too little care of this!
60. Or Tom might mean: life is no more than the time of dying.[3]
61. Not death, but dying, the constant process, such that living is to be in death.[4]

---

3. Maurice Blanchot: "Not just when they die but apparently while they are alive Kafka's heroes carry out their actions in death's space, and . . . it is to the indefinite time of 'dying' that they belong.' . . . Kafka is in a sense already dead. This is given him, as exile was given him; and this gift is linked to that of writing." *The Space of Literature*, trans. Ann Smock (Lincoln: University of Nebraska Press, 1982), 92.

4. Augustine: "No one . . . is dying unless living. The same person is . . . simultaneously dying and living. . . . If a man in whose body death is already at work should rather be called dying, and if no one can be living and dying simultaneously, I do not know when he is living. For from the very beginning of our existence in this dying body, there is never a moment when death is not at work in us." *The City of God against the Pagans*, ed. and trans. R. W. Dyson (Cambridge, U.K.: Cambridge University Press, 1998), XIII, 9–10.

62. Or if not dying, then undead, strung in that stretch between real and symbolic death.[5]
63. Which means, for Tom, that death is dead, it can arrogate no more than it has.
64. Which means, again, Tom is the unkillable life of theater.
65. Tom is recessive mirrors, one image opening onto another, none of them quite substantial.
66. Tom is a shuttered sequence, the briefest window before the shutter comes down again.
67. Tom is a sequence in scenes: here, then gone, here, then gone, here—and gone.
68. Tom is whatever it means to enter this gone. Is Tom ever anywhere but there?
69. Once Tom enters this gap, does he exist at all?
70. If Tom does exist, then how?
71. If Tom doesn't exist, then where did he go?
72. And if Tom doesn't, did he ever?
73. But if Tom didn't, then who did?
74. Tom is living *King Lear*.

---

5. What Eric L. Santner calls the "ultimate domain of creaturely life": *On Creaturely Life: Rilke, Benjamin, Sebald* (Chicago: University of Chicago Press, 2006), xx.

※ 8 ※

SCENE 3

Tom's Voices

The Edgar-part has the second most lines in the play, close to half of them in the voice of Tom (the proportion is impossible to measure). But remarkably little attention has been paid to what Tom says, as distinct from the figure's effect on or relation to others. There are limited exceptions, but in the main Tom is heard rather than truly attended to.[1] Onstage, offstage, even in the time-straddling world of reading: the odd plaintive refrain aside, his discourse tends to be passed by as "lunatic irrelevancies"[2] or a "string of nonsensical phrases,"[3] or else it is heard en masse as symbolic white noise.

But let's do something different. Let's not be like Kent, who hears a noise in the straw and dismisses it as a mere "grumble."[4] Listen closer—

---

1. See William C. Carroll, "'The Base Shall Top th'Legitimate': The Bedlam Beggar and the Role of Edgar in *King Lear*," *Shakespeare Quarterly* 38, no. 4 (1987); Kenneth Gross, *Shakespeare's Noise* (Chicago: University of Chicago Press, 2001); Grigori, Kozintsev, *King Lear, the Space of Tragedy: The Diary of a Film Director*, trans. Mary Mackintosh (London: Heinemann Educational Publishers, 1977).

2. G. Wilson Knight, *Wheel of Fire* (1930; reprint, London: Routledge, 2001), 188.

3. Michael E. Mooney, "'Edgar I Nothing Am': Figurenposition in *King Lear*," *Shakespeare Survey* 38 (1985): 158.

4. See Romans 8:22-23: "For we know that everie creature groneth with us also, and travaileth in paine together unto this present. / And not onely *the creature*, but we also which have the firsts frutes of the Spirit, even we do sigh in our selves, waiting for the adopcion, *even the redemption of our bodie*" (1560 Geneva edition; italics in original).

turn the sound up—and the grumble becomes something other. Here are all the words spoken by Tom in his first scene:[5]

> Fathom, and halfe, fathom and halfe: Poore Tom.
> Away, the foul fiend follows me, through the sharp hawthorne blow the winds [Quarto: cold wind]
> Humh. Goe to thy bed and warme thee [Quarto: cold bed]
> /Who gives any thing to poore Tom?
> Whom the foule fiend hath led through Fire, and through Flame, through Sword, and whirle-poole, o're Bog, and Quagmire, that hath laid knives under his Pillow, and Halters in his Pue, set Rats-bane by his Porredge, made him Proud of heart, to ride on a bay trotting Horse, over foure incht Bridges, to course his owne shadow for a Traitor. Blesse thy five Wits. Toms a cold, O do, de, do, de, do, do, de. Blisse thee from Whirle-Winds, starre-blasting, and taking. Do poore Tom some charity, whom the foul fiend vexes. There could I have him now, and there, and there again, and there.
> /Pillicock sat on Pillicock hill, alow, alow, loo, loo
> /Take heed o'th'foule Fiend, obey thy parents, keepe thy words Justice [Quarto: justly], sweare not, commit not with mans sworne spouse, set not thy Sweet-heart on proud array. Tom's a cold
> /A Servingman, proud in heart, and minde, that curl'd my haire, wore gloves in my cap, serv'd the Lust of my Mistris heart, and did the acte of darkenesse with her, swore as many Oathes, as I spake words, and broke them in the sweet face of Heaven. One, that slept in the contriving of lust, and wak'd to doe it, wine lov'd I deerely [Quarto: deeply], dice deerely, and in Woman, out-Paramour'd the Turke. False of Heart, light of eare, bloody of hand, hog in sloth, foxe in stealth, wolfe in greedinesse, dog in madness, lyon in prey. Let not the creaking of shooes, nor the rustling of Silkes, betray they poore heart to woman, keepe

---

5. I quote the Folio text; Quarto variations are in brackets. Each forward slash marks Tom's resumption after other speakers.

thy foot out of brothels, thy hand out of Plackets, thy pen from
Lenders Bookes, and defye the foule Fiend. Still through the
hawthorn blowes the cold winde. Sayes suum, mun, nonny,
Dolphin my Boy, Boy Sesey: Let him trot by.
/This is the foule Flibbertigibbet; hee begins at Curfew, and walkes
at first Cocke: hee gives the Web and the Pin, squints the eye,
and makes the Hare-lippe, mildewes the white Wheate, and
hurts the poore Creature of earth.
Swithold footed thrice the old
He met the Night-mare, and her nine-fold
Bid her a-light, and her troth-plight
And aroynt thee Witch, aroynt thee
/Poore Tom, that eats the swimming Frog, the Toad, the Tod-pole,
the wall-Newt, and the water: that in the furie of his heart,
when the foul Fiend rages, eats Cow-dung for Sallets, swal-
lowes the old Rat, and the ditch-Dogge; drinkes the green
mantle of the standing Poole: who is whipt from Tything to
Tything, and stockt, punish'd, and imprison'd: who hath three
suites to his backe, sixe shirts to his body:
Horse to ride, and weapon to weare:
But Mice, and Rats, and such small Deare
Have been Toms food, for seven long yeare
Beware my Follower. Peace Smulkin, peace thou Fiend
/The Prince of Darkenesse is a Gentleman. Modo he's called, and
Mahu.
/Poore Tom's a cold.
/How to prevent the Fiend, and to kill Vermine.
/Tom's a cold.
/Childe Rowland to the darke Tower came [Quarto: towne]
His word was still, fie, foh, and fumme
I smell the blood of a Brittish man (TLN 1819–968)

Shakespeare knew what he was doing here, what he was asking
of actor and auditor. Tom's idiom is radically indifferent to customary dialogical rules. It evokes some hobgoblin remainder, part ruined
prose, part ruined verse, part ruined song. Verse is the mode of gentles

like Edgar; prose of servants and beggars; song of the suprapersonal community—but all are at once recalled and scotched in Tom's vocative superflux. The effect is instantly to detonate decorum—sociopolitical, linguistic, and theatrical. Customary orders, customary affiliations, customary relations of word to person or to deed, are suddenly insecure. And a determining aspect of this shattered decorum is metaperformative. In having to juggle and switch between the scraps and splinters of various theatrical grammars, the Tom-part profoundly disturbs the recognitions upon which Shakespeare's actors habitually rely.[6] What is more, the scripting scrambles the usual decorum of cue and response, cause and consequence. He ends most of his allotted speeches with either a repeating cue-word or a song or a pantomime of action, all of which travel beyond the nominally cued response, strangely erasing his audiences. Who speaks? To whom does he speak? Whose actions are spoken? How possibly to tell?

❧

Tom speaks in a few recurring registers, one after the other, as though on three loops, played at different speeds, and intermittently cutting one across the other.

First, brisk accumulating parataxis, in which he lists examples of privation, punishment, vice, instruction, or degradation. The rhythms here are peculiarly strung between oral and textual: partly imitating

---

6. Compare Edgar and Tom with Valère Novarina's account of "The Flying Studio": on one side there is "Boucot" the manipulator, swallower of words, orator, "ceaselessly pierced, everywhere perforated," "wickedly attacking the word," fearful of death; on the other side are the "Employees," "suicidal, joyful. . . . Something that comes from elsewhere urges them on. . . . They develop nothing, possess neither tale nor discourse, have nothing to say. . . . The change of rhythm, of delivery, precedes meaning. . . . They are always bent forward, their words are ahead of their bodies or their bodies ahead of their words, as you wish. . . . Boucot speaks. It speaks in his employees. It comes out of their mouths, but it isn't their mouths that speak, because they have no mouths. . . . The employees ventriloquize, in front of Boucot the articulator. . . . What speaks within them? Reminiscences, bits of false infancy, fits, revolt, finagling, zigzag of hearts, impetus of false memories (a thousand lives), puffs of false reasoning, and especially, especially, especially swoons, syncopes, free falls, blanks everywhere, blanks in speech. Cyclothymia, suicide, electro-shock. They always faint, they always die. Boucot is always awake, and never dies." "Letter to the Actors," in *The Theater of the Ears*, trans. and ed. Allen S. Weiss (Los Angeles: Sun and Moon Press, 1996), 43–46. Edgar and Tom don't so much split neatly into Boucot and Employees: rather, the Tom-part introjects just such expenditure.

the muttered catechisms of frightened or bowed obedience, partly imitating the accumulating clauses and pleonastic iterations of nondramatic didactic prose. The imperatives build and build, uninterruptible, and all an auditor can do is wait.

Second, snatches of chant or song, as Tom drifts from all addressees, harmonizes with who knows what voices, and again his listeners are impotent to react. Even if the song or pantomime coincides with another actor's speech-cue—as it does no less than five times (six if we include Tom's exit-cue, closing the whole scene)—that actor cannot speak to the cue, or to Tom at all, but must instead act at an angle from his cuer, to all intents ignoring his continuing singing or babble or paroxysms.[7]

Third, the brief refrains in which Tom returns to intimate creaturely embodiment: "through the hawthorn blows the cold wind" (probably a floating quotation from a popular ballad[8]) and in particular, "Tom's a cold" (the standard cry of the Bedlam or Abraham man). Again, there is no clear address in these refrains; they can be played as an appeal, perhaps for pity, perhaps for an embrace—if so, an appeal that is certainly ignored once (by Gloucester, at TLN 1926) and quite possibly each time.[9]

The part's isolating effects are orchestrated at the most fundamental level. It is often uncertain whether it is Tom who speaks at all. Perhaps it is another, to whom he is hostage or which he hosts. Sometimes such stolen voice can be explained as demonic possession—as he says in the Quarto text, "The foul fiend haunts poore *Tom* in the voice of a nightin-

---

7. The exception to this is Lear: whenever the Lear-part is cued by the Tom-part, he speaks either to or about the beggar. But the others—first the Fool (twice), then Kent, finally Gloucester (four times)—do not respond to Tom at all.

8. The line appears in "The Friar of Orders Grey," in Thomas Percy, *Reliques of Ancient English Poetry* (London: J. Dodsley, 1765), Vol 1, 95. See William C. Carroll, "Songs of Madness: The Lyric Afterlife of Shakespeare's Poor Tom," *Shakespeare Survey* 55 (2002): 86. However, Percy admits to inserting "supplemental stanzas" of his own to connect the fragments, and the ballad as printed has so many Shakespearean touches—including Tom's "[See] through the hawthorn blows the cold wind," perfect in its numbers—that it must be doubtful which is drawing from which.

9. Importantly, however, these refrains are heard and understood by the offstage audience; whereas much in Tom's part resists or even repels understanding, the refrains speak a powerful sentimental challenge.

gale, Hoppedance cries in *Toms* belly for two white herring, Croake not blacke Angell" (III. vi. .34; italics in original). But demonic possession opens rather than ends the matter. There were demons for every occasion, an attendant for every passion: not least the passion of theater, the demonic stage par excellence, which the Tom-show vehemently concentrates.[10]

Another distinctive habit is Tom's rapid oscillation between speaking of himself in the first and the third persons, often in the same speech. The effect is to destabilize any notion of possessed identity, or to make the assumption of "I" or "my" seem like a beleaguered refuge from daily subjective dispossession. Of course we might say that Tom is not himself, he is Edgar; by the same token, the unstable shifts in self-reference actualize the fact that identity here is a multiparty struggle. No other name in the play is so repeated by its owner: this alone suggests a life lived in the second person, as though rented, or entered, rather than a simple predicative gift. But precisely the fact that he sees himself as though someone else—*Tom's a cold*—can bring home all the more pathetically the fact of lonely comfortless affliction.

Whatever Tom's discourse is, it is not as socialized as conversation—indeed it often barely deserves to be called dialogue. For instance, the questions addressed to the naked beggar repeatedly leave the Tom-actor with nothing to say. For all the part's garrulousness, it is written so as to be repeatedly dumbfounded by false cues, or by questions, directly addressed to Tom, that the actor *cannot* answer:

>   What art thou that dost grumble there I'th' straw?
>   Did'st thou give all to thy Daughters? (TLN 1832)
>   Ha's his Daughters brought him to this passe? (TLN 1844)
>   Could'st thou save nothing? (TLN 1845)
>   Would'st thou give 'em all? (TLN 1845)

---

10. Jan Kott: "Edgar's demonology is no more than a parody, a travesty of contemporary Egyptian dream books and books on witchcraft; a great and brutal gibe, in fact.... From the point of view of a Job who has ceased to talk to God, they are clowns. Clowns who do not yet know they are clowns." *Shakespeare Our Contemporary*, trans. Boleslaw Taborski (London: Methuen, 1964), 131.

> Is it the fashion, that discarded Fathers, Should have thus little mercy on their flesh? (TLN 1853-54)
>
> Is man no more then this? (TLN 1882-83)
>
> Thou ow's the Worme no Silke; the Beast, no Hide; the Sheepe, no Wool.... Ha? (TLN 1883-85)
>
> What are you there? (TLN 1907)
>
> What is the cause of Thunder? (TLN 1933)

Equally, it is often unclear to whom Tom speaks. Even simple statements, like "Blesse thy five Wits," defy illocutionary certainty. Who is he blessing? Does he remain trapped inside his torture, watched like dogs upon a bear? Are the five wits his, as in five minds (or as he says in the Quarto text, "Five fiends have beene in poore Tom at once" IV. i. 61). Or does he escape his specimen bottle, if only for a moment, glimpse the men around him, perhaps recognize them, and share the blessing around: a blessing for the King, another for the Duke, a third for the terrified Fool? Or consider this:

> Humh
>
> Goe to thy bed and warme thee [Quarto: cold bed] (TLN 1828-29)

These words cue Lear, but do they address Lear? If so, are they a savage irony, in the way of Lear's later imprecation for the blind Gloucester to use his eyes? Are they solicitous, taking their cue from the "poore naked wretches" speech, which the Tom-actor has just heard? Is it perhaps Edgar's voice, plaintive upon sight of the draggled king? Or is it Tom's, seeing the same thing, and saying that you do not belong here in my open? Are the words rebuking and dismissive? Or are they spoken to the fiend, a pitiful cry to be left alone? Again and again Tom's script gives no answers to such questions.

Even apparently direct answers are nothing of the kind:

> *Lear.* Did'st thou give all to thy Daughters? And art thou come to this?
>
> *Edgar.* Who gives any thing to poore Tom? (TLN 1830-32)

Tom's answer flips the agency on its head. He answers as the abandoned child, rather than the discarded father—unless the voice that answers isn't Tom's at all, but the hostage-taking fiend's ("who gives anything to that little creep . . . ?"). The king sees him as a fellow lost patriarch; Tom sees himself as a lost child. It is as though he hears but refuses the question, or doesn't recognize it as a social illocution—which perhaps it isn't. Of course in many plays Shakespeare leaves such things ambiguous, giving choices to actors while at the same time ensuring that such choices cannot finally decide the matter. These ambiguities speak to questions of theme, purpose, motive, and affect; the choices made will shape this or that particular stage-incarnation if nothing more. But the unresolved choices that frame Tom are at heart curiously aloof from any such regulating interpretive effects. Whatever choices performance brings, theme and emotion are in basic ways unaltered. Instead, the ambiguity here is *ontological*. It only accidentally organizes how Tom is perceived or treated, or even how he feels. Much more essentially, it scores what he is.

Because Tom's speeches do not really answer to interlocutors or to visible immediacies, it can seem as though they are already here, just waiting to be heard. "Away," he says to Kent, before even emerging from the straw: the king's scene interrupts an ongoing battle. The voices have been going on forever, and will continue to go on, and what we get is the briefest witness of this interminable sentence: a lid lifts, aurality is happening; the lid closes, the sound stops or is suppressed to a murmur; and instantly another lid pops open. One phrase seems to hatch another: a phrase-egg breaks and another is nestling, ready to fall and break; and so it goes on. Speech demarcations merely mark the scene's tuning in and tuning out of incessance: Tom's extreme experience, long-brewed and inescapable, turning on a loop. We catch him in flagrante, in process, on a wheel that he may never get off.[11]

Much of the work here is done by rhythm as much as semantics.

---

11. Eric L. Santner: "Unconscious mental life gets mobilized around such enigmatic signifiers that can never be fully metabolized, translated into the projects that make up the life of the ego. They persist as loci of signifying stress, excitations linked to but not absorbed by our life in the space of meaning. It is the excess of pressure that emerges at such sites— really a kind of life in excess both of our merely biological life and of our life in the space of

Prosody is fundamental in timing how an actor breathes, his flows and pauses. This in turn organizes social relations, particularly through the intervals in which other players can be noticed and addressed, in which they can move or be moved toward. At the same time prosody calibrates how the actor inhabits his own body: it supplies a rhythm that is intuited infinitesimally before semantics, before volitional or witnessed actions. It is thus a crucial instrument of self-presence, and for the easy cohabitation between speaker and audience. Even densely allusive prose such as Falstaff's is paced so that it always brings the audience with it.

This is palpably not the case with Tom. The songs apart, almost all of what he says is prose. But we do not keep up, and so cannot assume a shared place and time. What is more, there are no openings for other characters to enter. It is never clear whom Edgar addresses, or where or whether there is a switch of address. The audience onstage, like the audience offstage, can do little but be a mute witness to Tom's histrionics. But then at any moment Tom might draw in his external auditory, by way of direct address, by blessing or insult or touch. He can be embroiled in his schizophrenic frenzy, then suddenly face a face and implicate it. The same potential exists at every moment. But there is no absolute need for any such greeting; it is always contingent on decisions of the Tom-actor, whether extemporized or rehearsed. All of his audiences remain on the outside, watching and waiting, as though Tom has weaved his own circumambient magic circle, preventing ingress.

Uniquely, his songs have much the same effect. It seems that song was one of the most memorable aspects of the part's first performances: William Carroll has documented how representations of Poor Tom were "radically transformed" after Shakespeare's play, such that the figure was immediately identified with singing.[12] But it isn't that Tom is some kind of Autolycus-figure, entering in song, breaking into melody as his trade or calling card. He isn't a ballad monger. His relation to song is instead scrupulously keyed to his suffering: the songs come as fragments, barely recognized, and less the sound of freedom than of unsleeping

---

meaning—that I am calling *creaturely*." *On Creaturely Life: Rilke, Benjamin, Sebald* (Chicago: University of Chicago Press, 2006), 34; italics in original.

12. Carroll, "Songs of Madness," 83–84.

vocative competition or taunting, as though he constantly has an Ariel in his ear, a jangling, banging tinnitus, with tabor and pipe keeping him from sleep and issuing in this aural overflow.

Carroll notes how in the post-*Lear* afterlife Tom's songs quickly became sentimentalized, evoking a picturesque pathos or romanticized sublime.[13] This speaks the songs' assimilation into essentially ameliorative popular memory. But as much as it is true that Tom's songs link to some such communal wellspring, they are anything but happily flowing with it. The songs are touched by community but also severed from it. Certainly there is a germ in the part of later works, like Brome's *Jovial Crew*, or Gay's *Beggar's Opera*, perhaps even something like Jonson's *Bartholomew Fair*. But Tom does not stop the show, or beg for attention, or address a song to the other exiles around the fire, or receive anyone's thanks or harmonies. His songs cannot be shared; no one can join in; on every occasion they irrupt from nowhere and vanish unresolved, without accompaniment or applause. Their only accompaniment, in fact, is Tom's own discourse: in particular, the recitative prose that the songs break off and back into. In a sense, then, these saturating enumerations become the source of the songs; in turn, the songs disappear into silence, or pantomime, and then the voice returns with further harried list making. The effect is double: to desentimentalize the songs, and to decertify the catechisms. The songs lose their connection to an appeased community. The catechisms lose their authority as a moral map.

Indeed we might understand all of Tom's discourse as a kind of scrambled madrigal, one whose vertical harmonies have been cut and flung into tortured, interruptive horizontality. Tom's clauses are often arranged in apparently formulaic syntactic series—a little catechistic, a little euphuistic—but always lacking the context or symmetries that might settle the emotion or make the formulas more than an emptied observance. Consequently, we hear the *fact* of formulas, swallowed and refluxed like a child might medicine.[14] Occasionally a phrase scans as

---

13. Ibid., 90–93.
14. Bridget Gellert Lyons: "The contrast between Edgar's stock of formulations and the language of Lear's visions in their respective madnesses is as striking as the general difference . . . between an imitated role and an involuntary condition. As a madman, Edgar invokes the most familiar moral formulas. . . . The formal structure of Edgar's syntactic series and

a pentameter, the subject-matter betraying the distance from more formally organized times: "Drinkes the green mantle of the standing Poole" (TLN 1912-13); "The Prince of Darkenesse is a Gentle-man" (TLN 1921). More often the idiom is incantatory, or like hurried intervallic recitative, anxious to catch up to songs that have already been and gone and can be claimed now only as snatched echo.

Our own critical taxonomies are lacking here—the word *prose* applies to Tom's discourse only in the absence of some better alternative. I don't know of another part like it: denied the line, denied the comforts of prose. We might even say that Tom exists—virtually, literally—*at the end of the line*. Think of that ghostly space at a line's end, alive with memory and imminence; think of the possibilities glimpsed or intuited but unspoken; imagine living at that space, in it, as it: and find Tom. He is at that prosodic no place, allegory of a life marked by privation and waiting.

---

parallels . . . illustrate[s] exemplary couplings." "The Subplot as Simplification in *King Lear*," in *Some Facets of King Lear*, ed. Rosalie Colie and F. T. Flahiff (London: University of Toronto Press, 1974), 29-30. I think Lyons simplifies the subplot, though her larger argument that the Gloucester-plot is structured by way of repeated morality devices is pertinent.

9

INTERLUDE

To Be Allegory

With a figure like Tom, allegorical inferences often enter before the person, before even the name: "the name of loss and exile, of suffering and abasement, is poor Tom."[1] But perhaps this can be taken further. Perhaps he isn't just an allegory of something, but an allegory *tout court*.

For Angus Fletcher, "allegories are the natural mirrors of ideology," the "monuments to our ideals."[2] Before experiences can be personal, they have to be tagged with their exemplary purpose:

> The allegorical hero is not so much a real person as he is a generator of other secondary personalities, which are partial aspects of himself.... A systematically complicated character will generate a large number of other protagonists who react against or with him in a syllogistic manner, ... and the finest hero will then be the one who most naturally seems to generate subcharacters—aspects of himself—who become the means by which he is revealed, facet by facet.[3]

---

1. William C. Carroll, "'The Base Shall Top th'Legitimate': The Bedlam Beggar and the Role of Edgar in *King Lear*," *Shakespeare Quarterly* 38, no. 4 (1987): 430.
2. Angus Fletcher, *Allegory: The Theory of a Symbolic Mode* (Ithaca, N.Y.: Cornell University Press, 1964), 368, 360.
3. Ibid., 35–36.

This suggests the habitual limitation of allegorical writing, which Fletcher sums up in a single word: "anesthesia." Allegory presupposes a "ritual order."[4] The reader is distanced, and experience is witnessed as though through glass: it isn't quite real.

But is this adequate to Tom, or indeed more broadly to Edgar? Noting how the word *daimon* (almost a synonym of allegory) derives etymologically from *daiomai*, meaning to distribute or divide, Fletcher suggests that the "allegorical agent . . . is always a division of some larger power"; "a specific Idea possesses him and governs all he does."[5] This in turn links to the agent's place within a fixed celestial hierarchy, whether a ladder or a circle, assigning the figure his position in an unalterable progress toward God. Tom clearly enough evokes some such model—he can seem fixed to a purgatorial wheel, exiled from grace, on the lowest rung of choiceless perdition, and so on. But he also profoundly escapes it. Shakespeare generates a kind of concentric reversal, whereby the outer circle moves to the centre. Accordingly, Tom isn't so much a thin fragment of some organizing whole as a concatenation of numerous such divisions in one. What is more, Tom does not obediently serve his maker's purpose, or return for definition to him. He must be distinguished from figures like the Dwarf, Palmer, or Talus in *The Faerie Queen*, or Sancho Panza in *Don Quixote*, who "arise to help the hero" in a "process of fractionating personality." Fletcher writes that "by splitting off these chips of composite character, the author is able to treat them as pure, isolated, personified ideas, and they lend themselves better, as a result, to the overall aim of system and 'consistency.'"[6]

In fundamental ways Tom neither helps Edgar, nor derives from an idea, nor returns to a ritual order. The Tom-part is repeatedly wracked by ideological and institutional violence, and yet it doesn't come home to such things; it isn't settled or explained by them. Instead it exists in constantly resistant and asymmetric relation to all such coercion. A principle of Tom's role, in its voice as much as body, is that things jut

4. Ibid., 367.
5. Ibid., 60.
6. Ibid., 37–38

out and deconnect, like straw or nails or digits, each a sticking point for harmonious allegorizing.[7]

Tom is a figure beyond socialized belonging: this is the most basic implication of the uncertainty as to who or what he addresses. The institution, epistemology, and indeed time to which he belongs is radically unclear. In this way Tom might evoke what Emmanuel Levinas calls the "absolutely foreign," which "alone can instruct us." The experience of such a thing, says Levinas, would be *"a traumatism of astonishment"*: "refractory to every typology, to every genus, to every characterology, to every classification—and consequently the term of a 'knowledge' finally penetrating beyond the object. The strangeness of the Other, his very freedom!"[8]

The freedom appealed to here is nothing to do with liberty or choice. It refers to "a being that stands beyond every attribute"—beyond any attributes that would "qualify him," or "reduce him to what is common to him and other beings." This sort of nakedness is not "absorbed in the accomplishment of the function for which they are made: when they are subordinated to their own finality so radically that they disappear in it." Instead, it stands out in itself, "rending forms"; it is not resolvable into "the relations that link up to the totality."[9] Similarly, Tom cannot be plugged back into a defined place or parentage, the kind of connection that allows effective domestication, and so conceptual vanishing. Instead, he is all surplus, all remainder. His is the least beautiful figure imaginable—as in neat and elegant, the perfect size for the appreciative mind to grasp: "The thing is always an opacity, a resistance, a ugliness."[10]

---

7. Walter Benjamin's model of allegory is at times more pertinent: "Linguistic virtuosity, word, syllable, and sound are emancipated from any context of traditional meaning and are flaunted as objects which can be exploited for allegorical purposes. The language of the baroque is constantly convulsed by rebellion on the part of the elements which make it up." *The Origin of German Tragic Drama*, trans. John Osborne (London: Verso, 1998), 207.

8. Emmanuel Levinas. *Totality and Infinity: An Essay on Exteriority*, trans. Alphonso Lingis (Pittsburgh, Penn.: Duquesne University Press, 1999), 74-75; italics in original.

9. Ibid., 74.

10. Ibid. Compare Timothy Morton: "The ecological thought contemplates a subaesthetic level of being, beyond the cute and beyond the awesome. We can't call it beautiful (self-contained, harmonious) or sublime (awe-inspiring, open). This level unsettles and disgusts. It doesn't mirror our fantasies." *The Ecological Thought* (Cambridge, Mass.: Harvard University Press, 2010), 91.

You can turn your gaze away—as Kent and Gloucester do—but the thing will remain to be accounted for. This means that the flotsam and jetsam of his display—even considered as waste, as the effluvium of sunk or swallowed or never-been lives—presents itself as possibility: not only a buried or prevented past, but a counterfactual future and memory: "They are always in some respect like those industrial cities where everything is adapted to a goal of production, but which, full of smoke, full of wastes and sadness, exist also for themselves. For a thing nudity is the surplus of its being over its finality."[11]

Tom is no synecdoche of a settled ritual order. He carries a supercharge of allegorical possibility, but also of the possibility that *is* allegory: an allegory as yet unclaimed; an allegory without a narrative to cleave to; an allegory defined by the fact of allegory, of *being allegorical*. We can return here to Tom's first words: "fathom and half," and recall that *fathom* is also a verb, meaning to understand or ponder. These annunciating words herald the epistemological challenge of his presence. Perhaps Poor Tom is himself a figure for *allegoria*, or for *aenigma*: one whose surface covers untellable depths. As ever, Shakespeare makes the subjunction real: allegory suffers a kind of exposing verisimilitude. And one effect, likewise characteristic, is that totalizing systems shrivel, and we are left with the pathos of particularity.

And so what can it mean if a life *is* allegorical: consciously experienced, moment by moment, precisely as allegory? Perhaps this:

If we were to meet an allegorical character in real life, we would say of him that he was obsessed with only one idea . . . or that his life was patterned according to absolutely rigid habits from which he never allowed himself to vary. It would seem that he was driven by some hidden, private force; or . . . controlled by some foreign force, something outside the sphere of his own ego.[12]

This touches part of Tom's valency, but still it is too monothemed, too tied to the presupposed ruling idea. Tom is certainly compelled and

11. Levinas, *Totality and Infinity*, 74.
12. Fletcher, *Allegory*, 40.

spoken, but multiply so: he is not so much an allegorical figure as a figure of frangible, fungible allegory.[13]

Such a figure will always be delivered from elsewhere, and yet pushing somewhere else. Its apparent actions—words, movements—will instantly produce supplements. Each move will generate a remainder, and beg rather than satisfy interpretation. It will be a shadow and shadowed, an echo and echoed. It will travel in parallel or tangential paths, or be a symptom of some prior or succeeding cause. Any present voice and body may derogate from the origin, or seek to attain it. It will be a ruin or a fragment, implying but not delivering a whole. It will be ever-contingent, ever-dependent—but a dependence which can do nothing to protect or secure it. Equally, the dependence will never quite claim it. To be an allegory begins to suggest the most alarming kind of freedom: *to be an allegory!* To be an allegory, without a securing connection to ideology; without a frame or a hierarchy on which to peg one's movements. It begins to suggest the simplest modern pathos.

---

13. Compare Bernard Spivack's suggestion that allegorical figures possess *esse* rather than *Existenz*: "What it does is what it has to do by virtue of what it explicitly and indivisibly is." *Shakespeare and the Allegory of Evil: The History of a Metaphor in Relation to His Villains* (New York: Columbia University Press, 1958), 127.

10

SCENE 4

Tom's Places

Tom speaks the poor creature of earth. It could be anyone at all:

> The foul fiend follows me
> Through the sharp hawthorne blow the winds [Quarto: cold wind]
> (TLN 1827-28)

The poor thing is cowering: feel the flesh quiver from the cold, flesh which hides in the hawthorn and gets cut for its pains. There is no release, no comfort, no worst. The winds blow through the hawthorn and sharpen its spikes. Violence begets violence. The bristling hawthorn is also a subject: everything is tensile with its own pain. The bush is passed through, but the winds too are cold; they need shelter. The weather is alive. Place feels.

> Whom the foule fiend hath led through Fire
> And through Flame [Quarto: Foord]
> Through Sword
> And whirle-poole
> O're Bog
> And Quagmire (TLN 1832-34)

These are Tom's places, an unremitting torture, in life and after it, without hope of rest:

> That hath laid knives under his Pillow
> And Halters in his Pue
> Set Rats-bane by his Porredge (TLN 1835-36)

He is forever tempted by death, in sleep, in church, at breakfast. The fiend is despair, telling him he has failed, beckoning him to vice.

> Made him Proud of heart
> To ride on a bay trotting Horse
> Over foure incht Bridges
> To course his owne shadow for a Traitor. (TLN 1836-38)

Not a fidget in this living is free; everything is precarious, a tiny bridge over the whirlpool. He chases himself, like a dog its tail, accusing himself, feeding upon phantoms. His shadow is as substantial as his body. He is immersed in place, remade as it, his substance the flame and ford and quagmire:

> Blisse thee from Whirle-Winds,
> Starre-blasting
> And taking
> Do poore Tom some charity
> Whom the foul fiend vexes.
> There could I have him now
> And there
> and there again
> And there. (TLN 1840-43)

The speech ends, but it doesn't end; it can never end: the cue words echo and repeat, the show goes on, and Tom is in his suffering. This is no complacent naturist, happy for the dangle, briefly at one with what he can pretend is his origin. The exposure is alarmingly denaturing, such that a diabolic new nature is revealed, like some hideous holographic under-truth: "Pillicock sat on Pillicock hill (TLN 1857)."

It isn't only that he sees himself as a shrunken or severed penis, or as the lost son, even homunculus, cast out from family and generation and his own body.[1] He imagines the entire scene as composed of such, millions before him, reduced as he is now, the hill an accumulation of biodegraded remnants: fossils of pillicocks from which he arises, to which he will return, and upon which he now sits, watched by all, cursed with the brief and unwanted eminence of exposure. And exactly such a life sentence can be heard in the sound with which the speech ends—or does not end:

> Alow
> > Alow
> > > Loo
> > > Loo (TLN 1857)

Again Tom's cue is no cue, it defers to nothing but its own inescapability. It is a call, a wail, a lament, a hunting cry, with Tom both hunter and hunted: "Take heed o'th'foule Fiend (TLN 1860)."

Perhaps he ventriloquizes, repeating the words of his master. Or perhaps he says beware the fiend; give him no room for entrance; he feeds on sin like a puttock:

> Obey thy Parents
> Keepe thy words Justice [Quarto: justly]
> Sweare not
> Commit not with mans sworne Spouse
> Set not thy Sweet-heart
> On proud array (TLN 1863-63)

Do none of the things that I have done and for which I suffer:

> A Servingman
> Proud in heart
> And minde
> that curl'd my haire

---

1. See Peter L. Rudnytsky, "'The Darke and Vicious Place': The Dread of the Vagina in *King Lear*," *Modern Philology* 96, no. 3 (1999): 291-311.

> wore Gloves in my cap
> serv'd the Lust of my Mistris heart
> and did the acte of darkenesse with her
> swore as many Oathes
> as I spake words
> & broke them in the sweet face of Heaven (TLN 1865-69)

His torture is confession, the unremitting memory of chosen vice. He saw it, he knew it was false, and he did it, over and over and over again:

> One
> That slept in the contriving of lust
> And wak'd to doe it
> Wine lov'd I deerely [Quarto: deeply]
> Dice deerely
> And in Woman
> Out-Paramour'd the Turke (TLN 1869-72)

His story comes as snatched memories, partly in a lost moment, partly the judgment upon it:

> Let not the creaking of shooes
> Nor the rustling of Silkes
> Betray they poore heart to woman
> Keepe thy foot out of Brothels
> Thy hand out of Plackets
> Thy pen from Lenders Bookes
> And defye the foule Fiend. (TLN 1874-78)

He has been places, soft, luring, courtly places; he has fallen for luxurious fabric, and that fabric's falling; he has listened as they have come to him, creeping along the floorboards after dinner; he has been in private chambers with beauty that turned treacherous. They came to him, and the betrayal once achieved, they left. He went searching for them, down into stews, grabbing at passing women, a lewd fist, a spiral into dispossession, and into the deepest debt, deep existential debt. And the devil arrived to exact his charge.

Perhaps he has learned his lessons; perhaps he merely recites them, in neurotic terror; perhaps they possess him, and he is their amanuensis, the vehicle of apodeictic ethics.[2] And perhaps precisely this is his torture, to be the bounded host of allegories, that shoot and sizzle and die and repeat inside him, the windowless house of eternal return:

> False of Heart,
> Light of eare
> bloody of hand
> Hog in sloth
> Foxe in stealth
> Wolfe in greedinesse
> Dog in madnes
> Lyon in prey. (TLN 1872–74)

The accusation is at once escalating and revolving, always supplementing but never truly changing. To recognize another sin, a new sin, is to do little more than locate yet another metaphor for his vice: and the metaphor instantly transmutes to metonym because the thing he resembles is in him, at him, burrowing and biting, an inextricable part of his composition. Resemblance is substance. Tom enters a place and becomes it; he eats a thing and it alters him: and so too the other way around, as place and things are engrossed by him. This is his constitution, words as thing, things as body, body as place, place as mind. His words become a metonym, as Lear has it, of "plagues" in the "pendulous ayre" (TLN 1848). Two of Tom's long speeches end with the stage direction, *"Storm still"*: the words come from and return to weather.

To the extent that the lid lifts on brimming appetites and episodes and preventions, it clearly isn't only the one life that we hear.[3] Often

---

2. Harry Berger Jr. notes that Tom's "list of commandments has the ring of a parental catechism, and therefore helps target the father's hypocrisy." *Making Trifles of Terrors: Redistributing Complicities in Shakespeare* (Stanford, Calif.: Stanford University Press, 1997), 57.

3. Grigori Kozintsev: "Edgar . . . was no longer, he did not exist: he had been taken away from the world and his shadow remained—poor Tom. . . . The human features had disap-

Tom cuts himself off, severs a rhythmic riff, as though with some shard cut from another tale. The sense is of a swirl of attenuated or forgotten or emergent lives: stone-age or myth-aged, yesterday or tomorrow, overlaying and segueing and overtaking, even nipping each other quiet, like puppies:

> Poore Tom
> That eats the swimming Frog
> The Toad
> The Tod-pole
> The wall-Newt
> And the water
> That in the furie of his heart
> When the foul Fiend rages
> Eats Cow-dung for Sallets
> Swallowes the old Rat
> And the ditch-Dogge
> Drinkes the green mantle of the standing Poole (TLN 1908–13)

There is descent and ascent, ascent and descent, the self-same acts able to be seen as either. Tom eats the creatures, and he is what he eats. It is at once exiled degradation and a palpable evolution, from tadpole to amphibian to mammal. One man's disgust is another man's food; one man's food is another thing's life; one thing's condition is another thing's future; one thing's future is another thing's past—and one thing's past may be the same thing's future. There is no such thing as the worst. There is instead a bodily memory of tracks and sources, of deep creaturely interconnectedness, not such that we love all things but that we house all things, if not as microorganisms than as the quarks of returnable memory:[4]

---

peared. But this had happened to others as well. . . . People like him, faceless shadows of people. People who had been flung out of life, had ceased to be human. And this was reality. . . . Many voices have merged into one voice; Poor Tom is the leader of the chorus." *King Lear, the Space of Tragedy: The Diary of a Film Director*, trans. Mary Mackintosh (London: Heinemann Educational Publishers, 1977), 192, 197.

4. Donna Harraway: "Organisms are ecosystems of genomes, consortia, communities, partly digested dinners, mortal boundary formations. . . . To be an organism is to be the fruit of 'the co-opting of strangers, the involvement and infolding of others into ever more complex

> Who is whipt from Tything to Tything
> And stockt
> Punish'd
> And imprison'd
> Who hath three Suites to his backe
> Sixe shirts to his body
> Horse to ride
> And weapon to weare
> But Mice
> And Rats
> And such small Deare
> Have been Toms food
> For seven long yeare (TLN 1913-18)

His voices are turbulent with staggered or anachronic simultaneity. At times the voices gather escalating momentum, but even here it can seem that the rhythms are taking the speaker, as one phrase vents another, and then another, as though a sonic translation of sessile proliferation. He cannot move; he is stuck to his rock, like a punished clump of mussels. And yet he is condemned to relive the immemorial fact of reproduction, past and continuing. The germens spill, and Tom is at once the mess and the upsurge from it. A single possibility can perhaps be wasted: but others will mutate from the spillage.

It isn't that *Lear* presents human life as no different from animal or vegetable life. Caroline Spurgeon long ago noted the preponderance of beast imagery in the play, much of it shocked or disgusted or cursing.[5]

---

and miscegenous genomes.' . . . Yoking together all the way down is what sym-bio-genesis means. The shape and temporality of life on earth are more like a liquid-crystal consortium folding in on itself again and again than a well-branched tree. Ordinary identities emerge and are rightly cherished, but they remain always a relational web opening to non-Euclidean pasts, presents, and futures. . . . These are the contagions and infections that wound the primary narcissism of those who still dream of human exceptionalism." *When Species Meet* (Minneapolis: University of Minnesota Press, 2008), 31-32. Haraway is quoting in the middle of this excerpt from Lynn Margulis and Dorion Sagan, *Acquiring Genomes: A Theory of the Origins of Species* (New York: Basic Books, 2002), 205.

5. Caroline Spurgeon, *Shakespeare's Imagery and What It Tells Us* (Cambridge, U.K.: Cambridge University Press, 1935), 339-42.

By the same token, *Lear* does not foreshadow a Heideggerian worldview, in which a profound gap separates the "world-making" of humans from animalistic "captivation" in environment.[6] Tom is both of these things: existing on a subcreaturely continuum with the mantle of the pond and the wind-shivered hawthorn; wracked by the pathos of remembered possibilities, regretted in their commission or in their absence, testifying to his mutating life amid historical human community.

It won't do to sentimentalize any of this: to sentimentalize Tom, or his suffering, or nature, or the ecology to which all things contribute. Or rather: yes, let's sentimentalize, but as they might have done in pre-Romantic days—as the great suffering poet William Cowper might have done, feeling for every fold of earth, every suffocating weed, but never forgetting that the same earth will cover him when he is dead—and not think twice about it, just as these same seasons can turn in a moment from supplicating breeze to killing cold, or the sun can suddenly twist you to a distended shadow, a limbed fork or digital attenuation, reminding you that you are never more than an existential renter, fugitive imposter in the stranger's body that others, careless and preoccupied, assume is yours. Nature is no model for a man. But then, inevitably, it *is*.

---

6. Martin Heidegger, *The Fundamental Concepts of Metaphysics: World, Finitude, Solitude*, trans. William McNeill and Nicholas Walker (Bloomington: Indiana University Press, 1995).

11

INTERLUDE

History Man

It is well known that in speaking Tom, Shakespeare draws erratically but repeatedly on Samuel Harsnett's *Declaration of Egregious Popish Impostures*.[1] Harsnett's pamphlet is a lengthy exposure of bogus exorcisms, the "tragicall comedie" in which the "Romish" frauds seize upon any misfortune and symptom, especially in young women (a slip in the kitchen, a fright from a cat), impute it to the busy insinuations of the devil, then liberate the poor fools from possession via flagrantly theatrical "legerdemain." Harsnett's multiple victims all seem to speak through Tom, as though he collects in himself a gullible collective passion. Body becomes demonically expressive, almost cosymptomatic with language, as a sleepless, writhing, rented physicality speaks the fury of possession: "Here be certain actions, motions, distortions, dislocations, writhings, tumblings and turbulent passions fitting a devil's part . . . not to be performed but by the supplenesse of sinews, pliableness of ioynts, and nimbleness of all parts."[2]

---

1. See Kenneth Muir, "Samuel Harsnett and King Lear," *Review of English Studies* 2, no. 5 (1951): 11–21; Stephen Greenblatt, *Shakespearean Negotiations: The Circulation of Social Energy in Renaissance England* (Oxford: Oxford University Press, 1988), 94–128; Meredith Skura, "Dragon Fathers and Unnatural Children: Warring Generations in *King Lear* and Its Sources," *Comparative Drama* 42, no. 2 (2008): 133–40.

2. Samuel Harsnett, *Declaration of Egregious Popish Impostures* (London: James Roberts, 1603), 23.

In Shakespeare and Harsnett alike, one senses the intense vulnerability of social being; the fragility of decorum and self-possession; the permeability of mind and body; the capacity of apparently histrionic or formal gestures, as one might see in a theater, to come horrifyingly true; the heteroglossic, almost schizophrenic porosity of public discourse, which at any moment may flood the mind of a single subject. But Tom's subjection to such things is different: a subjection not to be exorcized, never to abate. Tom certainly speaks multitudes, but he is also left over: bereft of collective worshiping rituals; bereft of the permission to forget and move on; bereft, perhaps most strikingly, of judgment, whether dismissive, punitive, or exonerating. And if he is left over, it is because he is unrecuperated; more simply, he is still happening.

The reluctance of Tom is of the essence. He doesn't choose his presence; he doesn't choose his words. Both his words and his presence, consequently, are already taken; already subject to allegory. This is his passion, to be taken, over and over, as an example. And this is also his magnetic historicity. Edgar's experience is extreme, extremity piled upon extremity. But still it is in a known world, where the body feels and love hurts and families eat each other up. Whereas Tom? To adapt what the doctor says of Lady Macbeth: "Heaven knows what he has known."[3]

This makes him the most historical figure in the play—perhaps the only figure in the play who truly feels history in the making. Tom's schizophrenic vocatives repeatedly replay the passage between unfinished, unregulated, in-the-moment experience, and disciplined retrospective narration. They even speak the pain of this movement, as appetite or joy is suddenly swamped by post facto judgments; or a prescriptive and punitive litany is escaped from, and moral laws give way to childlike laments or games, or to renewed cohabitation with the agents of confusion.[4] Tom is not simply some haunted demoniac, wrig-

---

3. *Macbeth*, 5.1.50.
4. Kenneth Gross: "This landscape is archaic, yet full of contemporary detritus, things reified, accumulated, and dispersed all at once—soaked and decayed in the aftermath of the storm, like the contents of a drowned man's pockets. . . . Tom's memories also suggest fragments of a picaresque romance, a story like that of Thomas Nashe's 'unfortunate traveller,' who thinks of travel itself as a primal curse. . . . Each demonic name—Hoppedance, Smulkin,

gling with the undead or pricked by sleepless sin. Shakespeare burdens him with a kind of intermitted history, not so much national (as in British) or corporate (as in a particular group or vested interest) as folk. I mean folk history in various senses: retailing of mythic or legendary material, often precivil or prechronicle; bringing into the playworld otherwise excluded common people, beggars and servants, of city and court and country; reliving different subordinacies, as he either reports his subjection to some superior's imperative (his mistress's lust, the foul fiend) or rehearses, usually ventriloqually, the lessons he has learned.[5]

This posits something more faceted than a simple idea that Tom stands for houseless poverty, the disenfranchised, those left shivering outside the magic circle. Of course this is Tom's basic home register. But if Tom were simply the Bedlam Beggar, he would be sociologically placed: and he isn't. He is a multiply sourced, mannerist, even baroque construction. He is a made thing, a kind of consciously inflicted injury—but one that claims a status as natural, somehow more indigenous and independent than anyone.

This instantly ups the ante. In a sense our witnessing of his making—and how his made-ness then becomes automatized (it acts on its own, unplugged from its supposed source) and unclaimable (it will not return to its maker)—tears the veil from what we habitually take to be the natural mysteries of creation, or the inheritable orders of history. Instead Tom embodies the play's mutagenic historicity: a world crawling toward death, stuck on a primitive loop, as though whims and choices do no more than iterate an irreducibly determining Nature; a world of panoptic cultural alteration, in which any number of repairs

---

Flibbertigibeet, Frateretto—is a wound laid down upon the skin of air. The names are also games, a relief from other more coercive or frustrated vocatives in this play. . . . They conjure a non-existent or lost childishness. . . . Each bit of nonsense is a way of hearing experience, naming its troubled parts. The nonsense translates words whose own meanings are themselves desperate, lewd, infantile, residual, and mad." *Shakespeare's Noise* (Chicago: University of Chicago Press, 2001), 183–85.

5. Of course Tom also concentrates the play's own histories, echoing and animating most of the play's protagonists: Edmund (fox in stealth, wolf in greediness), Gloucester (the foul Flibbertigibbet), Kent (stocked and punished), Oswald (duteous to his mistress), Cordelia (who gives anything to poor Tom?), the bad sisters (false of heart, light of ear), Cornwall (bloody of hand), and Lear (bless thy five wits).

and institutions can seem latent, choking for oxygen as they seek the air; a world of sudden recombinations and interruptive mutations, neurotically alert to momentary chance, as though destiny may truly be accidental and the smallest heartbeat a kind of gamble.

And so in this section I want to take seriously the question of Tom's historicity: how he bears the past and promises the future; how he mediates the possibilities of historical understanding. But to do this it is imperative that history be given its proper scope: a scope as vast and as microscopic as the lives that make it. The historicity of *Lear*, as of Edgar/Tom, far exceeds merely civic measurements. More than one frame is needed to tackle this question.

Frame 1

Tom calls, at least in part, from the deeps of dark, unpermitted knowledge. How aboriginal a figure is Tom? Or, from the other end of the telescope, how degraded? Is he a snapshot of bare life? Of unaccommodated man? Of man as brother to the worm? Or might he be less even than this?

One of the truly strange, truly wretched conceptions is Plotinus's bare matter. He identifies such matter, bereft of soul and intellect, as "privation," and thereby evil:

> [It] goes out from itself because it is not perfect or primary but is a sort of ghost of the first soul, is filled with indefiniteness and sees darkness, and has matter by looking at that which it does not look at (as we say that we see darkness as well as the things we really see).[6]

Plotinus evokes here a condition of absolute exile from the Good, beyond helpless, beyond all possibility of action: it "has matter by looking at that which it does not look at." This impossible-sounding paradox suggests some kind of zombie condition, a hyperallergic passivity, where looking is bereft of all associations with the sovereign light-filled

---

6. Plotinus, *Enneads*, Vol 1, trans. A. H. Armstrong (Cambridge, Mass.: Harvard University Press, 1966), 287.

eye and becomes instead a blank face into a void, a faceless face, turned to shapelessness, descrying nothing, without traction or relief, without even the release that might come from being recognized by or subjected to another. Instead, this matter is constituted as negativity, as though by ontological infection.

This is surely the territory of nightmare. Perhaps prenatal memory, when the not-yet nonchild is sentient in the shapeless dark, the known world like the belly of a whale, without even the dream of egress. Or in previsions of death, where there is no ground beneath feet, no stop to the fall, and life gets slowly flushed down a weirdly waterless drain into an end that is no end.

What can it mean, to be "a sort of ghost of the first soul"? It was there at the beginning: this intimacy to origins, one might surmise, will bring some whiff of prestige or affinity to truth. Or so it might do, for something other. But not for this sort-of ghost, which haunts but is left irrecoverably behind. Perhaps the first soul has whistled away, has gone into commission, and now is at one with the Good; or perhaps it is busily aspiring toward it in the healthy world, the world beyond the sort-of ghost that is boiling with aspirant life. Or perhaps this first soul has gone, is dead, and all that is left is its sort-of ghost, with neither a life to remember nor a body to haunt. Or perhaps this sort-of ghost is a botched creation, a remainder from when the gods were hard at their lathes, turning material into form, one of the sundry scraps that didn't make the cut. Or it is the incompossible, a sort-of ghost lacking even a simulacrum. Whatever it is, it can have no part in a well-ordered world:

> The principle of becoming is the nature of matter, which is so evil that it infects with its own evil that which is not in it but only directs its gaze to it. For since it is altogether without any share in good and is a privation of good and a pure lack of it, it makes everything which comes into contact with it in any way like itself.[7]

The "evil" here is not active satanic malevolence. It is far more lost than any such interfering ego-fueled demonism. Likewise it is much

---

7. Ibid.

farther beyond recovery than Augustinian evil, in which no human condition, however corrupted, is beyond the healing power of God.[8] It is privation: a pure lack of the good, of all things that constitute life in the greater theater. It is "the principle of becoming"—but not some existentially romantic notion of becoming as desire, as a liberating absence of fixity. No: this is becoming as a condition of confounded nonarrival. This matter never quite *is*. It has no form, no soul, no place, no mind. If anything comes into contact with it, that thing becomes like it, instantly deformed. Avoid it, therefore, or if once you come upon it, hasten to leave it behind.

How possibly to put such a thing in a story, or on a stage?

Perhaps start with something that is not, and make it move; and then watch as other beings, the ones that have verifiable face and mind and shape, slap it away, with instinctual aversion, like they might a leech.

But what if it has latched on, is sucking from your stock, and you have neither salt nor fire to repel it? Perhaps the therapy is good.

Frame 2

A word that comes to mind, almost as the principle of Tom's presence, is *shattering*: a shatter that attended his conception; a shatter necessary for his becoming. He carries the shatter with him as his own particular radiance or radiation. The shatter moves from large to small, small to large. It is the predicate of his arrival. No arrival, no survival without

---

8. Augustine sees evil as doubly insubstantial: at a deep ontological level, necessarily incommensurable with God's perfection; at an experiential level, a contingent disharmony that waits on the healing of God. The fact of a perfect God means that all corruptible things remain in part good: they may be deprived of some goodness, but not all, because to be without goodness is to be without being. So Augustine, through the love of God, praises all things in the creation. God is immutable perfection, and no life can be finally beyond God's. Augustine, who establishes the essential terms of the existentially vulnerable, radically guilty early modern self, Christianizes Plotinus's privation and understands it as living without God—an evil that can be repaired by the light of God. So there is no evil in God's creation, just things we "call evil because they do not harmonize with other things." But even these disharmonious things harmonize with some things, and therefore they are good. Essentially, then, evil is *not*; it is privation; it is not a substance. See *Confessions*, 2nd ed., trans. F. J. Sheed, ed. Michael P. Foley (Indianapolis: Hackett, 2006), 129–30.

the shatter. And this shatter, among other things, is precipitous death, but a death that will not be buried; a surrendered child who yet will not quite pass.

I have said that Tom suggests El Greco's hanging man. But he equally evokes those nameless cherubs and putti and baby skulls in Renaissance pictures, floating in clouds, merging in and out of vapor, neither of the world nor gone from it. In that world vanishing was never quite complete. Children died, but it was too much to accept that they died into nothing. Parents lived to see their children dead. The precipitous departure was not, of course, just that of infants. Whatever age they reached, children kept on dying. An estimated 60 percent were gone before they attained adulthood. It is hard to imagine this today, when the death of a child seems such a scandal to order and sense, a grief never to be overcome. The insult was once less exceptional. That it hurt, and bewildered, and sent survivors into guilty rage is not to be doubted. Think of Ben Jonson's elegy—his failed epigram—to his first son; think of Macduff pulling his hat over his eyes, unable to speak in the face of his pretty chickens' slaughter. We can only imagine the mothers. Who knows, perhaps the grief was worse, the insult more absolute. Dead kids were the way of the world. But because of this they were also the measure of any theology. In the face of this daily existential insult, only prayers and fiction are of any use, and then perhaps not much.

Deep in the bowels of *King Lear*, we find these insults turning—the fact of young death, the fact of impotent survival. The play is headed, of course, to drama's most infamous instance of a child predeceasing the parent. English popular tragedy in a sense began with one such child-death—that of Hieronimo's son, Horatio, in *The Spanish Tragedy*—and it just about ends with Cordelia's. But if the play is premised on this culminating example, the horror it embodies is immanent throughout—the horror of wasted life, of being born to die, of never really getting to live.

We get numerous images of conception and delivery, all threatened by wastage: the first scene, when the bastard Edmund is both the accidental issue of his parents' "fault" and already there, waiting behind the star of his nativity (TLN 457-61); the various "parings" and split eggs and spilled germens (TLN 670-701; 1663); Lear's curses upon the womb and his prayer that if his child should "teem," she will vent a child of spleen, diabolically resolved upon turning the mother into a dissolving statue of tears (TLN 789-804). It is this world that discharges Tom—the retched-up wretch who collects in himself all such febrile waste, strangely blessed in his persistence. He is the undead child, clamoring in the between spaces; the prevented child, spending curses upon the living; the returned child, dizzily spinning in sin; and the dying child, because all are alone, and none can be protected, and parents are helpless beneath the skies. He is all of these children, and none of them close enough to comfort.

Frame 3

A striking fact of Tom's speech in his first scene is that for all its molar uncertainty—uncertainty as to where the words come from or go to, uncertainty as to the stories they tell—at the molecular level the words are simple. Tom doesn't really pun.[9] He is not a fool; he is not a professional; he is not speaking to instruct or to entertain. But still more suggestive is the absence from the Tom-part of latent wordplay—surprising when the words seem so hurly burly, so random and firing. Surely, one might think, Shakespeare would find punning irresistible.

But—almost uniquely—resist it he does. Recall the usual effects of Shakespeare's buried puns. They can suggest a mind at odds with itself, and speak repressed or unadmitted emotions; they can ironize or judge intended meanings; or they can produce alternative scenic snapshots, recalling the past, projecting into the future, generating possibilities through recessive or layered space-time. But Tom has none of Shakespeare's layered metaphors, no future-hearkening metalepses, no subdued paronomasia.

Perhaps he doesn't speak these things because he already lives them. Tom enjoys no repression, no happy self-ignorance. All that is

---

9. There is perhaps one half-instance—"Pillicock sat on Pillicock hill"—but even here the effects are at once strikingly on the surface (an aural ricochet from Lear's cue of "Pelican daughters"; a plaintive self-observation) and lacking any appeal to the audience. For interpretation of the line see the previous chapter, Scene 4: Tom's Places.

normally pressed down has irrupted into air. This is the exposed life, the scandal of an absolute now, of imminence as inescapable repetition. There is nothing pending because judgment is here: past and future are here, now, on a terrible loop of warring simultaneity. Perhaps this is what it means to speak of theater's fabled present tense. History isn't so much abated or escaped as contracted into a single shatter, a single shiver, here christened Tom.

Frame 4

The effect of Tom's hurly-burly discourse, one mode cutting across or echoing into another, is that no voice is either forgotten or sovereign. Nothing he speaks, or that speaks him, has yet carried the day. In this context, the notion of historical progress is at best dubious, perhaps little more than one mode (and hardly the only) of hopeful violence. Consider this snatch of song:

> Swithold footed thrice the old
> He met the Night-mare, and her nine-fold
> Bid her a-light, and her troth-plight
> And aroynt thee Witch, aroynt thee (TLN 1900–903)

It is scraps like this that give the sense that Tom has been everywhere, been around for thousands of years. These reports seem to echo through him, as though he is a country ruin, whistling with immemorial winds. But they are also his own experiences, his own place: he was there when the demon met the witch, spying into secret congresses. It is as though Tom, more so even than the aged titan Lear, traverses vast historical time. And this in turn makes him familiar with principles of life making, or conditions of production, that are far distant from the aspirational sin-haunted city that his scraps of memory also at times evoke.

The world of this song is before all cities, or at least beyond them. The Night-mare, with her brood of nine, evokes some kind of ur-mother, like one of the dinosaurs in Spenser's *Faerie Queene*, slouching across hill and plain, obliviously awaiting the human contract. She is the gigantic succubus, draining sleeping men dry for the hell of it. But she is also the original single mother, her children a type of world-historical accident, the spawn of efficiently dead men, of suffocating dream and supra-civil desire. Odd how community is born and sociality conferred.

Editors usually gloss the song as a cryptic swearing off of sin, but more immediately the song depicts some sort of precontractual sex. "Bid her a-light / And her troth-plight": the demon-saint bids her ride him, as she is wont to do; this done, perhaps another bairn seeded, he asks for her pledge of betrothal ("troth-plight"). Here, perhaps, glimpsed as she is dismissed, is the play's notoriously absent lawful mother—the one Shakespeare does not allow either Gloucester or Lear to remember (as he does in the earlier *King Leir*).[10]

The busy "Swithold," circling the barren lands as though hunting for a future, confers an evolutionary leap upon the burdened mare. But progress in *Lear* is never assured for long. The very moment that her "troth-plight" is spoken, she is whipped into oblivion: "aroynt thee Witch, aroynt thee." The snatch of song gives an elliptical history of community, offered as though by metaleptic narrative flashes: chaos, appetite, life, law, and then the same law's failure to hold things together. And then once more the unending end, as the speech will not finish, and instead devolves into an unanswerable repeating cue-phrase ("aroynt thee"), deferring to no decorum but that of the scene his song has just evoked, one of tail-biting violence and ineradicable haunting. Tom returns into his echoing, ricocheting aurality, as though into memories that are happening still, happening now, happening never endingly.

Frame 5

Long before political struggle turns to military conflict, life for Edgar is essentially war. He embodies an extreme form of Hobbesean "dif-

10. See Coppelia Kahn, "The Absent Mother in *King Lear*," in *Rewriting the Renaissance: The Discourses of Sexual Difference in Early Modern Europe*, ed. Margaret W. Ferguson, Maureen Quilligan, and Nancy Vickers (Chicago: University of Chicago Press, 1986), 33-49.

fidence," in which personal conation, one's most basic address to the world, becomes a sleeplessly vigilant resistance to the hostile arrogations of strangers. But the resistance, however tenacious, is also in part futile. For Edgar is repeatedly invaded—indeed, can be understood as a site of invasion: an invasion symbolized by Tom, turning inside or upon Edgar like the very spirit of historical anguish. This captivity suggests Emmanuel Levinas's notion of the "permanent possibility of war":

> In war reality rends the words and images that dissimulate it, to obtrude in its nudity and its harshness.... When the drapings of illusion burn war is produced as the experience of pure being.... The trial by force is a test of the real. But violence does not consist so much in injuring and annihilating persons as in interrupting their continuity, making them play roles in which they no longer recognize themselves, making them betray not only commitments but their own substance, making them carry out actions that will destroy every possibility for action.[11]

Understood in this light, Tom per se becomes an effect or symptom of Edgar's inescapable condition of war. However—and this is the radical thing, the reason the figure is so much the augur of possibility—Tom is also the agent of alternatives. To see how this works, we need to recognize that Tom's world is not simply identical to Edgar's. He develops his own distinctive relation to others, to past and future, to the intimate rhythms and instants of the playworld. In this, Tom's curious insubstantiality—his negative or bracketed ontology—is a gift as much as a peril. For it removes Tom from preempting teleologies, especially the kinds of expectation attendant on being in a tragedy: that you will suffer heroically and die; or that you will witness this suffering and survive. Tom is not bound upon either wheel. He is not preemptively claimed by a generic teleology, in which, as Levinas has it, "the meaning of individuals (invisible outside of this totality) is derived from the

---

11. Emmanuel Levinas, *Totality and Infinity: An Essay on Exteriority*, trans. Alphonso Lingis (Pittsburgh, Penn.: Duquesne University Press, 1999), 21.

totality."[12] Against this, Levinas advocates "the eschatology of messianic peace," a "breach of the totality," heralding a "beyond" of history that is yet reflected "within experience":

> Submitting history as a whole to judgment, exterior to the very wars that mark its end, *it restores to each instant its full signification in that very instant*: all the causes are ready to be heard. It is not the last judgment that is decisive, but the judgment of all the instants in time, when the living are judged.[13]

Tom's irruption from the straw produces something very like this. It is a provocation, an advent, an instantaneous call to judgment—but an instantaneity that irrupts at every instant, ever new, ever scandalous. This means, for instance, that the mock trial of Lear's daughters—and implicitly of all justice—is at once a logical and an unnecessary follow-up to Tom's "breach." Shakespeare can safely cut the scene from the Folio version of the play because the mere fact of Tom has already arraigned the guilty. And his presence can achieve this precisely because he cannot be pinned down to a place or trade or even a name ("Tom" was a generic label for vagrants):

> The eschatological vision does not oppose to the experience of totality the protestation of a person in the name of his personal egoism or even of his salvation. Such a morality based on the pure subjectivism of the I is refuted by war, the totality it reveals, and the objective necessities.[14]

Consequently:

> We oppose to the objectivism of war a subjectivity born from the eschatological vision. The idea of infinity delivers the subjectivity

---

12. Levinas continues: "The unicity of each present is incessantly sacrificed to a future appealed to to bring forth its objective meaning." Ibid., 22.
13. Ibid., 23. Italics are mine.
14. Ibid., 25.

from the judgment of history to declare it ready for judgment at every moment and . . . called to participate in this judgment, impossible without it.[15]

This is Tom: more radically opened to judgment than any normative character could possibly be, ready for it at every moment, restoring to each instant its signification. Clearly this openness is aided, indeed allowed, by Tom's partially spectral constitution: the immanent knowledge that he is at once here and not here; that he can be mercurially or even virtually judged, as he can be mocked, ignored, whipped, or indentured—because he is not absolutely here and is not to be pinned down by sensory or quantifying measures; because his advent is imagined or ambiguous; because he has been effectuated without necessarily having been exposed; because he has been brought to light without fully being *revealed*. But still it is an awesome taking-on of historical possibility.

Frame 6

The Tom-part imports the most basic questions of origins, both personal and civic: questions about the persistence or recurrence of what seems past: memes, genes, stories, lives. In this he epitomizes Shakespeare's age, in which almost all claims of truth, fair or foul, advertised connection to a determining origin. I want to invoke just two: one political, one religious—usually kept apart, but alive and at war in Tom.

First, origin as law. This is the argument of political legitimacy, exemplified in the question of sovereignty. So, if kings come from the decree of God, origin argues for an untrammelled prerogative and against the requirement to take counsel; if they come from a contract among the people, it argues for something more contingent, accountable, and perhaps even revocable (of course, Hobbes's *Leviathan* in some ways welds the two models together). This way of thinking puts the stress upon agreed discourses and laws. Origin is written backward from the present, invariably by those who possess property. This child is legiti-

15. Ibid.

mate because her parents are married; this king is legitimate because the line of succession can be articulated; and so on. Origin is determined by persuasive sentences (legal, punitive, grammatical); rhetorical power gets reified as law. In a basic way subjects live under the law. They are happiest when the law doesn't touch them; they are always aware that it may; and sometimes it does, savagely, and the origin is scolded in the skin.

Second, origin as sin. This is the argument of religion, especially reformed Christianity. Humankind is a living result and repetition of original sin, a fact that embodiment, desire, sex, decay, and death everywhere make manifest. Original sin—as a scene (of a garden, a woman, a serpent), as a choice (to listen, to be tempted, to take the fruit), and as a chain of consequences (shame, painful childbirth, death)—discovers repeated, horribly pregnant distillation in untold numbers of subsequent events and substances: each cast of an eye, each bit of sperm, each newborn's ineluctably human constitution. Original sin thinking is thus radically immanent. Traces of this origin are in everything. In turn, each such thing is this origin, intact and hell-bent on the future. Anything might be guilty; by the same token, anything might be responsible. So we get a neurotically split dispensation. On the one hand, a determining event and ideology, active in everything, speaking of a univocal authority from and to which all things move; on the other hand, the atomized dispersal of making energy, such that the tiniest motion or corpuscle is a world unto itself, creating anew the direction of history—and yet with absolute responsibility, if not because prescribing the terms, then certainly because suffering them.

As law, sovereignty, or sin, Tom is written and rewriting. He is the tortured subject of renaissance and reformation.

Frame 7

More than any other figure in the play, Tom bears the marks of subjecthood, in particular its origins in subjection: wearing the words, enduring the diktats of his master or mistress in a manner that has precious little of the participatory dignity associated with citizenship. But at the same time this subjected subjecthood is brewing with alteration. Partly this is because he animates multitudes—in the storm, after the blinding, at the "cliff"—a demographic far beyond any putatively established institutions (court, feudality, church, family). This multitude doesn't stand for a defined social body; it isn't really the commonwealth or the crowd or even a loosely atomized collective we might associate with city or village or countryside. As ever, Tom doesn't quite resolve into corporate allegory.

And yet Tom also remains a single body, and in animating such extraordinary variety of desire and fear—popular and private, shareable and not—this body generates an anticipatory charisma, as of civic mutations that Tom's barely communicable pain make as necessary as they are presently impossible. In other words, political recognition of this ill-defined multitude is incipient even as it is not quite happening. And this, in turn, relates to Tom as the play's most symptomatic figure: a kind of shattered augury and consequence of the playworld's exploded authority. Partly this explosion means anarchy; partly it means too many authorities, partial or illegitimate (including Tom's foul fiend and mistress dominatrix). And if sovereignty is up for grabs, then it is also warring in or as Tom.

Here we need to recall some basic medieval-cum–early modern thinking. Once upon a time, the King owned a sublime "second body," whatever the frailties that youth, age, or madness delivered to his "first" one.

> For the King has in him two Bodies, viz., a Body natural, and a Body politic. . . . His Body politic is a Body that cannot be seen or handled, consisting of Policy and Government, and constituted for the Direction of the People, and the Management of the public weal, and this Body is utterly void of Infancy, and old Age, and other natural Defects and Imbecilities, which the Body natural is subject to.[16]

---

16. Edmund Plowden's *Reports*, cited in Ernst Kantorowicz, *The King's Two Bodies: A Study in Medieval Political Theology* (Princeton, N.J.: Princeton University Press, 1981), 7.

It is pretty much the premise of *King Lear* that this "political theology" is a fiction. The natural body of Lear—as though by design—suffers all the grievous insufficiencies listed here by Elizabethan lawyer Edmund Plowden. And yet—the irony is deep and serious—his wracked mind and body seem to have far *more* perdurable substance than the magical flesh-beyond-flesh of monarchical ideality. This second body is as good as dead, having been frittered, bartered, ransacked into oblivion.[17] But this doesn't mean that the idea of a magically legitimate sovereignty has simply expired: of something sublime, beyond mortal measurement, demanding awe, and in that demand paradoxically dignifying those humbled by its truth.[18] It just means that it doesn't inhere in any present monarch.

And so the action plays out variations upon the possible consequences of this predicative death. One of the possibilities, powerfully foreshadowed, is of this magical body's royal resurrection. This is part of the burden of Cordelia. Her murder doesn't murder the idea of the monarch's two bodies; it doesn't murder the possibility, or still less the hope, that it might return. Indeed it may well be that some such nostalgia is already at work in the play: that it apprehends a state without king or queen, and yet far removed from the pithy order of any republic known to history, and simply shivers at the thought. But still Cordelia is wasted. Consequently, the potential of this second body is passed onto Edgar and Tom.[19] And thus it may well be Tom's detonated sublimity

---

17. Lori Anne Ferrell sees this "ruling metaphor" of the king's two bodies as being tested "to the breaking point." She identifies a double suicide of monarchical ideology and person: "*King Lear* is about the consequences of what.... James VI, and I, would surely have condemned as a uniquely monarchical act of self-murder.... With the division of his kingdom that is his body politic, ... Lear has committed suicide outright." "*King Lear* and the Suicide-Trick," in *King Lear: A Critical Guide*, ed. Andrew Hiscock and Lisa Hopkins (London: Continuum, 2011), 110, 114. Ferrell unfortunately doesn't expand or test her striking conclusion, that Lear is "a vexed ghost traversing a blasted landscape."

18. Much the same language attaches to the reification of democracy in modern polities (whatever it actually means, as process or praxis).

19. Eric L. Santner: "What appears with the emergence of the stateless is not simply the wretchedness of the human animal stripped of his or her social insignia; what appears is rather a bit of the *flesh* of the social bond itself, the stuff that the body of the sovereign was formerly charged with figuratively—and often theatrically—incorporating." *The Royal Re-*

that promises most true—promises, that is, a future time (a time perhaps already belated) when the unquiet multivoiced body will become the origin of sovereignty.[20]

Frame 8

For all that Tom is as stripped as a twig, at one with thorns and mud, he is not reducible to "bare life," if we mean by that some condition before or without political orders, common to all living beings, a kind of pure objecthood. Lear perhaps thinks he sees some such thing, the base mettle of man beyond institutional inclusions: but this is not true. Giorgio Agamben elsewhere defines bare life as suffering the "fracture" of voice (which it possesses) from language (which it does not). This is pretty much how Tom has usually been understood: a vocative torrent without meaning other than some blanket allegory of exclusion. But this is to put interpretive refuge before the actual thing in motion. Tom is voice, its bodied, primordial, supralinguistic pathos; but he is also, at every point, language. This is the unique thing. In much the same way, he is closer to pure flesh than perhaps any other figure in drama. But this flesh is also always riven through with script: this of course is the most basic fact of Tom, insofar as he is a constructed thing, ontologically factitious. But it is equally a fact of his existing, whether understood as objecthood, or subjecthood, or something moving between the two. At every turn Tom suffers and reproduces ideas, ideologies, institutions, a moment-by-moment living of the political. More broadly, Tom either eludes or preempts the genealogy proposed by Agamben, in which bare life, or what he also (somewhat nebulously) refers to as "private life"

---

mains: *The People's Two Bodies and the Endgames of Sovereignty* (Chicago: University of Chicago Press, 2011), 58. Italics Santner's.

20. Richard Halperin: "The dispossessed classes had a strong anticipatory force; by 'mirroring' the decoding effects of capital in a way that overstepped the structural limitations of late feudal production, they became a precocious and nightmarishly exaggerated image of *modernity*. They were a kind of volatile fluid coursing irregularly through the social body and visible everywhere in it, representing the possibility of a total and anarchic breakdown of the existing mechanisms of order and control": *The Poetics of Primitive Accumulation* (Ithaca, N.Y.: Cornell University Press, 1991), 74. Italics Halperin's.

and "biological life," is gradually removed from the margins of the political order into "a zone of irreducible indistinction" with it.[21]

For Agamben, it was only with the Nazi death camps that "the possibility of differentiating between our biological body and our political body—between what is incommunicable and mute and what is communicable and sayable—was taken from us forever," issuing too often in "a life that has been deadened and mortified into juridical rule."[22] But Tom already endures this, already embodies it. The immanent violence of his being, in which inside and outside blend and crack in an unceasing gyre, makes a mockery of the supposed "classical distinction" between *zoe* (bare life) and *bio* (political life). Whether Tom points farther ahead into a new politics, beyond modernity's "biopolitical" deployment of the body, is more difficult to say. But one thing, I think, is sure. Whereas Agamben defines *homo sacer*, the sacred man of bare life, as one who can be killed but never sacrificed, Tom foreshadows a strange spectral inversion of this deracinating fate: he can be sacrificed, but never killed.[23]

Frame 9

Tom's voice is beyond rhetorical orders. His speech is more like a shattered mime—a mime shattered into sound—than an understood illocution. What with one ear can sound like the lexicon of multitudes, string upon string of curling, suspended life, can with another ear seem noth-

---

21. Giorgio Agamben, *Homo Sacer: Sovereign Power and Bare Life*, trans. Daniel Heller-Roazen (Stanford, Calif.: Stanford University Press, 1998), 8–9. Robert Esposito writes that "we need to speak of the spiritualization of *zoe* and the biologization of the spirit." *Bios: Biopolitics and Philosophy*, trans. Timothy Campbell (Minneapolis: University of Minnesota Press, 2008), 142; quoted in Santner, *Royal Remains*, 28.

22. Agamben, *Homo Sacer*, 187–88.

23. Eric L. Santner: "Because human beings have not only natures but also *second natures*, when an artefact loses its place in a historical form of life—when that form of life decays, becomes exhausted, dies—we experience it as something that has been *denaturalized*, transformed into a mere relic of historical being.... Natural history is born out of the dual possibilities that life can persist beyond the death of the symbolic forms that gave it meaning and that symbolic forms can persist beyond the death of the form of life than gave them human vitality, ... this space between real and symbolic death, this space of the 'undead.'" *On Creaturely Life: Rilke, Benjamin, Sebald* (Chicago: University of Chicago Press, 2006), 17. Italics Santner's.

ing but an inarticulate white noise, or the cry of a dying bird or mammal. It can seem like no sound at all, and rather a wound, an image, as the words manufacture their very own body, understood by no one anywhere, horribly stillborn. The words are dropped so as to die, voided and then avoided; or they are heard instantaneously as frozen silenced muteness, and instead of listening we simply look, and wait for him to stop, and be silent, and disappear.

It is as pure surplus that Tom is often heard in performance, as his barrage of words is received en masse, a single, barely decipherable speech act, signifying little but a hunted form of suffering or schizophrenia. This is much to do with the visual assault of his presence. Tom's words have to catch up with, in a sense translate, this more primary and immediate reality: the vision of him, his face and limbs transfixed to the gaze, a body suddenly exposed. The combined effect is a kind of garrulous mime: the words not only generate, but somehow *are* histrionic physical gestures.[24] Face and voice combine to form a single compound violence.[25]

Consequently, much of Tom's allegory-rich suggestibility comes not from words, but from his startling physicality. Tom brings the body, as

24. Bruce Smith notes that the play seems to recover a primitive physical language, as though hacking back to dramaturgical as well as moral-social roots. Smith stresses that gestures such as Lear beating himself on the head with his palm do not represent a single passion, such as fury, but rather "multiple, indeed *contradictory* passions" in a "layered" rather than sequential "schema." This is part of a "kinetic" theatre, far more physically dynamic than the head-obsessed, inwardly accented performances of post-Stanislavski theatrical or film and TV acting. This works in tandem with words that are themselves tactile, often assaulting or piercing, and often come literally true. Linguistics needs to take into account "touch as well as speech, seeing as well as hearing, feeling as well as decoding." *Phenomenal Shakespeare* (Chichester, U.K.: Wiley-Blackwell, 2010), 160–61, 166. Poor Tom embodies this. Italics Smith's.

25. Referring to torture, Elaine Scarry writes: "The translation of pain into power is ultimately a translation of body into voice.... This dissolution of the boundary between inside and outside gives rise to ... an almost obscene conflation of private and public.... Eventually the pain so deepens that the coherence of complaint is displaced by the sounds anterior to learned language. The tendency of pain not simply to resist expression but to destroy the capacity for speech is in torture re-enacted in overt, exaggerated form.... It eventually occupies the entire body and spills out into the realm beyond the body, takes over all that is inside and outside, makes the two obscenely indistinguishable, and systematically destroys anything like language or world extension that is alien to itself and threatening to its claims.... In prolonged and acute pain the body often begins to interpret all sensations as pain." *Body in Pain*, 53–55.

image and as mime: others offer their gloss. The Fool's nervous joke is typical: "he reserv'd a blanket, else we had bin all sham'd" (TLN 1846-47). Tom's body here evokes nothing less than original sin, straddled between fait accompli and imminent threat. Tom is Adam, and the hovel the flooded Garden, but exactly when in the terminal succession is open to doubt. He is clothed, therefore ashamed, therefore already fallen; equally, the Fool jokes that only exposure will produce shame, an exposure that has not yet occurred: his blanket "reserves" his innocence. And yet Tom is also Everyman, struggling in the wake of the original malediction. Lear's response, neurotically alert, picks up both the Fool's Adamic allusion and its uncertain place in a dreadful succession:

> Now all the plagues that in the pendulous ayre
> Hang fated o're mens faults, light on thy Daughters. (TLN 1848-49)

Lear sees him right at the cusp: when the storm is about to break, the plague about to infect, and the poor man—already in fault, already at fault, already a fault—will suffer ineradicably for what he is: "Now all the plagues that in the pendulous ayre / Hang fated o're mens faults" (TLN 1848-49). Every word here is grave and weighted, but none more so than the first: *now*. Now is what Lear sees before him: right "now," all of the plagues "hang fated." There is no escaping what shall happen, but it hasn't happened yet; or it hasn't happened yet this time; or it is about to happen, as though for the first time, yet again, to this sot before him, with his arms and legs and fingers and cock, each digit a spoke on the suffering wheel.

Lear wants to save the boy from this plague, and for the storm instead to light on his daughters. Clearly the identity exchange feared by the Fool is already at work. But more than refracting Lear's experiences, the curse upon "Daughters" reinforces Tom's uncanny temporality. In Lear's antiprayer, mothers have already suffered the curse of childbirth. Tom is a father and a boy; he is before any revealed fault, and yet this fault has delivered children.[26] So Tom is both before and after this even-

---

26. The fault/woman metalepsis carries through the play, from its first chortling invocation by Gloucester in 1.1.

tuality: indeed he might be called eventuality per se. He exemplifies the punishments consequent upon an event; he exemplifies the same event yet to come and its punishments. History is on the shortest imaginable spool, recurring with barely a remission. And yet each remission holds open the possibility, if only a whimsical or retaliatory glimmer, that the cycle might abate and a different dispensation take its place.

Frame 10

Tom's allegorical susceptibility is redoubled by this straddling, here-and-there temporality. For the effect is always to render him incomplete, as though waiting to resolve. What is more, it opens him to resolutions that can only arrive through the inferences of others. In this sense, his very ontology is hermeneutic. It depends upon translation, or upon cultural analogue and appropriative comparison. And this in turn produces Tom's nervous futurity: by definition, Tom waits upon what has yet to come. For all that he takes the stage and speaks and speaks and speaks, Tom remains beyond all efficient transactions, abandoned by the present economies of both theater and Lear's Britain.

Inevitably, as is often the case in Shakespeare, this can take the form of seeming to predict historically subsequent forms of living—events and institutions that have emerged in the years since the play was first produced. But Tom incarnates a far more profound historical supplement than this. It is to do with the figure's constitutive anachrony: the way he is layered simultaneously with different historical times; the way he is composed on a principle of recessive action, a recessiveness that has neither endpoint (in past or future) nor defined beginning (ditto), and therefore seems to be generated from some unreachable virtual date, parallel only to imaginative or sympathetic possibility.[27] Tom is removed from local, named, material specificity, and

---

27. Jacques Derrida: "Without this *non-contemporaneity with itself of the living present*, without that which secretly unhinges it, without this responsibility and this respect for justice concerning those who *are not there*, of those who are no longer or who are not yet *present and living*, what sense would there be to ask the question 'where?' 'where tomorrow?' 'whither?' . . . Turned toward the future, giving toward it, it also comes from it, it proceeds from the future. It must therefore exceed any presence as presence to itself." *Specters of Marx:*

this renders him *allegorically prone*, waiting to be supplemented by the desires or violence or memories of his witnesses. The sum effect is a kind of absolute futurity, a constitutive not-yet-ness that no historical actuality can claim.

Walter Benjamin is suggestive:

> Thinking involves not only the flow of thoughts, but their arrest as well. Where thinking suddenly stops in a configuration pregnant with tensions, it gives that configuration a shock. . . . In this structure he recognises the sign of a Messianic cessation of happening, or, put differently, a revolutionary chance in the fight for the oppressed past. He takes cognizance of it in order to blast a specific era out of the homogeneous course of history—blasting a specific life out of the era or a specific work out of the lifework.[28]

Tom is such a blast, or the shard or fragments that result, every one of them a crystal of unfinished history. Is it any wonder that Tom evokes futures of which Shakespeare knew nothing?

Frame 11

I dwell on the arrested pathos of his body, Tom stunned in his secrecy like a deer, the species-memory of danger, the urge to run or dive. I see him so thin and pale and naked, as though prematurely buried. I picture this figure, frozen in the torchlights, skeletal and chattering. I imagine broiling punishment in his every move, the contorted, bestialized, excruciated body familiar from Bosch's or Durer's visions of hell. I see all this, and the most awful image comes to mind. It is an image of extermination camps: not of living figures herded and whipped or reduced to dumb obedience, but of the piled-up dead, somehow clattering into motion and voice.[29]

The State of the Debt, the Work of Mourning, and the New International, trans. Peggy Kamuf (New York: Routledge, 1994), viii–xix. Italics Derrida's.

28. Walter Benjamin, *Illuminations*, trans. Harry Zohn (London: Fontana, 1992), 254.

29. Kozintsev's visual rendering of the huddled "Toms" in his film of *King Lear* might appear to be informed by the same image. But it is similar, not the same. He was inspired by Dos-

The thought may seem barely admissible. But it is there. And it is there because Tom is an ontological and ethical scandal—and, in a way that is difficult to account for, a historical scandal too, repeating into the future. Tom never sleeps; he hasn't died: something about the figure forbids it. Of no other character in Shakespeare, in all of early modern literature, am I tempted to say this: that he prefigures Holocaust, or Shoah; he haunts it, expects it, is unsurprised by it.[30] No one else—not Hamlet, revolted by the very smell of life; not Macbeth, razing children from a whim; not Edmund, happy to be handsome and allowing *anything*. Only Tom.

Western modernity's worst offense is prefigured and remembered in Tom's decreated presence. Some correlations are simple enough to list: systemic institutional guilt; the antinomian self-permissions of genre, or of government, as modes of formalized cruelty; the willingness, unremarked by anyone, to let the sufferer pass, to allow the disappearance, to pretend that it hasn't happened even as it is happening, even as it happens over and over again; an imperfect vanishing, a vanishing that keeps on being reinforced by intentions to be rid of the vermin once again (a bitter irony that Tom's avowed "study" is "prevent the Fiend, and to kill Vermine"; TLN 1938).

---

toevsky's account of the penal baths in Siberia: "Imagine a room some twelve paces in length and the same in breadth, into which was packed . . . upwards of a hundred men. . . . Steam that half blinded the eyes, soot, filth, a press so thick that there was nowhere to put one's foot down. . . . They were all whipping themselves into a frenzy. . . . The whole place roared with shouting and laughter, to the accompaniment of a hundred chains dragging on the floor. . . . Everybody was in a state almost of intoxication, a kind of violent mental stimulation; there were shrieks and cries all about. . . . When a back is swollen with steam, the scars of blows inflicted at some time with whips or rods usually stand out clearly, so that now all the backs seemed newly injured. . . . Through the mist of steam glimmered scarred backs, shaven heads, crooked arms and legs . . . If we should ever be all together in the fires of Hell, it would be very like this place." Fyodor Dostoevsky, *Memoirs from the House of the Dead*, trans. Jessie Coulson (1861–1862; reprint, Oxford: Oxford University Press, 1956), 145–46. Kozintsev comments: "The penal settlement wash-house is a model of life itself. It is the fate of those whom life has banished from its systems." *King Lear, the Space of Tragedy: The Diary of a Film Director*, trans. Mary Mackintosh (London, Heinemann Educational Publishers, 1977), 193.

30. Agamben refuses the false veil of the word *Holocaust*, which pretends religious sacrifice when the fact of the matter is state murder. Hence his "bare life"—when you can be killed, but you cannot be a sacrifice. There is no redemption, no cleansing, no shoring up of community from the reek of your passing: just extermination, like a rat. The epitome of this ("the privileged negative referent of the new biopolitical sovereignty") is the Jew killed by Nazis. *Homo Sacer*, 114.

More specifically, the reminder is rooted in the namelessness; in its lack of public record, and its effective erasure; in the numberless many who seem to inhabit the stark horror of this example; in the divested civic dignity; in the fact of being sacrificed to an idea—call it the theme, which calls these things forth, and names them, and winds them up to confess, and then discards them. Then there is the blank impossibility of assimilation. Such lives—such deaths—will not be explained by any rational or symbolic order. Conventional epistemologies cannot reach to them; nor can given historical narratives; nor can the culture's ruling metaphors: bits of them, yes, but not the whole phenomenon, not one thing without leaving others adrift.

Hence, perhaps, the ensuing silences once Tom appears to have gone: the silence of those in the play; the silence, in the main, of critics and commentators through the centuries. Of course it won't do to compare such a turning away with the infamous silences that attended and succeeded the gas chambers. And yet is there not something, some sort of dark politics, in the too-easy raking of the sands? Something rooted in the fact that Tom, from the start, is not really heard; that his voice, for all its pitch and loquacity, is experienced as a kind of white silence? He was barely heard then, and he is barely heard now, other than as an approximate synecdoche of something else. But this something else is never enough. Specular relationships with Lear or Edmund or Cordelia explain a little, Jacobean vagabonds and demoniacs a little more: but not the central provocation, the overburdening persecution, the terrible hostage taking and superconscious mania of the role's specific dynamics. Perhaps he is still roaring, a single wave in the sea, and no one is alert to notice.

Here is Primo Levi:

> Hurbinek was a nobody, a child of death, a child of Auschwitz. He looked about three years old, no one knew anything of him, he could not speak and had no name.... He was paralyzed from the waist down, with atrophied legs, as thin as sticks; but his eyes, lost in his triangular and wasted face, flashed terribly alive, full of demand, assertion, of the will to break loose, to shatter the tomb of his dumbness.

The speech he lacked, which no one had bothered to teach him, the need of speech charged his stare with explosive urgency.[31]

But then this boy is nursed, fed, and spoken to by an older boy, and eventually he speaks a word: "It was certainly an articulated word; or better, several slightly different articulated words, experimental variations of a theme, on a root, perhaps even on a name."[32]

No one can decipher it: "mass-klo," "matisklo"; perhaps it means "bread," or "eat" or "meat"; perhaps it is his name. No one will know, because Hurbinek, who "had never seen a tree," died in 1945, and now bears witness only through these words of Levi's.

Can something similar be imagined of Tom? That he gives his secret cue, his single indecipherable word, to Edgar, who bears witness in the form of his Tom-act, which is a dilated translation of Tom's lost prompt word? If so, the Edgar-role becomes an amanuensis of the beyond-world, the survivor who himself has never touched the worst and is instead cursed to report what he cannot finally experience:

> We survivors are not only an exiguous but also an anomalous minority: we are those who by their prevarications or abilities or good luck did not touch bottom.
>
> The survivors speak in their stead, by proxy, as pseudo-witnesses; they bear witness to a missing testimony. And yet to speak here of a proxy makes no sense; the drowned have nothing to say, nor do they have instructions or memories to be transmitted.[33]

Or is Tom the revealed thing itself? After all, we might think that his verbal cavalcade is hardly less impenetrable than those syllables of Hurbinek. The crucial point is that the voice, even when it is listened to, is not understood. That for all its noise, it translates as horrifying mute-

---

31. Primo Levi, *If This Is a Man*, trans. Stuart Woolf (London: Abacus, 1987), 197.
32. Ibid., 198.
33. Primo Levi, *The Drowned and the Saved*, trans. Raymond Rosenthal (New York: Vintage, 1989), 63–64.

ness, the paroxysmal mouth behind glass, at once a museum exhibit and the creature pushing for the sun.

Tom's voice and body incarnate the paradoxes in the word *history*. He is past events, but he is also a barely discovered archive; he is neither seen nor heard sufficiently, a failure that inhibits his action in the world; he is charged with too much past, and is consequently out of time, in no place; he is history's castaway, and yet also its repository.[34] He doesn't seek asylum; he has no status as refugee, being everywhere stateless, belonging to no group or sect or nation. He is the exception: not the "state of exception": the exception, in irredeemable exile.

> Those who did so, those who saw the Gorgon, have not returned to tell about it or have returned mute.... We who were favoured by fate tried, with more or less wisdom, to recount not only our fate but also that of the others, indeed of the drowned; but this was a discourse "on behalf of third parties," the story of things seen close at hand, not experienced personally. The destruction brought to an end, the job completed, was not told by anyone, just as no one ever returned to describe his own death.[35]

---

34. Compare Giorgio Agamben: "The assistant is the figure of what is lost. Or, rather, of our relationship to what is lost. This relationship concerns everything that, in both collective and individual life, comes to be forgotten at every moment. It concerns the unending mass of what becomes irrevocably lost. Throughout our lives, the measure of oblivion and ruin, the ontological waste that we carry in ourselves, far exceeds the small mercy of our memories and our consciousness. But this formless chaos of the forgotten that accompanies us like a silent golem is neither inert nor inefficacious.... It is a force and almost an apostrophe of the forgotten that, although it can neither be measured in terms of consciousness nor accumulated as a patrimony, insistently governs the hierarchy of all knowledge and all consciousness. ... He spells out the text of the unforgettable and translates it into the language of deaf-mutes. Hence his obstinate gesticulations coupled with his impassive mime's face." *Profanations*, trans. Jeff Fort (New York: Zone Books, 2007), 35. Agamben adapts this figure from Benjamin, who calls the assistant "crepuscular" and incomplete, half celestial genie, half demon: "None has a firm place in the world, or firm, inalienable outlines. There is not one that is not either rising or falling, none that is not trading its qualities with its enemy or neighbour; none that has not completed its period of time and yet is unripe, none that is not deeply exhausted and yet is only at the beginning of a long existence." Benjamin, *Illuminations*, 113–14.

35. Levi, *Drowned and the Saved*, 63–64.

Shakespeare is fascinated by this sublime possibility—of hearing from beyond, being blinded by the Gorgon and yet continuing to see,[36] hearing from a before that may still become, or from a future whose impossibility is only too possible.

※

Can we enter any of this as a lived existence? Or does it demand to be taken as allegory, because it is too weird or too horrible to take for real? Perhaps this is also where the Holocaust returns. We cannot enter into its experience, not that of the hunters or the hunted, not even that of the bystanders, the mute permitters. Or if we do, it is difficult to do so for long, without lying, or taking refuge in excoriation or pity or sententiae, by which time we are gone into the comforts of normative allegory. In time we turn our minds away from all of it because it is simply too accusing, or if not accusing then presumptuous, or if not presumptuous then bathetic. What else can be done but to shake the head free of the thought, and turn the horror into an example? And so both Tom and Holocaust, to the extent that they can be thought, become events for the future: one that exists as a warning of what must never be allowed to occur; one that exists as a promise of life that can never come true. But of course the pressure of both thoughts insists on the opposite conclusion: Holocaust will come again; and so will Tom.

And in doing this, perhaps we arrive at a further dismaying thought: that allegory is the real; that all we are, if not an accident, is an example. Or we are each an accident, always, and we are redeemed, if we are extraordinary, to be made into an example.

---

36. "Approach the chamber, and destroy your sight / With a new Gorgon. Do not bid me speak: / See, and then speak yourselves" *Macbeth*, 2.3.70-72.

12

SCENE 5

Lurk, Lurk

Tom's shattered cavalcade refracts every single figure in the play, while being claimed finally by none of them. The same applies to the most famous such claiming: which is of course Lear's, seeing in the naked boy exactly what he needs. It is a beautiful thing when Lear takes the beggar into his care. It is one answer, at least, to Tom's inescapable "cold." It pays on the promise of the "naked wretches" speech, and helps to make Lear worthy again of his good daughter's faith.

At the same time Lear's attention to Tom, poised between that of a parent, a child, a student, and a fraternal confederate, shifts a questioning and perhaps accusatory light onto the actions of the other present father. Gloucester mainly wishes the beggar would go away. He resists bringing him along to where "fire, and food is ready" (TLN 1931) and demurs to Kent's plea to humor the king by telling the unsavory vagrant to "hush" (TLN 1965). Or so the action seems to say. But in fact the scripting of this scene is much more delicate than my bald summary allows. Shakespeare is already working at a more subterranean level, one where emotions churn. And here this means at the level of actorly recognitions, ones that are for the moment not quite expressible.

The Gloucester-part has a sequence of cues that either come from or allude to Tom: "thou Fiend," "Tom's a cold," "Tom's a cold," "take the Fellow," "Come, good Athenian." (TLN 1919-64), Likewise, his own words either clearly do or may speak of or to Edgar-Tom: "I had a Sonne, Now out-law'd from my blood . . . I lov'd him (Friend) / No Father his Sonne dearer"; "In fellow there"; "Go in with me"; "keep thee warm"; "Take him you on"; "No words, no words, hush." (TLN 1946-65) If the part is studied in isolation, it may seem that at least some of these caring words are directed to the one who cues them— Edgar/ Tom. But performance will reveal that such care is in fact for another, leaving Tom explicitly without the comfort that Gloucester's words speak: " Go in with me" (TLN 1926) is spoken to Lear, and " In fellow there" (TLN 1955) probably to Kent or Fool.

The scripting is clearly focusing on the most difficult questions of notice and recognition. The actor has to experience such questions *for* his character, and trust that his own instincts (for justice, sympathy, recognition) will in due course be satisfied by the script. Right now the Gloucester- actor must do what he can with what he has: among other things, decide whether to pay the beggar—his son—any attention at all, and if so of what kind.[1] Perhaps he remains stonily removed from the "Swine" (TLN 2787); equally, the briefest touch or beckoning will speak volumes. As so often, the spaces between words, or between speeches, may be the most promise-crammed of all.

And Edgar? Talk about being an existential renter: because what else is he right now, crunched somewhere inside Tom's pyrotechnic display? Who can say what he is thinking?[2] He certainly cannot. He is given nothing, not the tiniest aside, still less a parting soliloquy, to assure the audience that he knows how big and strange this moment is, or that he might have things under control. And yet at every moment we may hear the man crouching inside the Tom-body; hear the fury or misery of the

---

1. For a fuller reading of the meticulous part-scripting here see Simon Palfrey and Tiffany Stern, *Shakespeare in Parts* (Oxford: Oxford University Press, 2007), 250–55.

2. However, compare Harry Berger Jr.'s psychological reading. He sees Tom as an expression of Edgar, with inferable continuities between this scene and what follows: "The rapid oscillation of cross-purposes evident in his Poor Tom language, the sense of betrayal and rejection that circles from retributive anger to guilt to sympathy to new anger engendered by the feeling that the sympathy is undeserved—these keep him from confronting his father, and produce the diffidence on the heath." Berger identifies an R. D. Laing-like progression of tail-chasing paranoia: Gloucester pursues Edgar, Edgar pursues Gloucester, a fiend within Gloucester tempts him to punish Edgar, a fiend within Edgar tempts him to punish Gloucester. *Making Trifles of Terrors: Redistributing Complicities in Shakespeare* (Stanford, Calif.: Stanford University Press, 1997), 61.

abandoned child; hear the hateful memory of violence that even an Earl's legitimate child might suffer, as he bursts into accusation when his father appears, gruesomely haloed in his torch.

> *This is the foule Flibbertigibbet*
> > Here comes his father in the guise of a fiend:
>
> *Hee begins at Curfew*
> > Never a peaceful sleep in that house:
>
> *And walkes at first Cocke*
> > We were always woken early:
>
> *Hee gives the Web and the Pin*
> > Lessons were torture:
>
> *Squints the eye*
> > The teacher malevolent, candlelight dim:
>
> *And makes the Hare-lippe*
> > His ghoulish face distorted as it loomed:
>
> *Mildewes the white Wheate*
> > Breakfast was mean:
>
> *And hurts the poore Creature of earth.*
> > You made us to mar us. (TLN 1895-99; italics mine)

Or so it might be construed, in the same way that much in the Tom-show might be imagined as fractured confessions of the young noble. We might say that Tom has never been more necessary than now, when Gloucester arrives, and it is only through Tom that Edgar can let loose his barbs. The Edgar-actor has little more to go on than we do. And Edgar has little more to go on than his actor. He is clamped inside Tom—Granville-Barker calls it an "arbitrary bondage"—guarded by him, armored by him, in some implacable way prevented by him.[3] Life is at once ratcheted to barely bearable intensity and tantalizingly on hold.

---

3. Harley Granville-Barker: "Edgar also is drawn into Lear's orbit; and, for the time, to the complete sacrifice of his own interests in the play. 'Poor Tom' is in effect an embodiment of Lear's frenzy, the disguise no part of Edgar's own development." *Prefaces to Shakespeare*, Vol 1 (London: B. T. Batsford Ltd., 1930), 273-74. But compare Granville-Barker's later observation: "Through the ravings of Poor Tom we can detect something of the mind of Edgar with its misprision of the sensual life—of his father's life, is it?" (319).

Edgar is held inside Tom, forced into deflection, seeing and not-seen, excited in a state of waiting. And what is worse: just like his father, with his wistful address to his lost son ("I had a Sonne, Now out-law'd"; TLN 1946–47), Edgar is possessed by love and hurt that are expressible only through apostrophe. For surely this is the key to Tom's parting chant, with its darkly poignant infantilism:

> Childe *Rowland* to the darke Tower came [Quarto: towne]
> His word was still, fie, foh, and fumme
> I smell the blood of a Brittish man. (TLN 1966–68)

Tom resists Gloucester's thrice-spoken demand for silence ("No words / No words / hush" (TLN 1965) as the child is led by the smell of blood and climbs the "darke Tower" to where the ignorant "Brittish man" lays. The song perhaps harks back to childhood in the castle; perhaps it echoes a fanciful dream. But above all Tom's rhyme, characteristically, will not be bound by the occasion. He does not stop when Gloucester tells him; his voice floats beyond the moment, across the gap and into the scene that immediately takes the stage: where Bastard and Cornwall vengefully plot the very same British man's destruction. The scripting is devilish and heart-breaking. Because these are apostrophes to apparent absence—to the son, to the revenge—that are in fact terrifyingly imminent.

❧

There is a marked difference between every one of Tom's appearances. In his first scene "Edgar" barely gets a look in. Tom carries all before him, is the focal point of endless questions: indeed, he or it in many ways *is* the question. It is little wonder that the Quarto text notates the king's party's next appearance on stage thus: *"Enter Gloster and Lear, Kent, Foole, and Tom"* (III. vi). The stage direction is no error. Tom is. Edgar has vanished.[4]

But the second Tom-scene is different. He struggles to get Lear's

---

4. Compare here Qs entrance direction for the Dover cliff scene: "Enter Gloster and Edmund." This is no doubt a mistake; but not entirely inapt.

attention. And as Lear ignores Tom, Edgar re-emerges: as though issued precisely from Tom's loneliness or his redundancy. In the Folio version Edgar seems to say goodbye to Tom halfway through the scene: "poore Tom thy horne is dry" (TLN 2032). We might hear in this a reemergent Edgar, perhaps quoting a proverbial lament: the horn is the vessel in which the beggar-man carries his drink; and it is his voice, his music. Taken as one (drink, voice, music) the horn compacts or perhaps compensates for Tom's elusive virility. A dry horn speaks the emptying of inspiration, and so the need to move on to find refreshment. The horn must be filled; a new patron found. But for Edgar, it seems, the lament is valedictory. His Tom is done.

At the end of the scene everyone else simply leaves the vagrant behind, without so much as a word. There is a litter prepared for Lear, and "welcome, and protection," promised at Dover. "Come, come, away," says Gloucester, and the king's party departs (TLN 2049-56). But what of Poor Tom? Where does he go? He is left by his maker (Edgar), apparently because he is alone and disregarded: no longer noticed or useful, and so dispensable. Secretly, surreptitiously, Edgar leaves Tom. Then less secretly, and with far more carelessness, everyone else leaves Tom too. No one sees this happening, of course, because no one can see the difference between Tom and Edgar. But in Shakespeare sight is not always the measure of truth or existing. Has Tom then vanished? Is he annihilated, rendered null, by this withdrawal of attention?

But if so, what happens if we decide to renew our attention?

※

Edgar's next appearance takes place only in the Quarto text. He is alone, marooned on stage after the others leave. Edgar is trying manfully to cheer himself up, to be a loyal subject and faithful godson, to frame a catechism whose repeated uttering might carry him across present doubts and turmoil:

> Exit [Lear, Gloster, Kent, Fool]
> *Edg.* When we our betters see bearing our woes, we scarcely
>   think our miseries our foes.
> Who alone suffers suffers, most i'the mind,

> Leaving free things and happy showes behind.
> But then the mind much sufferance doth or'e scip,
> When griefe hath mates, and bearing fellowship:
> How light and portable my paine seemes now,
> When that which makes me bend, makes the King bow.
> He childed as I fathered, *Tom* away;
> Marke the high noyses and thy selfe bewray,
> When false opinion whose wrong thoughts defile thee,
> In thy just proof repeals and reconciles thee,
> What will hap more to night, safe 'scape the King.
> Lurke, lurke.
> *Enter Cornwall, and Regan, and Gonorill, and Bastard.*
> (III. vi. 109-23)

The speech happens between two scenes – one in which Gloucester leads the king and his party away, the next in which Gloucester is hauled in to be tortured by Cornwall and Regan. This interstitial placement is crucial. Perhaps Edgar's soliloquy expresses something quite different from anything in the Folio text; or perhaps it provides a text for the dizzying transvertebrations to come. The decisive couplet is this:

> He childed as I fathered, *Tom* away;
> Marke the high noyses and thy selfe bewray (III. vi. 117-18)

He has been badly fathered (poorly treated by Gloucester), just as Lear has been badly "childed," or cruelly treated by his progeny.[5] Conversely, Lear has been made a child ("childed"), and Edgar has been made a father ("father'd"). So who has Edgar been made a father to? One answer is about to become apparent: he will father his own father, caring for the blind man's life like a parent might a toddler. Another answer is Tom, insofar as he is Edgar's own creation. But if Tom is Edgar's

---

5. Harold Bloom sees this couplet as the key to the play, and the Edgar-role as afflicted by "an excess of love." *Shakespeare and the Invention of the Human* (London: Fourth Estate, 1999), 480-84.

child, then the chiasmic inversions of the phrase also insist that Edgar is Tom's child. Each is responsible for the other's creation and sustenance; each seeks to mold, prescript, discipline the other; each cares for the other; each potentially seeks to annihilate the other.

None of this is to the exclusion of already-established "family" relationships. So, both Edgar and Tom are in some sense poorly "father'd" by Gloucester. This, I take it, is the point of Gloucester's carelessness or negligence toward Tom in the storm—it repeats his earlier treatment of Edgar (with Tom now his exiled ward). Having the same father, Edgar and Tom are also brothers. The relation is filial and fraternal and narcissistic. Tom recalls both Gloucester and Edmund: it is as though he was there all along, the ghost in the troubled household. Fates and allegories begin to morph: parent and child, maker and made.

The inextricable complicity of Tom and Edgar is reinforced by the couplet's ambiguous address. "*Tom*, away" might be a dismissal, an admonition for Tom to leave and for Edgar to resume his "just proof." Equally, it might speak a renewed girding of the loins—"let's go!"—with Tom retaining his role as the disguised Edgar's barrier-breaking avatar. Decisions about this—whether Tom is being dismissed or employed—duly inform our sense of the couplet's second line. What does it mean to "thy selfe bewray"? Which self? And why "bewray"—a word that usually implies the exposing of secrets, often with malign or betraying intent. Perhaps Edgar (or Shakespeare) is picking up Lear's earlier dare, to "Expose thy selfe to feele what wretches feele" (III. iv. 34 in the Quarto text). The phrases echo each other: Expose thy selfe / thy selfe bewray. As Lear recommended, Edgar is immersing himself in "grief" and "sufferance," a horrible but therapeutic sentimental education.

But surely this interpretation is too sentimentalizing, and misses a crucial difference in the two statements. Lear's "selfe" is single and presupposed: it is just such presupposition of comfort and possession that argues the necessity of exposure. Edgar's "thy selfe" is dizzyingly uncertain: not only because it is unclear whether "thy" is Edgar or Tom, but because to "bewray" this "thy" is to reinforce, even to thematize, the same agential ambiguity. That is, the very assumption that "thy selfe" is a clearly possessed thing is a lie, a pretense demanding exposure. In turn, to persevere in this immersion in grief and suffering is itself a betrayal of any prepossessed self: not because it is false to this self, but because this self is false. Social identity, the assumed self, a proper name: each is deconstructed, vertiginously groundless: "*Tom*, away"; "thy selfe bewray": both phrases are as foundationally ambiguous as a statement can be, meaning opposite things equally, abandoning any vestige of referential hierarchy. It is as though Shakespeare is set upon embarrassing the pretensions of all clarifying, summative discourse—of the kind precisely epitomized by end-of-scene couplets. And in place of summation, we have probation. Hence perhaps the rarely noticed fact that—contrary to expectation—this rhyming speech does not end with a parting rhyme of affirmation, but with a short line consisting of a single repeated verb: lurk, lurk.

At times like this the Edgar-part, under extremity of duress, can seem to float almost schizophrenically above both of its selves, with "Edgar" and "Tom" equally distanced and synthetic. There is a curious sense that the part—an uncertain amalgam of part-text, actor, Tom, Edgar, and some abstracted persona that is not quite any of these units—is being forced to rethink the smallest movement, that nothing can be taken for granted, and that the automatic instincts of customary body have been atrophied or paralyzed by trauma. Consequently, the part has to tell this body what to do, instruct it like an apprentice or a doll. But which is the master, which the doll? Who is told to "Lurk, lurk"? Who is doing the telling? It sounds like Tom: the creepy verbal repetition is often played as a return into the guise and voice of vagrancy. But this morphing has been going on for at least three lines. Again, neither origin nor target of the speech can be pinned down. To lurk is to be concealed and furtive. But it is different from the "happy hollow" in which Edgar earlier hid himself. For lurking suggests an active, perhaps surveilling observation of others. The lurking precedes an ambush; it is an act of waiting as much as hiding: its true secret is latency, and therefore imminence. He is waiting; he is gestating; and when he comes, he will have secret and usable knowledge. Clearly the verb applies as much to Edgar (lurking inside Tom) as to Tom (for whom lurking is vocation and ontology).

Clearly Shakespeare is worrying hard at the relation between the two identities, the permeability of which begins to threaten genuine ego loss.[6] The rival arrogations of purpose, where we cannot quite know which of them speaks, or which, if either, is the object to the other's subject, suggests something captious and misprisioning for both of them in their compact. Is it a relation of possession? If so, which possesses which? Tom is host to a changeable parade of demons, but he may be such a demon himself. And yet if one them here "lurks" in the other, it is primarily Edgar: making him the demon, lodged in the suffering of Tom.

Perhaps the exchange enters the uncanny territory of transferred possession, where the man becomes the shadow of the robot he creates.[7] Or is it better understood as a relation of substitution—or rather as a struggle to substitute for the other, in the Levinasian sense of being taken hostage by another, such that the self-conscious will becomes as though nothing, a trivial and deflecting egotism, and ethical truth is found in the absolute taking on of another's misery. This posits the most intense adoption of "persecution": beyond the persecution of the skies, beyond the persecution that the despised and homeless suffer daily, it becomes the permitted persecution of full ethical recognition of the other. We are taken hostage; we have no will other than this taking-on. And if this is the case, then yet again it is impossible to tell one apart from the other. Edgar substitutes for Tom; Tom substitutes for Edgar. And thus they both suffer a kind of subjective annihilation, an annihilation repeatedly experienced and repeatedly revoked—because final annihilation would mean the substitution was over, the suffering at a cease. This is the base import of the agential ambiguity that racks every clause. There is no end to it.

Indeed, this soliloquy itself reaches not so much an end as a forced suspension: for its final words are in fact a repeated cue: "Lurk, lurk.".

---

6. Michael E. Mooney identifies a more ordered progression of voices in the speech than I do. He thinks the first six lines are "purely choric" and the next six "personal and reflective"; and then "Lurk, lurk" marks "reinvolvement" in the "illusion" of Tom. "'Edgar I Nothing Am': Figurenposition in *King Lear*," *Shakespeare Survey* 38 (1985): 159.

7. A staple of fantastical allegory and science fiction: see Angus Fletcher, *Allegory: The Theory of a Symbolic Mode*. (Ithaca, N.Y.: Cornell University Press, 1964), 55–56 *passim*. William C. Carroll sees Tom as both embodiment and cause of Edgar's suffering: "To be Poor Tom is Edgar's trial." "'The Base Shall Top th'Legitimate': The Bedlam Beggar and the Role of Edgar in *King Lear*," *Shakespeare Quarterly* 38, no. 4 (1987): 436.

The implications of this are potentially stunning, giving decisive point to the speech's uncertain closure. So the soliloquy's terminal prosodic swerve (from couplet to half-line) doesn't imply merely irresolution or frustration. *Edgar is interrupted.* He hears something or spies someone; he is stopped in his tracks. The speech's closing couplet is thus sacrificed to the scene about to happen. The cue is half stolen (the first "lurk" claimed by the invading party) and half returned to sender (Edgar can say the second "lurk" whenever he likes, with no one left to listen). The ensuing action, then, may darkly supply the soliloquy's otherwise missing closure. It may condemn it to eternal suspension. More fundamentally, it suggests that the days of adequate soliloquizing are done, because summative wisdom cannot possibly keep up with the unprecedented suddenness of stage action:

> Lurke, lurke.
> *Enter Cornwall, and Regan, and Gonorill, and Bastard.*

The repeated cue—both an exit and an entrance cue—invites the evil party to enter at the first "lurk." This would leave Edgar remaining on stage, with his second "lurk" still on his lips, yet to be released. It is like a nightmare return to the storm scene, when Edgar-Tom was surprised in his hiding place, captured in the act of who knows what. But this time, instead of being heard and then seen, the horror is being forced to hear and see. For what can be done, if the others enter and the Edgar-actor is stuck on stage? Can he calmly depart, secure in the conventions of stage and fiction, confident that no one, onstage or off, will trouble themselves to notice? Will he slope away, obscurely late, obscurely guilty? Might he hang at the margins, neither offstage nor on, paralyzed in the antinomy between an allowed invention and its suddenly exposed instruments? Or must he remain on stage and allow his character—perhaps his characters—to witness all that follows?

Of course mimetically this last is impossible. Edgar cannot get inside the "dark tower" (he cannot get home). Dramaturgically, too, it might seem impossible. The actor either exits or remains; he cannot be strung between the two. But is it so simple? Perhaps Edgar exits: but perhaps Tom, as licensed by the repeated cue, *lurks*. Perhaps Shakespeare is orchestrating—for this boundary-haunting, inside/outside, here-and-not figure—a correspondingly penumbral location, spatially ambiguous, haunting and haunted, neither in the scene nor out of it.

From its very beginning the Edgar-role straddles doorways, is swung between scenes and identities. Consider Edgar's very first entrance cue: "my bastardizing" in the Folio, "my bastardy Edgar" in the Quarto, followed by Edmund's "my Cue is villainous Melancholy, with a sighe like *Tom* o'Bedlam" (TLN 462; I. ii. 144–45).[8] Edmund claims Tom as his cue: at once Edgar morphs magically into action, as though by demonic incantation. Or recall Edgar's initial passage into Tom: as the stocked Kent "*sleepes*," Edgar steals onto stage and speaks his "happy hollow" soliloquy. He rises from the gap between scenes, as though carceral imagination made manifest (TLN 1251; II. ii. 180–II. iii *Entrance*).

Later plays show comparably inventive stage sectioning: *Antony and Cleopatra* uses repeated cues to split the stage into rival camps, one speaking, both seen; *The Tempest* often has actors present on stage *before* their characters are, or asks the character's presence to lapse into abeyance and wait for a decisive cue to fully reenter the fiction. And so there is nothing dramaturgically unlikely, or still less metaphysically unthinkable, about the Edgar/Tom-actor being strung across scenes. Perhaps Edgar cannot get home to his childhood castle. But through the haunting repeated cue "Lurk, lurk," his part, or part of his part, can. The consequence is truly shocking: he is given a phantom presence at the scene of his father's blinding, hung there like a specter on a stick, embodying the fact that the curtain will not be drawn upon atrocity. Like us, he is forced to bear witness.

No doubt Edgar's situation can be understood—not for the first or last time—as parricidal rehearsal. The audacious scenography itself tempts or teases Edgar, a bad angel surprised in his darkest desires. Another way of seeing it is as a staging of memory, or memory of a particular kind: the memory of a trauma at which the boy was not; the replaying of a horror he could not prevent. At the same time, he was, he *is*, exactly there. He was present, and he did nothing. His haunting at-

---

8. The Quarto text has "mine is villainous melancholy, with a sigh like them of Bedlam" (I. ii. 146–47).

tendance at the scene fixes him in a condition of painful remembrance, rehearsing, replaying, witnessing over and over the scene of violation. One might infer a guilt that cannot speak its name, which has to be consigned to spectral, barely adumbrated, here-not-here surrogacy. Equally one can intuit the simplest grief: the scene that will not shut down—that is always there, waiting to be shamefully revisited.

In a dark, barely fathomable sense, Edgar-Tom's correspondent place—the place of his births, his departures, his waiting, his mutating—seems to be precisely in scenic clefts: if not the clear breaks between scenes, then cracks within scenes, such as the straw beneath the stage from which Tom first irrupted. It is a horrible privilege. To experience such cracks is to foretaste death; to assay the normally unknowable. The scenic break is theater's black hole: the event horizon of thought and action; the cuspal space of perfectly full possibility. Perhaps there is no peace in this nonbeing, just agitation and vulnerability and helplessness; perhaps this place bears no consciousness whatsoever. Either way, the break between scenes epitomizes Tom's home: his alpha and omega, the place where his energies are garnered, stored, and protected. And if indeed Tom is discovered here, at this no place, it will not be for the last time.

13

INTERLUDE

Living *King Lear*

What would it be truly to live a tragedy such as *Lear*? Not just to be in a tragedy, as Lear or Gloucester are. But to experience it, awake every inch of the way. To give body and mind to this experience, unremittingly trace its passage, however sudden or vertiginous or strange?

It would mean being at once in the play and apart from it; in the moment and apart from it. It would mean being on both sides of the glass, witnessing that separation, knowing the hopelessness it presages, that of being unable to alter a thing. Can this be imagined? Can we imagine this mental travelling, this horrible trapped voyeurism, inside and outside the test tube, as a person, or as a life story? As a multiform dramatic part? As a moving passion, doubly suffering the action of the playworld?

This character will be in part a child of the tragedy. But as such it must be disobedient. As the true act of interpretation, it will enact filial trespass. It will not return obediently to the maker. The character will have to be let go, allowing the germ of a thought, a fugitive association, to grow up into its own fullness, however flawed or wayward. It will not remain single or unified. It cannot: the experience is too multiple and mutable. One of its parts might challenge another part. It might spawn self-surrogates. It might be doubled, or drowned, or reborn. What others understand as accidental or mistaken, this character will absorb as the very substance of possibility. It will voyage this way and that, unfaithful to any absolute identity, however it commits to a single purpose. Whatever it endures, it must outgrow any single idea. And because it is always on the outside, watching, it can never quite rest in the thing it also is.

And this figure's tragedy, its nontragic tragedy, is inescapable: it must remain to repeat the experience. It shall survive.

14

SCENE 6

Shuttered Genealogy

A proposition: let's stop for a moment thinking of the men and women of *Lear* as being much like us. They are radically foreign: if not from long ago, then from far elsewhere. They are un-made-up, or abortions; they are animals, hunger-beasts, compositions of little more than vile jelly. And here is the tagline of this strange world: "Where is thy luster now?" (TLN 2159).

In a different mouth, this question could be the most plaintive lament. But the question is Cornwall's, spoken jeeringly to Gloucester, the moment after he gouges out Gloucester's remaining eye. Can there have ever been a sentiment more vicious, more inhumane, more un-Christian? It is a question that says: the eye was always a deceiver; it never shone, never emanated a thing; it was always degraded material, accidental slop: and even if it wasn't it must be.

Cornwall's question—it isn't a question, but a triumph—seems to revel in the same loss of quintessence bemoaned by Hamlet. But imagine Cornwall as a primitive, without a glimmer of anything but appetite, and the vengeance upon "luster" might seem almost fearful, an animistic exorcism of mystery. Regan's mind is a lynch mob, in Stanley Cavell's words, but even this may be too civilized.[1] All of them are half-

---

1. Stanley Cavell, *Disowning Knowledge in Seven Plays of Shakespeare*, updated ed. (Cambridge, U.K.: Cambridge University Press, 2003), 63.

conscious brutes, stupidly self-certain, their vision as though occluded by heavy lashes or hanging brow—even Cordelia, blind as a child to what her bluntness unleashes. The characters that seem closest to modern reference-points, principally Edmund and Kent, are in most things atavistic. Consider Edmund's superstitious harping upon his and his brother's nativities; his appeal to the goddess Nature; the automatism in his passive receipt of the sisters' love or his father's maiming. Or consider Kent's gratuitous decision for loutishness, his attacking Oswald for laughs, so that even this role, whose main purpose is to balance the anarchy all around, to recall normative measures of order and authority, is threatened by overspilling libidinal appetite. This world is thousands of years before any other play of the period.[2] *Hamlet*'s Denmark, drunkards and all, is an experiment in postmodern sophistication next to *Lear*'s Britain.[3]

In such a world, Poor Tom is less the exiled stranger than a figure of talismanic verisimilitude. Throw out the BBC accents and instead imagine weathery vowels and consonants like tree trunks; picture them fresh from the hunt, feel a culture of dyed-in-blood custom and savage peremptory suddenness, in which a life truly can be leveled like a flower's—and a thing like Tom will feel like the merest decorum.

---

2. August Wilhelm von Schlegel: "To save in some degree the honour of human nature, Shakespeare never wishes that his spectators should forget that the story takes place in a dreary and barbarous age. . . . From this point of view we must judge of many coarsenesses in expression and manners: for instance, the immodest manner in which Gloster acknowledges his bastard, Kent's quarrel with the Steward, and more especially the cruelty personally exercised on Gloster by the Duke of Cornwall. Even the virtue of the honest Kent bears the stamp of an iron age, in which the good and the bad display the same ungovernable strength." *A Course of Lectures on Dramatic Art and Literature*, Vol. 2, trans. J. Black (London: Baldwin, Cradock, and Joy, 1815), 207. Schlegel is right that the personal cruelty of Duke to Earl is the alien thing; had he employed a servant it would have been more civil, strangely more evolved. But this in turn suggests that Shakespeare is really questioning the remit and possibility of service.

3. G. Wilson Knight: "Those daughters, and Edmund, are human beings, yet cruel as beasts that have no sense of sympathy. They are therefore throwbacks in the evolutionary process: they have not developed proper humanity. They are 'degenerate.'" He sees Edmund being of the past, Lear of the present, Cordelia of the future dispensation. "There is thus an implicit suggestion of a time-succession about these three. They correspond to definite layers. . . . She [Cordelia] is of the future humanity, suffering in the present dispensation for her very virtue. Nor is this evolution-thought an irrelevant imposition: it is throughout implicit." *The Wheel of Fire* (1930; reprint, London: Routledge, 2001), 210–11, 228–29.

But of course all of these figures are also scarily close—or can suddenly become so. This is one of the keys to the play's rare power. The action is at once eons away and whisperingly imminent. And this means that it really can dramatize the fact, concentrated into lightning epiphanies, of necessary historical transformation. Consider this brutal juxtaposition:

> A pezant stand up thus?
> *Killes him.* (TLN 2155-56)

It isn't just the lack of due process. Even virtue comes as a kind of creaturely shaking off, like a dogman, kicked too many times, waking to an alternative:

> *Serv*. I have serv'd you ever since I was a Childe:
> But better service have I never done you,
> Than now to bid you hold.
> *Reg*. How now, you dogge? (TLN 2146-49)

The waking is slow. The servant is still in mind "a Childe"; his working category is "service," against which he checks his movements for meaning; he is ever a "dogge" to his mistress. And yet there *is* movement, the slow simplicity of which garners strange permanency, as of emergent allegory. For the servant's resistance is clearly meant to show a kind of mutation or evolution in the exchange's foundational terms. He is now a man who was once a "Childe"; he remains a servant, but the service too must bear the trace of the years: rather than stay the same, on an oblivious loop, the service is getting reborn as self-conscious, sympathetic, ethical witness.

The power of the moment comes not only from the stirring sight of resistance to evil, but from the fact that the servant is performing *for others*, and in doing so surviving beyond his own extinction. It is an act of intervention, of interruption ("take the chance of anger"; TLN 2153) that transforms him from mute observer to active player— indeed to multiple active players. Of course he acts on behalf of the helpless "host," Gloucester, and for the watching audience. But he is also strangely acting for Cornwall, protecting him against himself. The resistance thus has exemplary and telepathic force: it demands imitation. And as we have seen, it may well be that the primary witness—hovering on the skirts of the stage, horrified but impotent, enacting our own sinister attendance—is Edgar/Tom.

It is precisely to bed down these transferred responsibilities that Shakespeare returns in the scene after the next to the servant's act of resistance. A messenger enters to report big news: the death of Cornwall, the blinding of Gloucester, Gloucester's betrayal by Edmund. Or so we might think. But he spends far more time detailing the actions of the servant:

> A servant that he bred, thrill'd [Quarto text: thrall'd] with remorse,
> Oppos'd against the act: bending his Sword
> To his great master, who, threat-enragd [Quarto text: thereat-enraged]
> Flew on him, and among'st them fell'd him dead. (TLN 2317-20)

The links to the world of Regan and Cornwall are clear in the messenger's language. The servant has been "bred," like a dog for purpose. The sense is of a barely human species mutating beyond expectation (in another of the play's telepathic surprises, we might recall its very first conversation, in which Gloucester harped blindly upon the "breeding" of the primal rebel, Edmund). But it is more than a one-off upsurge against cruelty or caprice. It has deep political import. The movement is institutional, the servant a figure for a whole emergent rank of men and women. The crucial word is "thrill'd." The *Oxford English Dictionary* tells us that the word means to "be moved with sudden emotion"—noting this instant as the first example of such use. But Shakespeare has exacter applications in mind. More primarily, "thrill'd" means two things. It means to pierce or penetrate; and it means to be "in thrall" (which is indeed the verb in the Quarto). That is, to be a bondman. The servant's actions, then, are defined precisely as service. The thrill he experiences *is* his thraldom.

This is the heart of the moment's allegorical reach. The servant embodies service as one might an abstraction or ideal, here discovered in the act of its own transformation. This, in turn, is shaped and moved by the verb's complementary meaning: to be pierced. So, the servant is pierced by emotions (anger, remorse, compassion); he bears them like a wound, which invokes an acceleration in the blood, a pulsing flow like never before, at once through his veins (impelling his "act") and from his veins (causing his death). The sense is of accelerated physiological alteration, provoked by the occasion's violence, which generates the suddenly possible virtue of remorse.

The metaleptic leaps in the key words thus transfer to those in the scene. The "pezant" is pierced, and in being so he pierces his master; the servant discovers remorse, both a suffering and a serendipity: but so too should authority. There is similar electrical movement from internal to external, invisible to visible, personal to public, actors to audiences— and precisely because of this, in due course from one character (the servant) to another (Edgar). So the image sends us initially inside the body, indeed inside very particular movements of the body. But these movements in turn generate correlative external acts: "bending his Sword / To his great Master," in which the shape of the sword traces that of the arm, which mimics that of the servant's uprising ("A pezant stand up thus?"). The movements derive their own singularity, and get magnified into allegory by the fact: an allegory that it is up to the beholders to make something of. Because what we are witnessing—in a sense more deeply even than in Lear's earlier prayer to the homeless—is the birth of political sensibility, in the fullest sense of both words. After all, what else justifies the big nouns, like law and government, than the simple experience of feeling in one's body, like a phantom organ, the suffering of another? (Abstractions are as untrue as flattery, which is made up of them.) Gloucester's eye always has magical metonymic capability, and nowhere more so than here. You could just about start to build a world from such hideous connections.[4]

---

4. Maynard Mack: "*King Lear* . . . is a vale of soul-making, where to all appearances the will is agonizingly free. As if to force the point on our attention, almost every character in the play, including such humble figures as Cornwall's servant and the old tenant who befriends Gloucester, is impelled soon or late to take some sort of stand. . . . Choice remains in the forefront of the argument, but its psychic antecedents have been so effectively shrunk down

Albany's reaction, typically, is useless ("This shewes you are above / You Iustices, that these our neather crimes / So speedily can venge"; TLN 2323-25). But the play is already far ahead of his ever-belated reactiveness. For this is the point: the affective claims and scenic connections of theater model those of politics. And remember: for better and worse, Edgar is present.

This presence duly feeds into the moment's forward memory. This kind of rebellion sticks, even as the slain fool is thrown, like a failed Job, "Upon the Dunghill" (TLN 2175). So the "Dunghill" returns in a conflict that is clearly companion to this scene of uprising: the killing of Goneril's Steward by Edgar, disguised as the yokel, and abused in exactly the same terms ("bold Pezant," "Slave," "Villain") as Cornwall's dead retainer:

> *Edg.* Nay, come not neere th'old man: keepe out che vor'ye, or ice try whether your Costard, or my Ballow [Quarto text: bat] be the harder; chill be plaine with you.
> *Stew.* Out Dunghill.
> *Edg.* Chill picke your teeth Zir: come, no matter vor your foynes.
> *Stew.* Slave thou hast slaine me (TLN 2692-99)

Edgar-the-yokel has become the dunghill onto which Cornwall's slave was thrown, like some metamorphosis from Golgothan dead skulls or regeneration from a compost heap. The rebellious dog snarls still. The Edgar-part animates the servant's potential, in and beyond death.[5]

Here the Quarto text in particular is suggestive about Shakespeare's purposes. Witness this exchange between servants, cut from the Folio text:

---

in this primitivized world that action seems to spring directly out of the bedrock of personality.... The meaning of action ... appears to lie rather in effects than in antecedents, and particularly in its capacity ... to generate energies that will hurl themselves in unforeseen and unforeseeable reverberations of disorder from end to end of the world." *King Lear in Our Time* (London: Methuen and Company, 1966), 90. This is largely right: but the disorderly reverberations may also hold restorative possibility, if not yet.

5. See the chapter on Scene 10 ("Alive, or Dead?") for further discussion of Oswald's killing.

> *Servant.* Ile never care what wickedness I doe,
> If this man come to good.
> *2 Servant.* If she live long, & in the end meet the old course
> of death, women will all turne monsters.
> *1 Ser.* Lets follow the old Earle, and get the bedlom
> To lead him where he would, his madness
> Allows it selfe to any thing.
> *2 Ser.* Goe thou, ile fetch some flaxe and whites of egges to
> apply to his bleeding face, now heaven helpe him. (III. vii. 98–107)

The servants interpret the scene not only allegorically, but typologically. It is an example for all time, but the particular precedent it offers depends not on their judgment or on the too-evident horror of what we have just witnessed, but on as yet unrevealed lifelines. The future will interpret the past. These events will repeat, that is certain: but whether the imitation is of evil or good, of terroristic authority or resistant subjects, waits on scenes still to be played.

We shouldn't preempt the possibilities here envisaged. There really is a feeling for the perilousness of all dispensations, including one's own commitment to virtue. Anyone might give up; anyone might despair; there is no easy passage through misery and injustice. This is precisely the subject of those soliloquies of Edgar that frame this awful and inspiring scene. I have shown how the Quarto's cue scripting makes it possible for Edgar to be the phantom-witness at this scene. His philosophizing tops and tails the action, with the effect of relaying its potential consequences. He has experienced it as it happens, and his haunting suprapresence means he can continue to do so, living the scene's extrapolation into future-hearkening allegory.

There is no question that the world is hateful, or sponsors hatefulness, and that the resources of this hatefulness are extraordinary. The plaintiveness of the servants' coda comes from the evident struggle of these small men against the evil tide. They know they are in most things powerless. What can they do but wait and watch and hope for comeuppance? But they are also not impotent. This is very important, and partakes in the play's enduring interest in collecting from wreckages, in gathering breakages and spillages—as another nameless man might pick samphire off a cliff, trusting that sustenance may be scraped together from whatever unpromising cleft. Of course there is no simple trust that the breakage will not call forth monsters. This is exactly Servant 2's theme, repeating that of Lear's Fool earlier (on cutting eggs in the middle, paring wits on both sides, and so enter the daddy-destroying daughters, TLN 670–702). But the play also insists, at this moment and over and over again, that destruction may not be terminal, just as "nothing" is never truly empty. To think you are faced by nothing is not to be looking hard enough, or to be baffled by rage or nostalgia or pity.[6]

The message is this. Pick up the pieces and move, even if the only persisting unity is a fissiparous assemblage of fractures and bits. This, I take it, is one of the abiding principles of Tom's composition. And of course it is also a most basic lesson of Job, never very far from mind in this world. The servants appeal to theodicean logic here, as Albany does when he hears that Cornwall is dead: the logic of poetic justice, eye for eye, just desserts. We all know this is pig shit. The play knows it from the very start, when Cordelia is whipped out for not nearly enough—and of course the fact comes home with a vengeance at the end. But this is not the end of ethics or of care. Perhaps theodicy is a joke, an insult to the things lost, speaking nothing at all to suffering. But still you carry on, you persevere precisely as protest, even though all you have is a shattered pot with which to rip at your broken skin. *Lear* feels the life in everything, each weed and pebble a potential subject, a source or recipient of care. And so the thing really to attend to, in the servants' moral coda, is what their passion commits to.

Consequently, on this principle of building from the merest remains, of refusing to accept that ruins must equal an end, they will do their best to palliate Gloucester's pain. They will get flax (cloth) to clean

---

6. Grigori Kozintsev: "The texture of Webster's art seems elementary in comparison, not because there is less horror and darkness in Shakespeare's world (sometimes the darkness is even more hell-like than in *The Duchess of Malfi*), but because in this dimension, saturated with movement, nothing perishes without trace, and death is answered by birth, and when the darkness reaches its utmost limits, an almost invisible spark already begins to burn, and the darkness loses its power in comparison with this tiny fragment of light." *King Lear, the Space of Tragedy: The Diary of a Film Director*, trans. Mary Mackintosh (London, 1977), 222.

him up, and egg whites to ease the burning. It is more than nothing; it is the beginning of healing (if not of sight). Importantly, this is not the last we hear of egg whites. They recur as the conclusion of Edgar's cliff fiction: if his body had mass, it would have "shivered like an egg" upon impact. But (as we shall see) Edgar's counterfactual tale indeed does work as a coexistent truth: the egg is smashed, releasing the healing white and fertile yolk.[7] Edgar mightn't know it (even though he says it): but the play knows, layering divergent possibilities, none of them free from violence, but also none of them quite finished by it.

These scenic interconnections are reinforced by the servants' next resolve: to "get the bedlom / To lead him where he would." (III. vii. 103-4 in the Quarto text) That is, put the blind man into the care of Tom ("the bedlom"). It is a very strange, seemingly gratuitous decision. Presumably the servants mean by this that the beggar can be the eyes of the Earl. Tom can lead him (Gloucester) where he (Gloucester) wishes. But Shakespeare embeds a much stranger and more dangerous thought: the madman can lead him (Gloucester) where he (Tom) would. Shakespeare seems to copy a trick that Spenser often uses in the *Faerie Queene* (as Shakespeare does in his sonnets), using flatly ambiguous pronouns to allow bifurcated possibilities, at once incompatible and simultaneous. Rather than judicious palliation of suffering, it becomes a reckless resignation of the blind man to contingency and whim: "his madness / Allow it selfe to any thing." (III. vii. 104-5 in the Quarto) Again, the servants probably mean, "Tom is mad, he will do whatever he is asked." But the construction more pertinently seems to say that Tom allows himself any liberty, admits of no barriers whatsoever. The blind man will be taken into the unknown. And so, of course, he duly is. And this, precisely this, is the care from which futures, however trace-like or tenuous, might grow.

For there is something life-affirming—literally life-affirming—in Tom's persisting. Consider again Edgar's words upon first seeing his blinded father:

---

7. See the chapter on Scene 10 ("Alive, or Dead?") for further discussion of the smashed egg.

> But who comes here? My Father poorely led?
> World, World, O world!
> But that they strange mutations make us hate thee,
> Life would not yeelde to age. (TLN 2189-92)

He may mean we only live long (yield to age) out of hatred for life. He may mean we only die or commit suicide (yield to age) because we hate life. It means both, at equal odds, like locked beasts on a coat of arms. Either way, the words express a curious willfulness about the passage between living and death. If only life were sweeter, we might live forever! Death is a choice: a life choice. Immortality is only vitiated by our witness of injustice, suffering, cruelty. Inside the world hatred, then, turns a strange, tortured, but almost beautiful commitment to life's possibility. Perhaps it is this, deep inside Edgar's pain, as its symptom and release, that keeps Tom alive.[8]

---

8. Kenneth Gross: "In lieu of ban or curse, what emerges in Tom's speeches, heartrendingly, is blessing. Tom places for us the power to bless in this world." *Shakespeare's Noise* (Chicago: University of Chicago Press, 2001), 135.

15

INTERLUDE

Decreated

Let's think a difficult thought: Edgar's secret task—certainly often secret to him—is to allow that Tom truly is the outcome, the correlate, the *necessity* of his condition. Not some diversion or means to an end; not a mask to deflect from the silent truth of suffering. Tom is the necessary thing: a life profoundly removed from objects, human or nonhuman; from the pursuit of them or definition through them. And this includes oneself, considered as any such socially recognizable object.

If so, this takes Edgar-Tom into the rarefied, perhaps saintly possibilities foreshadowed by Simone Weil:

> Renunciation demands that we should pass through anguish equivalent to that which would be caused in reality by the loss of all loved beings and all possession, including our faculties and attainments in the order of intelligence and character, our opinions, beliefs concerning what is good, what is stable, etc. And we must not lay these things down of ourselves but lose them—like Job. Moreover the energy thus cut off from its object should not be wasted in oscillations and degraded. The anguish should therefore be still greater than in real affliction, it should not be cut up and spread over time nor oriented towards a hope.[1]

---

1. Simone Weil, *Gravity and Grace*, trans. Emma Crawford and Mario von der Ruhr (London: Routledge, 2002), 36.

This is very difficult, morally strenuous territory. But the question needs asking. Might Shakespeare be pushing at an idea similar to what Weil called decreation? Imagining it, testing it, perhaps feeling its astringent human terror?

Weil posits a creation that is permitted by God's original kenosis: "he who gives us our being loves in us the acceptance of not being."[2] God empties part of himself, withdraws from his own fullness, and this deficit produces human presence. The world is empty of God precisely to the extent that we *are*. As in *Lear*, it can seem that life itself is ineluctably guilty. Humanness is a sort of substantial inauthenticity: a negative arrogation; a robbing from divinity. To be in the world is to be some foreign substance: in pain, in the way, a coarse nodule necessary to emit. Consequently, the true thing must be to return to God what is God's: "Our existence is made up only of his [God's] waiting for our acceptance not to exist. He is perpetually begging from us that existence which he gives. He gives it to us in order to beg it from us."[3]

Weil writes of the absolute imperative to make ourselves nothing, indeed to recognize that we truly are nothing: "We possess nothing in the world—a mere chance can strip us of everything—except the power to say 'I.' That is what we have to give to God—in other words, to destroy.... I must love being nothing. How horrible it would be if I were something!"[4] This renunciation cannot simply be our flesh or any other accidental wretched object; nor can it be compelled by external circumstances: "Nothing is worse than extreme affliction which destroys the 'I' from outside, because after that we can no longer destroy it ourselves."[5] In a typical Weilian paradox, it must be a willed renunciation of our will: a choice to give over the spurious autonomy of choice. To renounce this is to be decreated. But the difficulty of the paradox is everything: it cannot be an action of the ego; it must be suffered, an absolute passivity.

2. Ibid., 32.
3. Ibid., 33.
4. Ibid., 26, 111.
5. Ibid., 26.

This is the dilemma suffered in Edgar's taking on of Tom. If he substantially preserves himself in a disguise, if he superintends the Tom-show, calmly awaiting his moment to reappear, then Edgar has not suffered what Weil calls a renunciation. However, in Tom's long first scene, we might indeed conclude that Edgar is renounced. Tom takes over, and Edgar suffers a more comprehensive renunciation than he ever chose. In subsequent scenes Edgar tries to claw something back, but the genie is out. Tom has existence, and Edgar cannot abrogate the fact. As a consequence, it is Tom who then incarnates renunciation: a walking nothing who calls the bluff of his maker's contingent kenosis, and proceeds to live the possibility of a truly decreated existing—an existing in which one's slice of creation, of time, space, and attention, is also always rescinded. We thus get a double movement of renunciation: Edgar's into Tom; Tom's as an existent nothing.

This moves into spiritual territory that Edgar's role until this point has hardly apprehended. If Edgar becomes the play's proto-Christian metaphysician, it is Tom who takes him there. For it is Tom who really moves the play into supra-secular experiential possibilities, making the most basic ontological contract a live issue: to be alive as privation, as an ontological *blanc*, as a figure with no foundation in agreed provenances. His life is knowingly inauthentic. But it is just this that brings his actions home.

It is no surprise that Weil, over a period of many years, so profoundly lived with *Lear*—with the world of the play, and with a world that is like the play:

> When I saw *Lear* here, I asked myself how it was possible that the unbearably tragic character of these fools had not been obvious long ago to everyone, including myself. The tragedy is not the sentimental one it is sometimes thought to be; it is this:
>
> There is a class of people in this world who have fallen into the lowest degree of humiliation, far below beggary, and who are deprived not only of all social consideration but also, in everybody's opinion, of the specific human dignity, reason itself—and these are the only people who, in fact, are able to tell the truth. All the others

lie. . . . Even Kent and Cordelia attenuate, mitigate, soften, and veil the truth.[6]

The play stands for her as one of the supreme examples not only of imaginative literature, but of words that can speak to the true "gravity" of life:

> To find the words which express the truth of their affliction, the words which can give resonance, through the crust of external circumstances, to the cry which is always inaudible: "Why am I being hurt?" For this, they cannot count only upon men of talent. . . . They can count only upon men of the very highest genius: the poet of the *Iliad*, Aeschylus, Sophocles, Shakespeare as he was when he wrote *Lear*, or Racine when he wrote *Phedre*. There are not very many of them.[7]

This may sound like a familiar cry, echoing the many who have found in *Lear* a profound pity for the poor and the outcast. But Weil's recognition is of something much more singular, less sentimental, nothing to do with essentially bourgeois constructions such as "rights" and "persons":

> To put into the mouth of the afflicted words from the vocabulary of middle values, such as democracy, rights, personality, is to offer them something which can bring them no good and will inevitably do them harm. . . . In order to provide an armour for the afflicted, one must put into their mouths only those words whose rightful abode is in heaven, beyond heaven, in the other world.[8]

Perfect truth doesn't come from—doesn't speak in the mouth of—a defined social individual. How can it when it is exactly personality which

---

6. Simon Weil, letter to her parents, 1943, in *Simone Weil: Seventy Letters*, translated and arranged by Richard Rees (Oxford: Oxford University Press, 1965).

7. Simone Weil, "Human Personality," in Simone Weil, *An Anthology*, ed. Sian Miles (London: Penguin, 2005), 87.

8. Ibid., 86.

must be divested, being the "part of us which belongs to error and sin"? What is needed is impersonality:

> Impersonality is only reached by the practice of a form of attention which is rare in itself and impossible except in solitude; and not only physical but mental solitude. This is never achieved by a man who thinks of himself as a member of a collectivity, as part of something which says "We."[9]

Now think of the *Lear* playworld: even the king, for all his isolation, always conceives of himself as connected to others, whether in degradation or exile or personal sovereignty. Only one figure truly enters solitude—Edgar. This solitude doesn't so much issue in Tom, as though an escape from it: solitude *discovers* Tom. And here is where Edgar-Tom's angelic wrestle over identity really comes home: Tom-as-Tom experiences impersonality as his immanent ontology; but so too does Edgar-in-Tom experience it, a shocked, reluctant, recoiling new entrant into this strenuous condition. This, I think, is what Weil sees when the play sends her into truth-raptures: she sees Tom-as-Tom, *and* she sees Edgar-in-Tom. And in doing so she sees the antinomies which this persona endures, rooted in this peeling away from all circumscribing collective belonging:

> The human being can only escape from the collective by raising himself above the personal and entering into the impersonal. The moment he does this, there is something in him, a small portion of his soul, upon which nothing of the collective can get a hold.... Every man who has once touched the level of the impersonal is charged with a responsibility towards all human beings; to safeguard, not their persons, but whatever frail potentialities are hidden within them for passing over to the impersonal. It is primarily to these men that the appeal to respect the sacredness of the human being should be addressed.[10]

---

9. Ibid., 76.
10. Ibid., 77–78.

This intimates a kind of protomessianic promise, sacred if not divine, that opens to the "frail potentialities" in all human captives. It is nothing to do with ascendance, and still less with transcendence. Instead, this impersonality implies exposure to our creaturely groundedness in affliction:

> The only way into truth is through one's own annihilation; through dwelling a long time in a state of extreme and total humiliation.... Just as truth is a different thing from opinion, so affliction is a different thing from suffering. Affliction is a device for pulverizing the soul; the man who falls into it is like a workman who gets caught up in a machine. He is no longer a man but a torn and bloody rag on the teeth of a cogwheel.[11]

Such affliction seems like a scrupulous gloss on Tom's enduring purgatory. But there is for him no saintly freedom from complicities, no thankful awareness, in the midst of pain, of having escaped from all collectivity. As much as Tom is a dehuman rag, torn in the machine, he is also repeatedly taken or spoken by the forces of the collective, by fearful iterations and anxious interpellations. But this, I think, makes his experience all the more faithful to spiritual struggle: after all, it is no passage to saintliness merely to be stripped of clothes and whipped into the weather. Equally, Tom cannot be approached as a single conflicted person. His tortured catechisms, for example, speak a collapsing public as much as a haunted subject. Tom lives the pain of systemic entropy, and of the shattering collective that is its symptom.

Here the particular form in which Shakespeare worked is crucial to the existential load it can carry. That is, this kind of living is the peculiar gift of dramatic technology. The Tom-part really can dissolve into separate persons, at the same time as it can resolve into a single overburdened victim. And it is just this that allows the part to embody the terrible processes recommended by Weil: "A collectivity must dissolve into separate persons before the impersonal can be reached."[12]

11. Ibid., 90.
12. Ibid., 76.

Again and again, Weil's most profound prescription for life doubles as an intimate window onto Edgar and Tom:

> Human thought is unable to acknowledge the reality of affliction.... "I may lose at any moment, through the play of circumstances over which I have no control. Anything whatsoever that I possess, including those things which are so intimately mine that I consider them as being myself.... It could happen at any moment that what I am might be abolished and replaced by anything whatsoever of the filthiest and most contemptible sort."[13]

Isn't this what happens to Edgar? Not when he loses his father, brother, home, respect and freedom: but when he loses himself to Tom. In doing so, Edgar enters the afflictive negativity that is already Tom's: "To be aware of this in the depth of one's soul is to experience non-being. It is the state of extreme and total humiliation which is also the condition for passing over into truth. It is a death of the soul."[14]

Tom is not. There is no ground for his being: it is weightless, vertiginous, in absolute existential freefall. But the audacious, awful thing is that just this condition is the truest truth of Edgar's immersive probation, its most necessary point of self-recognition.[15] Who would not shy away from such a recognition, as from a personal death?

> This is why the naked spectacle of affliction makes the soul shudder as the flesh shudders at the proximity of death.... Therefore the afflicted are not listened to. They are like someone whose tongue has been cut

---

13. Ibid., 90.
14. Ibid., 90–91.
15. Maurice Blanchot: "To write the decreated self is not to write the absence of self, but the very core of self. To understand oneself as an individual who cannot be revealed as such, and to communicate this with what remains of the outside world, is to approach the very limits of selfhood." *The Infinite Conversation*, trans. Susan Hanson (Minneapolis: University of Minnesota Press, 1993), 106. Also see Anne Carson, *Decreation: Poetry, Essays, Opera* (New York: Knopf, 2005); Timothy C. Baker, "Praying to an Absent God: The Poetic Revealing of Simone Weil," *Culture, Theory and Critique* 47, no. 2 (2006): 133–47.

out and who occasionally forgets the fact. When they move their lips no ear perceives any sound.[16]

This uncannily evokes the aversion to Tom expressed by the Fool, Kent, and Gloucester: the wish to hurry away, the failure to attend. And it is just this inattention that is for Weil the key to the play's revelatory extremity. As she writes in a 1943 letter to her parents:

> What makes the tragedy extreme is the fact that because the fools possess no academic titles or episcopal dignities and because no one is aware that their sayings deserve the slightest attention, . . . their expression of truth is not even listened to. Everybody, including Sh.'s readers and audiences for four centuries, is unaware that what they say is true. And not satirically or humorously true, but simply the truth . . . the bitterness of possessing the truth and having won at the price of nameless degradation, the power to utter it and then being listened to by nobody.[17]

No doubt she has Lear and his Fool partly in mind: both in some sense nameless or titleless, both in some sense ignored. But the foremost sufferers of a "nameless degradation" that will not be heard are Edgar-in-Tom and Tom-as-Tom. This is the recoil that needs repairing. For it speaks more than distaste, or a holding to personal or social dignity, such as concern the decorous Kent and Gloucester. The failure to hear, Weil suggests, is resistance to an ultimate substitution: "To listen to someone is to put oneself in his place while he is speaking. To put oneself in the place of someone whose soul is corroded by affliction, or in near danger of it, is to annihilate oneself."[18]

Lear moves toward something like this when he addresses the naked beggar in the storm. His famous recognition—"Is man no more than this?"—is undoubtedly crucial to Weil's immersion in the play,

---

16. Weil, "Human Personality," 90–91.
17. Weil, *Anthology*, 1–2.
18. Weil, "Human Personality," 90–91.

as it is to Shakespeare's purposes for the alarming figure of Tom. But still Lear doesn't quite get there—or if he does we do not witness it. The king never responds to Tom's answers (if indeed Tom gives any). After Lear's first searing recognition, distraction takes over, and the beggar is distanced, sentimentally instrumentalized; Tom morphs in the king's mind into a comical Socrates, addressed as "learned Theban," "good Athenian," and "Noble Philosopher," only without the dialogue that should follow (TLN 1936-64). And so as much as Lear's attentions point to Tom's thematic importance, they also fail to claim him. This instead is Edgar's private, incommunicable, annihilating burden. He cannot but attend to Tom; only he can finally claim him. It is the hardest thing. He resists it as if his life depended on it—which it does. But there is nothing more important than this attendance, if only it might be sustained: "Because affliction and truth need the same kind of attention before they can be heard, the spirit of justice and the spirit of truth are one. The spirit of justice and truth is nothing else but a certain kind of attention, which is pure love."[19]

It is the very hardest thing for Edgar to live up to his own part—which means living up to the kind of attention that the playworld at every point demands. That is, attention to Tom.

19. Ibid., 92.

16

SCENE 7

Fool to Sorrow

> It's suicide by waves: a man who disappears while speaking.
> VALÈRE NOVARINA, *The Theater of the Ears*

Is it possible for a phenomenon—or phenomena—such as Tom to die? If it is, when does he pass away? In a gap between scenes? Or onstage, visibly, as we watch?

The play is notorious for its unacknowledged passings. The Fool vanishes. So too does France—with the part's actor quite possibly passing into the role of Edgar.[1] What then of Tom? Where does he go? Shakespeare certainly seems aware of the problem. One sign of this is the evident strain felt by Edgar in keeping going with the Tom-show. After the exhausting adrenalin rush of Tom's first appearance, Edgar seems eager to give Tom up ("poore Tom thy horne is dry," "Tom, away"; III. vi. 77, 117 in the Quarto). But he isn't permitted to break free. As can be seen from an apparently trivial example such as Cornwall's servants, Tom's existence can be the predicate or consequence of others' needs or decisions, not necessarily Edgar's. Edgar doesn't want Tom, but others

---

1. This gives subperformative sense to Tate's decision to make Edgar the long suffering betrothed of Cordelia. Unless, of course, the Edgar-actor doubles with Cordelia (and France with the Fool)—less likely, perhaps, but either way suggesting the Edgar-part's deep-lying implication in Cordelia.

call him forth, recognize him, employ him. Nowhere does this happen more painfully than in the immediate aftermath of his father's blinding. Here is the scene in the Folio:

> *Edg.* . . . Welcome then,
> Thou vnsubstantiall ayre that I embrace:
> The Wretch that thou hast blowne vnto the worst,
> Owes nothing to thy blasts.
>   *Enter Glouster, and an Oldman.*
> But who comes heere? My Father poorely led?
> World, World, O world!
> But that thy strange mutations make vs hate thee,
> Life would not yeelde to age.
> *Oldm.* O my good Lord, I haue bene your Tenant,
> And your Fathers Tenant, these fourescore yeares.
> *Glou.* Away, get thee away: good Friend be gone,
> Thy comforts can do me no good at all,
> Thee, they may hurt.
> *Oldm.* You cannot see your way.
> *Glou.* I haue no way, and therefore want no eyes:
> I stumbled when I saw. Full oft 'tis seene,
> Our meanes secure vs, and our meere defects
> Proue our Commodities. Oh deere Sonne *Edgar*,
> The food of thy abused Fathers wrath:
> Might I but liue to see thee in my touch,
> I'ld say I had eyes againe.
> *Oldm.* How now? who's there?
> *Edg.* O Gods! Who is't can say I am at the worst?
> I am worse then ere I was.
> *Old.* 'Tis poore mad Tom.
> *Edg.* And worse I may be yet: the worst is not,
> So long as we can say this is the worst.
> *Oldm.* Fellow, where goest?
> *Glou.* Is it a Beggar-man?
> *Oldm.* Madman, and beggar too.
> *Glou.* He has some reason, else he could not beg.

I'th' last nights storme, I such a fellow saw;
Which made me thinke a Man, a Worme. My Sonne
Came then into my minde, and yet my minde
Was then scarse Friends with him.
I haue heard more since:
As Flies to wanton Boyes, are we to th' Gods,
They kill vs for their sport.
Edg. How should this be?
Bad is the Trade that must play Foole to sorrow,
Ang'ring it selfe, and others. Blesse thee Master.
Glou. Is that the naked Fellow?
Oldm. I, my Lord.
Glou. Get thee away: If for my sake
Thou wilt ore-take vs hence a mile or twaine
I'th' way toward Douer, do it for ancient loue,
And bring some couering for this naked Soule,
Which Ile intreate to leade me.
Old. Alacke sir, he is mad.
Glou. 'Tis the times plague,
When Madmen leade the blinde:
Do as I bid thee, or rather do thy pleasure:
Aboue the rest, be gone.
Oldm. Ile bring him the best Parrell that I haue
Come on't what will. *Exit*
Glou. Sirrah, naked fellow.
Edg. Poore Tom's a cold. I cannot daub it further.
Glou. Come hither fellow.
Edg. And yet I must:
Blesse thy sweete eyes, they bleede.
Glou. Know'st thou the way to Douer?
Edg. I Master. (TLN 2184-257)

"How now? Who's there?" says the Old Man when "Tom" is first latched upon, as though he's smelt some invisible spirit. And perhaps he has. Because what actually happens here is that first Edgar and then Tom is claimed by the two old men, in some basic dramaturgical and ethical sense brought center stage: Edgar by the overhearing of his father's apostrophe to him; Tom by Old Man's recognition. It is as though both Edgar and Tom are caught, like robbers, frozen with their guilty load and forced to come to account:

Old Man. How now?	*Edgar/Tom freezes*
Who's there?	*Edgar/Tom hides*
Edg. O Gods!	*Cursing because caught?*
	Or lamenting his father?
Who is't can say I am at the worst?	
I am worse then ere I was	
Old Man. 'Tis poore mad Tom.	*He says to Gloucester*
	Or to the audience, pointing at the cowering figure at the far end of the stage
Edg. And worse I may be yet:	*Is this general philosophizing? Or does he speak to the moment, aware that once more he "must play Foole to sorrow"?*
The worst is not,	
So long as we can say this is the worst.	*He starts to slope away*
Old Man. Fellow, where goest?	*Edgar-Tom is addressed, or called back from the edge of the wings*
Glou. Is it a Beggar-man?	*All eyes turn to Edgar-Tom. What is he?*
Old Man. Madman, and beggar too.	*He isn't one thing; he is two*

Tom is here not Edgar's choice, not his consoling fiction. Edgar wants to be rid of him. But Tom is insisted upon. Why is this? Who insists? For Edgar is almost forcibly conscripted into the Tom-part, as the two old men vocally surround him with assumptive, annunciating misrecognitions:

> Oh deere Sonne Edgar
> Might I but live to see thee in my touch

> How now?
> Who's there?
> 'Tis poore mad Tom
> Fellow, where goest?
> Is it a beggar-man?
> Madman, and beggar too.
> He has some reason, else he could not beg.
> I'th'last nights storme, I such a fellow saw
> Whch made me thinke a Man, a Worme. My Sonne
> Came then into my minde. (TLN 2202–18)

Edgar is called, and then Tom is captured. This is the slow burden of the whole scene. Each one of Edgar's speeches is an intermitted commentary upon his hateful part, and a graduated morphing into it. He enters philosophizing about "lamentable change" and the relativity of misery. He sees his father led in, savagely blinded. He expresses world-hatred and tries to leave, as though to depart the scene is the kind of proxy-suicide he needs, an immersion in oblivion he can suffer rather than be released from. But instead he is forced to remain. And so it is this remaining—on stage, in scene, and *as Tom*—that stands for Edgar's continuing subjective evacuation, even eradication.

The play is never more pitiless than right here: forcing Edgar to see his father like this, forcing him to stay, forcing him to remain hidden. But not hidden in the only way he could endure: out of sight. Of course he is out of his father's sight, his Tomness inferred precisely in sight's lack (another in the play's savage pleonastic ironies). But he can see himself in his father's presence. He can see his father's failure to see. The scene thus pitilessly stages the fact and the exposing of hiddenness. It is a recipe for paralyzed shame. By the same token, if identity depends upon recognition, Edgar truly is not here. So what Edgar must now suffer is both unseen visibility and visible unseenness. In a sense, then, Shakespeare is putting absence very directly on stage: Edgar tries to creep away, but his body is caught; Edgar is not called back, but Tom is. Consequently, Edgar is exactly where he was heading to before being arrested—offstage, in the cleft between scenes. Which makes Tom, once again, a figure exactly of this enigmatic space—a moving cipher for unfinishable annihilation.

There is something relentless and punishing about this, something inextricable in Edgar's complicity in the role: "I cannot daub it further.... And yet I must" (2241-43). The apparent gap on the stage between the old and the young marks something like the gap between Tom and Edgar. The closer he draws to the two old men, the more Tom mutates out of Edgar. The metabolism of Edgar and Tom is at once shared and radically distinct. Edgar belongs to the visible world, of normative cause and effect and summative philosophy. At this moment he is visible to us, invisible to Gloucester, and in the process of disappearing into Tom. Tom belongs to the invisible world, in which places and characters materialize out of the possibilities of words. The old men's words, then, have a strangely conjuring facility: rather as Edmund did at the start of the play, they summon not just Edgar (as the missing son) but Tom (as his avatar or medium). Mental visions are taking over as scenic predictors. Gloucester can no longer see: and so what he "sees" is a nightmarish thought derived from his final night of sight. This movement, from vision to possible judgment, not only remembers, but requires again the same metastable "fellow" that he saw. This fellow shall again be the genius of the imminent scene; the words cue and shape his emergence. Here is the Quarto text:

> *Old Man.* Mad man, and begger too.
> *Glost.* A has some reason, else he could not beg,
> In the last nights storme I such a fellow saw,
> Which made me thinke a man a worme, my sonne
> Came then into my mind, and yet my mind
> Was then scarce friendes with him. I have heard more since,
> As flies are toth' wanton boyes, are we toth' Gods,
> They bitt us for their sport.
> *Edg.* How should this be, bad is the trade that must play the foole to sorrow angring it selfe and others, blesse thee maister.
> *Glost.* Is that the naked fellow? (IV. i. 33-41)

The scripting plays remorselessly upon the Edgar-part's foundational duality. Gloucester makes the link that even Edgar wants to resist, summoning Tom and his son in the self-same movement, discovering one in the other.[2] Edgar has to hear the words, and their awful balancing of tender wish and depressive curse and baffled awakening. Their claim upon him is almost overwhelming. As always when Shakespeare is working at high intensity, the lines and rhythms themselves have an existential charge:

> Might I but live to see thee in my touch. (TLN 2204; IV. i. 25 in the Quarto).

Hear the optative plea at the start, addressed to he knows not whom; the modesty of "but," and its knowledge that to ask anything may be to ask too much; and then the triplet verbs, *live, see, touch*, ever more intimate, moving from the predicative and yet almost impossible gift (*but live*), to the central condition of his continuing existence, experienced now only as snapshots of memory (*see thee*), to the last remaining faculty, the only thing still his own, which is feeling (*in my touch*).[3] Similar movements mark another line a moment later:

> Which made me thinke a man a worme, my son. (TLN 2217; IV i. 35 in the Quarto)

---

[2]. William Empson: "He is himself forgiven—a fact which he hardly seems to realize, and indeed we must suppose he is now rather crazy because he doesn't." *The Structure of Complex Words* (London: Hogarth, 1985), 141. This reading is striking, but I think too tied to a single conception of the character.

[3]. Clearly the line is also powerfully proleptic, suggesting a possible model of therapeutic touch that others, and not only Gloucester, might discover. In this context the account given by Rachel Fensham, of Barrie Kosky's 1998 Bell Shakespeare Company production of *King Lear*, is very suggestive. Of this scene she writes: "Scapegoat and deject, Gloucester and Tom. In the theatre, in the anonymity of a transit space, these two, father and son, find each other. . . . In these scenes men are destined to admit permeability, and at least weep for the blindspots. Poor Tom feels tenderly for his blind father's eyes, touching the hollows. . . . It has a painful jouissance: the male bodies soften to one another—as the boy asks the father to feel him. . . . In this uncomfortable zone, masculinity feels like a surface of suffering. Through the touch of the boy child, a breach in the male body occurs and there is a movement toward healing. Now, the bloody father rocks the dirty son like a baby. . . . The son stretches a little, spasms, and then falls back into Gloucester's bare chest. Tragic masculinity becomes-mother, and I think of the soldier heroes who cradle the bodies of their dead companions after bloody contest. This image of father and son seems more peculiar than any war movie since neither are dead, and instead it has the quality of a new birth." *To Watch Theatre: Essays on Genre and Corporeality* (Brussels: Peter Lang, 2009), 92-93.

The prosody is typical of Shakespeare, overlaying competing forms, such that an actor can play only one idea, correspondent to the character's conscious intention, but we can see and hear two, speaking the situation's shimmering prehensions. So, the implied sentence is simple enough, and presumably the actor pauses to make it distinct. He saw a fellow who made him think a man was a worm. His son came into his mind. But the *line* gives us something more, produced by the three consecutive nouns, nesting together and qualifying each other. A man, a worm, my son. He takes responsibility, a biological and ethical paternity, for the worm. The noun seems to fall, only to rise again: *man, worm, son*; likewise, it moves from anonymity into personal possession: *a, a, my*. It is the line alone that allows this very beautiful thought. But at the same time Gloucester can barely admit it to cognition.

Such a thought should be impossible, or has always seemed impossible in the cosseted world of the Earl. For the thought is much more radical than some leveling notion that humanity is despicable or disgusting, undistinguished and undistinguishable. If the line ended with "a Worme" this might be all it meant. But it doesn't. It ends with "my son." He doesn't just think "a man is like a worm." He moves from "a man," to "a worm," to "my son": he *thinks* each one. At the same time, the worm is *itself*, blessed and named as "my son." It is ineffably humble, deep in earth, but as "my son" it is the channel to re-possession and inheritance.

Gloucester is seeing past the daily plane, with its deceiving opacities. His blindness is a visionary gift—suddenly intimate to Shakespeare's—in which reality is holographic: look more closely, shine the virtual laser, and the worm is in the man, the son the worm, just as the flies "bitt" by the "wanton boys" are also the boys killed by the gods: notice the same triplet rhythm—*as flies, to boys, to gods*. The fractals are getting larger, but the vision is affectively the same. There is no absolute size for life, just as there is no absolute power (the gods are plural, and subject to the reverse metonymic exchange). This is also the inward secret of the storm-creature he saw: deindividuated, fertilizing the dirt, feeding on the dead, posthumous—*surviving*.

Life has irreducible value precisely because it is fragile as grass.

Everywhere is this recognition of interconnectedness. If we are cruel, we are cruel to what we are. One thing inheres in the other; each thing returns to the other. It is not just that we should share in the gifts of life. Each of us is composed of recycled stuff; all things are metabolically exchangeable. It is the basic rule of this playworld, and incarnate in the storm-creature Tom.[4] Edgar both recognizes and resists the summons:

> How should this be?
> Bad is the Trade that must play Foole to sorrow,
> Ang'ring it selfe, and others. Blesse thee Master. (TLN 2223-25).

The imperative "must" has rare strenuousness, and there is bitter play on the word *trade*. He means a job, a base vocation. But he also means a swap: a swap, that is, precisely from himself to Tom. As with the "Lurk" soliloquy, the part is both reporting and captive to its ambiguating agency. Which of the two, Edgar or Tom, is the "selfe" that is angered by the trade? Who are the "others"? The scenes are portraying something like the torturous process of possession, as Edgar watches himself being taken over by Tom, against his will, for some purpose that he cannot yet, perhaps cannot ever, understand. A few speeches move between one voice and the other—"Ang'ring it selfe, and others. Blesse thee Master" (TLN 2225); "Poor Tom's a cold. I cannot daub [Quarto: dance] it further" (TLN 2241); "And yet I must: / Blesse thy sweete eyes" (TLN 2243-44)—and then it seems Tom takes over. It is a strangely cruel kind of differential repetition, almost a deconstruction of Shakespeare's own stratagems. Earlier, Edgar became Tom, for his own purposes, and then the simulacrum seemed to take over. Now, Edgar is told he must become Tom again, like some awful automaton pageant with a momentum all its own. But then without this act, without

---

4. Giorgio Agamben: "What is man, if he is always the place—and, at the same time, the result—of ceaseless divisions and caesurae? It is more urgent to work on these divisions, to ask in what way—within man—has man been separated from non-man, and the animal from the human, than it is to take positions on the great issues, on so-called human rights and values." *The Open: Man and Animal*, trans. Kevin Attell (Stanford, Calif.: Stanford University Press, 2004), 16.

the recognition accorded to Tom, Edgar would not have been called, and he would have slunk away in his confusion. If Gloucester is to be saved by Tom, then so too is Edgar.

The metadramatic reference ("play the foole") seems to look ahead to the part Edgar must "play" in this particular drama. The "others" he will "anger" are us, the spectators to the "trade" he is set to embark on: playing the fool for his father, pretending to take him to Dover, fabricating a redemptive miracle, and never once revealing that he is the very son whom Gloucester's speech so lovingly recalls. Any of this might, even should, anger us: the deception, its baroque extensiveness, and above all the refusal to give his father either of the comforts for which he longs: reconciliation or death. But it isn't just that Edgar's words, characteristically, seem inspired with supraconscious scenic telepathy. It is that this very telepathy, in all of its apparent seeing through to the part he shall perform, seems to be suggested, even commissioned, by the words of his father that cue him:

> *Glost.* As flies to wanton Boyes, are we to th'Gods,
> They kill [Quarto: bitt] us for their sport. (TLN 2221-22)

Whether or not Edgar hears these words, their import seems to lodge in the Edgar-part, uncannily cueing what he is about to be asked to perform. Either that or we witness the cold-eyed appropriation of a plot: Edgar seizes Gloucester's lament as a prompt and pattern for his own sadistic game. For isn't this exactly what Edgar goes on to do? The disguised fool, playing his "bad" trade, killing his father in sport? Edgar becomes the wanton boy, reliving juvenile sprees, taking revenge on daddy. Coterminously, Edgar is one of the gods, toying with life and with death like a fisher might his catch. "The Gods" are figured as the audience at the tragedy, looking down from the "heavens," requiring blood for their money; the actor is tied to his trade, playing the fool to "sorrow," now recast as the spectator's pity; and Edgar occupies all such stations.

The Edgar-part's "strange mutations" really do go beyond what we customarily understand as human. To the extent that it is prewritten, stuck on a train it cannot get off, a reactive instrument of theatrical technologies such as telepathic dialogue and deterministic cues, it is as fastened to its passage as a worm. But to the extent that these same technologies move sublimely beyond mere materiality, the Edgar-part can test godlike possibilities, where humans find or exceed their own limits. Edgar is all set to experience that spaciousness, those opportunities, those terrible, terrifying powers. But to be one with the gods, in cruelty and folly, is also to be one with them in pained self-contempt and a kind of ricocheting pain. Empson invokes a "suffering demi-urge,"[5] hurting others because itself hurt, but hurt even more because power is in truth prescripted servitude, its games the reflux of boredom or waste, even as those subjected to this service are no more than flies or worms. These are the paradoxes of agency that the Edgar-part's multiple misprisions can now assay. Edgar is here at the very limit point of possibility.[6]

Edgar needs Tom, just as Gloucester needs Tom, to find out these limits. For if Edgar is in part the wanton boy, mentally rehearsing his playact parricide, and partly the godlike subject, granted unwonted power over another, it is Tom, as the angel of the scene's transgressions, carrying across evidentiary boundaries, who might make this likeness real.[7]

---

5. *Structure*, 142.

6. Empson: "The gods are called fools both as lunatics (or malicious children) and as mockers; this is the trade Edgar has adopted, and he feels it is too bad a trade for the gods. . . . Perhaps he may have felt that to go on pretending madness was a sort of penance to bring good luck, but one may suspect darker feelings to be at work. . . . After Edgar has imposed a false death on the father who has wronged him he describes himself as he was till then as a sort of grotesque devil. . . . If we regard it as the root idea of tragedy that the sacrifice of the hero re-unites his tribe with Nature or with supernatural forces, then it is in these passages that we find the idea fully at work." *Structure*, 141–42.

7. August Wilhelm von Schlegel: "nothing can be more affecting than to see the good son become the father's guide, and the good angel." *A Course of Lectures on Dramatic Art and Literature*, Vol. 2, trans. J. Black (London: Baldwin, Cradock, and Joy, 1815), 205.

❈ 17 ❈

INTERLUDE

Humanist and Posthumanist: A Dialogue

Humanist. Account for Tom? It is self-evident. His travails are Edgar's. They are directed by him and answerable to him. The source of trauma lies in the past. This isn't Bradley, you understand. The text tells us. The family romance, I think someone called it. Trauma returns to events. In sublimated forms, of course. Tom is Edgar working out his repressions. Working them out, you see, in various senses. As I said, pretty self-evident.

Posthumanist. Lazy Freudianism! Family photos, childhood memories. Bin it all! Your fruit has shriveled on the arboreal vine! Clapped-out capitalist sentimentalism!

Humanist. It has nothing to do with capitalism, I assure you. It has to do with being a human being.

Posthumanist. Being a human being. Can you hear yourself? You freeze the verb in a noun! You are deaf to the interpellations! "You will be organized, you will be an organism, you will articulate your body—otherwise you're just depraved."

Humanist. I didn't say that.

Posthumanist. "You will be signified and signifier, interpreter and interpreted—otherwise you're just a deviant."

Humanist. Have you finished?

Posthumanist. Sentimentalists! Embrace instead the Body without

Organs! Not the child before the adult, or the mother before the child—their strict contemporaneousness!

Humanist. There is no such thing.

Posthumanist. Contagion, molecular multiplicities, a worldwide intensity map! Tell me, where does a body begin and end? When does becoming cease, and your *being* take over? Planes of intensities!

Humanist. This is errant nonsense. A person is. A body has organs. That is why human beings can feel pain.

Posthumanist. Forget your hierarchical organisms!

Humanist. Like the brain, do you mean?

Posthumanist. If we were faithful to the brain, so much the better! A brain is a barely imaginable sensorium! But you are no more than filers, filing things away.

Humanist. It isn't about filing things away. One's knowledge does not go into boxes.

Posthumanist. Disorganize! Pulverize! Sensual radiation! Life as effigy!

Humanist. No Dionysus without Apollo, my friend. No passions without form. This is what allows recognitions. And feelings. And the obligations that ensue. How not to infer and interpret? A play will not exist unless we do. Should one not feel for another human?

Posthumanist. They are not human! None of them! Least of all Tom! A field of intensities, merging and colliding and fissioning. Convulsive passions! Necessarily a Place, necessarily a Plane, crossing thresholds, assembling elements, things, plants, animals, tools, people, powers, and fragments of all of these!

Humanist. Granted, one's experience streams with confluences between oneself and others.

Posthumanist. Machines, technologies, virtualities!

Humanist. But they are not oneself.

Posthumanist. Weather, rumor, infection, smells, borders, packs!

Humanist. Is that what you see when you see another? Or when you see yourself?

Posthumanist. Maintain your Cartesian delusions! Your nostalgias! Tom is not a person. He—it!—isn't even a character! Rather—an abstract of radical susceptibility! A disobedient robot! A cross-wired artificial intelligence! No ruling organism, just organs of intensity—"a" stomach, "an" eye, "a" mouth. The indefinite article is the conductor of desire!

Humanist. The indefinite article is the what? What on earth can you mean? The human subject is irrelevant? No choice, no responsibility, no ethics? It is delirium.

Posthumanist. What are you afraid of! Losing your precious rational surveillance? Enter a playworld, and already you have renounced it!

Humanist. I haven't. Quite the contrary.

Posthumanist. Of course you have! Every one of your organs, eye and brain included, can be taken in a moment! They can take off on their own! They can join to unknown others and create new assemblages! Why else enter this place?

Humanist. Why else? To feel the truths that daily life neglects. To respect true mastery.

Posthumanist. Whose mastery?

Humanist. The artist's.

Posthumanist. Precisely! Radical passivity! It's the modern erotic. Don't you think?

Humanist. No, I don't. And I am not passive at all. I am an active reader. I recognize and appreciate aesthetic skill. I am moved by what I see, because I direct my attention toward it. There is no abdication of will. No abject surrender to others. No renunciation of family and order and common sense.

Posthumanist. Not Edgar then? Certainly not Tom!

Humanist. Certainly not. Sympathy, understanding, is not empathy. There is your sentimental fallacy.

Posthumanist. You are miles away from the event, old academician with your perspective-stick, measuring, measuring! You with your decorum, your discrete bodies, your settled notions of what a tragedy should be! Immerse yourself!

Humanist. Control yourself! Where is pity in your world? Where is awe?

Posthumanist. Didn't they kill Aristotle, 450 years ago?

Humanist. Art has its laws. However much you luxuriate in your ecstatic sublime. One wants to feel sympathy, the pleasures of pity, of moral wisdom, of resolve to make things better. Why should we not? It's called humanism. Why else do we have plays? Why else universities?

Posthumanist. To explode all such complacencies! Your pity is superiority and comfort! It is the collected protection of the patron!

Humanist. And what are you? Some kind of fugitive backstairs looter? You flatter yourself. Your philosophy is sophisticated exquisiteness. Abject desire, conducted without will? It isn't true. It isn't human.

Posthumanist. Forget your so-called Human. The play's the thing! The *thing!* And in being the thing, apprehending what we are!

Humanist. What we *are?* We are things? Who is the essentialist now? I am not a thing.

Posthumanist. Bodies without Organs. Concatenating virtualities! Machinic texts! Cyborgs!

Humanist. Try a man, with memories, who can imagine other minds.

Posthumanist. Renounce yourself! Risk anonymity! The truth of desire is to swing from the cliff! Exceed yourself!

Humanist. Do you mean end myself? I don't wish to. I don't wish to be no one. Nor does Edgar. Or even Tom, I dare say. He is cold! Such experience cannot be relished.

Posthumanist. Yes! He is cold! Relish its difficulty! Shiver like an egg!

Humanist. I don't even know what that means.

Posthumanist. Concatenate!

Humanist. As I shiver? Listen. One reads. One watches events on a stage. One doesn't experience those events oneself. There is no cliff. There is a play.

Posthumanist. There is nothing but such play!

Humanist. There is oneself. And there is a play.

Posthumanist. You call that realism?

Humanist. That is not a word I like to use. I call it sane.

Posthumanist. What is sane about devoting a life to studying things that don't exist?

Humanist. Well, they do exist, in a manner of speaking. They just aren't—alive.

Posthumanist. What is sane about devoting a life to studying dead things?

Humanist. I didn't say they were dead.

Posthumanist. Not alive, and not dead. What then?

Humanist. What then?

Posthumanist. What then.

Humanist. Well—art.

Posthumanist. Dead art? Live art?

Humanist. True art.

Posthumanist. Not dead, not living, just true.

Humanist. Well, art, of course—it is self-evident—it comes true, it has that kind of life in it.

Posthumanist. Becoming-true?

Humanist. Becoming? It has been here since 1605.

Posthumanist. Tom is becoming-true!

Humanist. He has truth. Like much else in the play.

Posthumanist. Has? Like much else? Wake up! Tom is becoming!

Humanist. He *is* becoming? I say again, who is the essentialist now?

Posthumanist. Wrong, old man! I didn't say I knew *what* Tom signifies—only that he is becoming. He is coming!

Humanist. Is, is, is.

Posthumanist. No! The copula is erased by the becoming! Don't you see? Verbs, not nouns. Proliferate!

Humanist. Well, if you will not stand by your own words there is precious little point in discoursing.

Posthumanist. There is an ecology beyond words! Words are indentured to law, to violence! Silence!

Humanist. Excuse me?

Posthumanist. Listen to the silence!

Humanist. To the silence?

Posthumanist. The silence!

[Pause]

[Long pause]

[Longer pause]

Humanist/Posthumanist. There's no such thing!

18

SCENE 8

To the Edge of the Cliff

I

The Old Man has left the scene, having been told by the blind man to go off and find the naked beggar-man some clothes and to deliver them a mile or two down the road. The blind man leaves the scene hand in hand with the naked man. The tableau is irresistibly allegorical. The stripped-down physicality makes the two figures nameless and unknown, in true existential solitude, as we must be when, alone in our brains, we are born or we die. Hence Gloucester's strange address to Tom: "this naked Soule, *Which* Ile intreate to leade me" (TLN 2232). The beggar is *naked*, a *soul*, and a *which*: not quite a human, but all the more intimate for the fact. The naked man is a skeleton, a *memento mori*, a newborn boy, and a bared soul on its way to judgment; a stranger, a kindred spirit, a son, and a memory; a prophecy, a ghost, a better-and-worse sufferer—and in all these things a walking surrogate of the blind man.

When next we see them, Edgar is clothed, but this supernal, posthumous, purgatorial vision remains active, as a kind of x-ray reality behind the simulacra: or rather the simulacra upon simulacra of the Dover cliff scene. We are in Dover, we are in some unnameable terrain, we are in the beyond, or the before, when souls enter and leave one world for another—or appear to, or think they have when they haven't, or think they haven't when they have.

❦

The tableau is moving into the passage between living and death. This is why Gloucester asks Tom to take him to the "very brim" of the cliff, from where he "shall no leading need." He is going to jump to his death. But notice what Tom says. He doesn't say, "Ay, master," as he does a moment earlier when asked if he knows Dover. He says "Give me thy arm, / Poor Tom shall lead thee." One "lead" directly takes up the other. Gloucester "shall no leading need," but "Poor Tom shall lead thee." There is terror in these competing, mutually annihilating modalities: Tom shall lead Gloucester, directly off the brim and into the "confined deep." Tom shall go off the cliff, a micro-moment before Gloucester tries to do the same.

❦

It is the imperative to "lead" Gloucester to suicide that forces Edgar to keep Tom alive. We might say that Tom is saved from extinction for the purpose of killing Gloucester. Equally, he is saved to save Gloucester, precisely by sacrificing himself, by doing the deed for him. The surrogacies are dark and twisting. Truly Edgar has no father, and Gloucester has no son, unless Tom can take them to the cliff.

❦

> There is a Cliffe, whose high and bending head
> Looks fearfully in the confined Deepe:
> Bring me but to the very brimme of it.
> And Ile repayre the misery thou do'st beare
> With something rich about me: from that place
> I shall no leading need. (TLN 2258-63)

The confined place is a borderland, a frontier, and a magnet. Beyond sight, beyond the verification of knowledge, this is the place to which they are unerringly headed, the very threshold of possibility: at once a public horizon, a metaphysical puzzle, and a deep inward journey.[1]

---

1. Maynard Mack: "As everyone knows, this figure [Lear] and his persecutors and allies move in a dense atmosphere of implication. . . . Is the hill that Gloucester is told he climbs

❧

In this context the trip to Dover, and indeed the leap from the cliff, expresses somewhat more than either irreligious despair or an ultimacy-evading trick. It is equally a blessing and a return: as Gloucester himself says, a "repayre" (TLN 2261). And it is also the most enormous spiritual risk. For we cannot take Christian proscriptions against suicide as the only frame in which to judge what Gloucester intends. He will head off the cliff into the thoughts that hang in the pending air. There is the largest sorrow in these spaces—memories of failed connections, unendurable regrets. But there is also an ecstatic abandonment to feeling, and to connections that Gloucester has only now begun to intuit: between himself, the superfluous and lust-dieted man, and the humbled and wretched; between man and boy; between the human and the nonhuman. He will leap not into forgetfulness, but into memory and recognition, and into the strangest connection with the anonymous atoms of existence.

❧

Because he do's not feele, feele your power quickly. (TLN 2254)

He has not felt enough. He will leap so as to feel it, quickly. It will give life, it will quicken.

❧

So distribution should undo excesse. (TLN 2255)

Distribution is not merely handing out rations. It is a winnowing away of excess. Gloucester is characterizing his leap. It is a distribution

---

a foretaste and brief map of Purgatory, as R. W. Chambers once suggested? . . . The play has qualities that seem to countenance our asking such questions, though nothing is clearer than the specificities by which at the same time it insists that Gloucester's cliff is neither in our own mythic imagination nor in his, but at Dover. . . . Here then are divided and distinguished worlds, bonded to each other in such an intimate way that it is idle to argue which takes precedence of the other. . . . The doctrinal relationship of one thing to another embraces almost every aspect of the play. It solidifies ideas into incidents. . . . Conversely, it bathes the literal event in figuration, so that Gloucester's imagined climb at Dover, to say nothing of his leap, teases the imagination." *King Lear in Our Time* (London: Methuen and Company, 1966), 48, 72.

of excess; an undoing of excess. The act is a protest in the name of life: "One flees life toward life."[2]

⁂

This is the direction Tom shall lead him: toward death; toward life.

II

A madman is leading a blind man. He has been paid to take the blind man safely to a cliff, from which the blind man can jump. The madman wants the blind man to believe that he shall soon be able to kill himself. He is anxious that the blind man should think him faithful. The madman supplies the blind man with his thoughts. He speaks of things, and as he speaks them the blind man sees them. He gives the blind man a scene, and as he gives it the blind man can enter into it absolutely.[3]

⁂

A son is lying to his father. He is lying about what he sees and where they are and who he is. He can do what every son longs to do, and get away with it too.[4] He can murder his father, and then enjoy the thanks

---

2. Emmanuel Levinas: *"One flees life toward life.* Suicide appears as a possibility to a being already in relation with the Other, already elevated to life *for the Other*. It is the possibility of an existence already metaphysical; only a being already capable of sacrifice is capable of suicide. Before defining man as the animal that can commit suicide it is necessary to define him as capable of living for the Other and of *being* on the basis of the Other who is exterior to him. But the tragic character of suicide and of sacrifice evinces the radicality of the love of life." *Totality and Infinity: An Essay on Exteriority*, trans. Alphonso Lingis (Pittsburgh, Penn.: Duquesne University Press, 1999), 149; italics in original.

3. Of "that grotesque guiding of Gloucester up no hill to no cliff to no suicide," Stanley Cavell writes: "It is grotesque because it is so *literal* a consequence of avoiding the facts. . . . That grotesque walk is not full of promise for our lives. It is not, for example, a picture of mankind making its way up Purgatory; for Gloucester's character is not purified by it, but extirpated. . . . To fill this scene with nourishing, profound meaning is to see it from Edgar's point of view; that is, to avoid what is there. Edgar is Ahab, trying to harpoon the meaning of his life into something external to it; and we believe him, and serve him. He is Hedda Gabler, with her ugly demand for beauty. In the fanciful, childish deceit of his plan, he is Tom Sawyer . . . enveloping Jim's prison with symbols of escape, instead of opening the door." *Disowning Knowledge in Seven Plays of Shakespeare*, updated ed. (Cambridge, U.K.: Cambridge University Press, 2003), 56; italics in original.

4. Harry Berger Jr. identifies a "symbolic parricide" in the cliff scene: *Making Trifles of Terrors: Redistributing Complicities in Shakespeare* (Stanford, Calif.: Stanford University Press,

of having saved him, of bringing him back into life, humbled and grateful and obedient. The father will be made the child.

※

The son has a duty of extraordinary delicacy. He must bring his father to his act of dying, and then take him away again.

※

An exiled noble has been told to be someone else: a poor, mad beggar. He doesn't want to, but he must carry on. He is sick of pretending to be mad, and he starts speaking in verse. The blind man notices, but the disguised man insists that nothing has changed. His clothes have altered, but he remains the madman. Disguise, it seems, doesn't even pretend to disguise. The gap between player and part has vanished. Here at the noncliff, there is nothing but disguise which is no disguise.[5]

※

Call him what you like—Friend, Fiend, Fellow, Nobody—he is always the beggar and always the son.

※

He tells the blind man that they have reached the edge of the cliff:

> Come on Sir,
> Heere's the place: stand still: how fearefull
> And dizie 'tis, to cast ones eyes so low,
> The Crows and Choughes, that wing the midway ayre

1997), 63. Likewise Meredith Skura sees an unconscious rehearsal of parricide: "Dragon Fathers and Unnatural Children: Warring Generations in *King Lear* and Its Sources." *Comparative Drama* 42, no. 2 (2008): 130–31.

5. Jan Kott: "This entire scene is written for a very definite type of theatre, namely pantomime. This pantomime only makes sense if enacted on a flat and level stage. . . . No other Shakespearian landscape is so exact, precise, and clear, as this one. It is like a Breughel painting: thick with people, objects and events. . . . Mime is the performance of symbols. . . . The Shakespearian precipice at Dover exists and does not exist. It is the abyss, waiting all the time. The abyss, into which one can jump, is everywhere." *Shakespeare Our Contemporary*, trans. Boleslaw Taborski (London: Methuen, 1964), 114–17.

> Shew so scarce so grosse as Beetles. Half way downe
> Hangs one that gathers Sampire: dreadfull Trade:
> Me thinks he seems no bigger then his head.
> The Fishermen, that walk'd upon the beach
> Appeare like Mice: and yond tall Anchoring barke
> Diminish'd to her Cocke: her Cocke, a Buoy
> Almost too small for sight. The murmuring Surge,
> That on th'unnumbred idle Pebble chafes
> Cannot be heard so high. Ile looke no more,
> Least my braine turne, and the deficient sight
> Topple down headlong. (TLN 2445–59)

❦

The scene's eye is split, crossing what is seen, its grid less a lattice window and more like drunken fractals, moving in and out of self-identity.[6] Every detail gathers crystal dimensions, turning in the air like a glistening aboriginal form. Every last particle has its own conatus.

❦

The end of each line is a precipice; the words stop, the eyes look over, the head swoons. It is fearful to stand still at this brim. The fearful thing isn't the height, but the drop; not the destination, but the interim. The line-ending phrases take us to the verge of the fear. Each one enacts a dizzying vertigo, each both a temptation to leap and an admonition to retreat.

> How fearefull
> Eyes so low

---

6. The speech poses different theories of perspective and pictorialism against one another, with particular attention to what Jonathan Goldberg summarizes as "anamorphic" or "illusionistic" perspective. Anamorphic perspective refers to pictures (they can be framed paintings, chapel frescos, even cave drawings) whose composition anticipates more than one viewing position, with objects appearing, disappearing, or changing shape according to the angle of vision or if the composition is viewed in a mirror. Clearly the whole cliff scene can be understood partly as such a consciously composed shape-shifting trick. But the anamorphosis goes much further, and indeed can be seen as a basic analogue of Shakespeare's art. The multi-angled, multiply imperfect perspective—in which each viewer's sight is at once admitted and in need of supplementation—informs at every move Shakespeare's compositions. Goldberg, *Shakespeare's Hand* (Minneapolis: University of Minnesota Press, 2003).

> The midway ayre
> Halfe way downe
> Dreadfull Trade
> Then his head
> Upon the beach
> Anchoring Barke
> Murmuring Surge
> Pebble chafes
> Looke no more
> Deficient sight
> Downe headlong (TLN 2445–59)

※

The eyes are "cast," as though on a fishing line. We enter one object and then another, each a cast into lives beyond the speaker's—bird, plant, insect, animal, rock, water, vessel. The world is large and alive with small things. The movement is away from delusions that only *my* pain or struggle or dread matters. And yet this same movement connotes the fact of loneliness, as each figure is in monadic isolation from the other. Solipsism opens to a world; a world returns to a self.

※

There is nothing there at all, and each of these things is the simplest self-projection. The recapitulations are compulsive: a mind that turns and returns upon itself, as though to its own scenes of trauma.[7] The speaker proceeds from creature to creature, one inside or birthing the next, like the nested toys of misery or madness. He moves from a larger blackness (crow, chough) to a smaller (beetle): the visible wings disappear, and the common blackness concentrates his shard-born element. He casts his eyes low into his own ignominy: the carrion hunting corvine, the larcenous jackdaw, the beetle feeding upon shit. Service gives way to abjection. The tall bark is reduced to a cock; the cock to a boy,

---

7. William C. Carroll notes in this scene a "process of self-return," but precisely to which self is hard to be certain. "'The Base Shall Top th'Legitimate': The Bedlam Beggar and the Role of Edgar in *King Lear*," *Shakespeare Quarterly* 38, no. 4 (1987), 437.

who in turn is "almost too small for sight." The theme, once more, is pitiably derogated masculinity. To enter these specters speaks a mind wracked in exile, searching for a home, unable to separate sympathy from self-pity, because whatever he feels for is also *him*.

❦

Each "cast" is a lifeline, or a possible life. Each object is a metempsychotic possibility, a potential house of soul.[8] Hence the enormous wistfulness of the fantasy. There are homes everywhere, in every cleft and cranny—only not for him, not any more, or not yet.

❦

The imaginary fall is not one continuous action.[9] It is slow motion and interruptive. It repeatedly clocks things on the way down, with each of which we can linger. The event is of conscious duration, but not unimpeded flow. We don't just see a bird no bigger than a beetle. We see a bird, distinct and named, and then we see a beetle. We see one turn into the other; we see the process of shrinking; we see the possibility of magnification. The beetle can become a bird, which it will if we fall right past its "midway" flight. The sight lines are not all one way. Each image is seen from the angle of the others, animate with recursive, cuboid movement, just as the experience is timed throughout by the "murmuring surge" of the tides that depart to return.[10]

---

8. Compare Giorgio Agamben on the zoologist Jakob von Uexküll's interest in amoebas, ticks, and sea urchins, and his "excursions in unknowable worlds": "the tick is immediately united to these three elements [odor, temperature, skin typology] in an intense and passionate relationship the likes of which we might never find in the relations that bind man to his apparently richer world. The tick *is* this relationship; she lives only in it and for it." *The Open: Man and Animal*, trans. Kevin Attell (Stanford, Calif.: Stanford University Press, 2004), 46–47; italics in original.

9. Samuel Johnson: "No, sir; it should be all precipice—all vacuum. The crows impede your fall. The diminished appearance of the boats, and other circumstances, are all very good description, but do not impress the mind at once with the horrible idea of immense height. The impression is divided; you pass on, by computation, from one stage of the tremendous space to another." James Boswell, *Life of Johnson*.

10. Herbert Blau: "The problem is the referent, we are never quite sure what it is, though it is right there in the text, like 'The murmuring surge / That on th'unnumb'red idle pebble chafes.' . . . I've often thought that the problem of textuality is summed up in those lines, with

❧

We zoom in; we zoom out. We see the fishermen, who turn to mice, who yet are fishermen. We see a man; we guess at his dread; we infer a home for which he risks his life. The man is no more than a head, a blot in the distance—but the head contains everything. And so we enter the head, which expands back out into the scene. The samphire gatherer sees the birds and the beach. He hears the water on the pebbles. The herb he picks is large before his eyes, green in his pan or satchel, but all the time he feels the length of cliff below him, the danger of a slip, the imminence of anything. Life is radically hazardous. This moment, like the play it distills, is imminent to crisis. It only takes a moment's decision, or a moment's slip, and it is over.

❧

The distant lives evoke a busy creation, everything in its place, small epicenters of sufficiency. The vision is of therapeutic community. Do not jump.

❧

The distant lives evoke the stunning vanity of creaturely endeavor; a leveling, multiplying anonymity.[11] The vision is a temptation in the wilderness. Jump.

❧

The distant lives are oblivious to yours. You may as well not exist. And so jump.

---

the uninterpretable immensity of that murmur in the surge nevertheless as particular as the unnumbered pebble being chafed." *The Dubious Spectacle: Extremities of Theater, 1976-2000* (Minneapolis: University of Minnesota Press, 2001), 300.

11. Stephen Booth: "Over and over again . . . throughout *King Lear*, an audience thinks in multiple dimensions—entertains two or more precise understandings at once, understandings that might, but do not, clash in the mind. . . . Each variety and each instance is one in which a mental boundary vanishes, fails, or is destroyed." *King Lear, Macbeth, Indefinition, and Tragedy* (New Haven, Conn.: Yale University Press, 1983), 33.

You are no longer oblivious to theirs: that is the living thing. Do not jump.[12]

❦

Each line is a temptation, at the very edge of sense, imagination, understanding:

> Almost too small for sight. The murmuring Surge
> That on th'unnumbred idle Pebble chafes
> Cannot be heard so high. Ile look no more (TLN 2455-57)

The surge is beyond empirical reckoning, present precisely as a disappearing. The "almost" waits for further movement, and the movement will erase it. But it is too simple, too ontologically coarse, to understand the movement as being from life into death, or from something into nothing. This is not how absence works. It isn't how *nothing* works. Absence teems with life. It moves *as* life.

❦

The progress is one of graded, graduated disembodiment, moving farther and farther away from physical form, moving closer to astonishment that anything exists at all. And the more the speech moves away from what can be sensed, the more intimate it becomes. It starts somewhere actual if unnamed (a "place"); moves to things that are not present but that it pretends to see; proceeds to things these inferred sights resemble; and finally arrives at things that even in the fantasy can be

---

12. Goldberg suggests that the cliff scene "implicates the audience in its annihilative vision" because Edgar's imagined Dover "is a working out of illusion that rests on nothing: silence, invisibility, blindness," offering "an anatomy of the techniques ... upon which Shakespearean theater depends." We are with Gloucester, passing through the vanishing point, toppling down into a double blindness, agreeing to see what cannot be seen: "the lines comment, in their visual form, on the limits of possibility in the real and on the impossibility of the realization of language and desire. The real rests on an insubstantial basis." *Shakespeare's Hand*, 142–43; 138.

neither heard (the surge of the waves) nor seen (the "idle Pebble"). But it is exactly the unheard and unseen, the elements beyond measurement ("unnumbred"), that most delicately touch upon possibility. He could not hear the murmur, even if he really were where he claims to be. And yet the fact of not-hearing draws the speaker still closer.

❦

A murmur can only ever just be heard. A surge is neither voice nor sound, is nothing acoustical per se. It is impelled movement, the soul-endeavor in natural things. The surge does not devolve into a single source. No noun takes possession of the unheard noise. The noise is movement. Things are movement. The world, all its atoms and participants, is dynamic with movement.[13]

❦

We enter the endlessly divisible constituents in any space, seen or unseen, heard or unheard. This multitude finds its echo and correlate—perhaps its *cause*—in the teeming illimitability of a mind. The pebbles cannot be counted. There is always another one. And yet he talks of the "idle Pebble," one pebble, nestled amid countless others. One pebble, rounded like a brain, uniquely shaped and marked, glistening from the salt and the brine; one pebble, at once prehistoric and just born, every instant fizzing with brand new tiny bubbles. A single pebble, to the eye idle and static, but generating through friction these sounds, the chafe that intermits and modifies the "Surge."

---

13. Christopher Pye says of the cliff speech's use of metonymy: "The conversion of whole to part sustains a purely self-referential and self-sustaining signifying chain on the condition of that chain's indefinite extension." Perspective, then, is generated rhetorically—a system of "proportional ratios oriented around limitless extension." In turn, this closed, self-referential economy "subjects the subject to the unchecked sliding of the metonymic chain"; it "subjects that masterful being to its own annulment," which "passage to the limit can be understood as the condition for that subject's supersensory mastery." *The Vanishing: Shakespeare, the Subject, and Early Modern Culture* (Durham: Duke University Press, 2000), 91-92. Pye understands the scene in terms of symbiotic absolutes. There is the self and the void, and in constructing this self along a metonymic chain, the subject both submits to the void and establishes an imaginative surviving of it. This is powerfully stated, but also, I suspect, too determined by a superstructuring conceit. In Shakespeare, the small things garner stubborn life.

❦

Stand at the imaginary cliff top, and go deep inside the tiniest nodes of belonging.[14]

❦

The speaker—beggar, son, player, played—is the unnumbered pebble. To be the pebble is to be anonymous, undistinguished, almost nothing. Almost nothing, but not. It is unseen, just as Edgar is right now by his maker; and just as Tom is right now by his. At the same time the pebble is the sole centered thing in the universe. All movement, of ocean and air, all the vectors in space, all the potential lines of perspective or address, all meet their point in this single thing, as though magnetized by it, the hidden prince of creation, the lodestone waiting patiently for recognition. Each thing is such a prince! And yet it is also not anthropomorphic at all. The speech gives life to the pebble. The pebble is. This one, and the next, and the next.[15]

❦

> Ile looke no more,
> Least my brain turne, and the deficient sight
> Topple down headlong.[16] (TLN 2457-59)

---

14. Leibniz could be glossing Edgar's speech, or indeed Shakespeare: "At every moment there is in us an infinity of perceptions, unaccompanied by awareness or reflection; that is, of alterations in the soul itself, of which we are unaware because these impressions are either too minute and too numerous, or else too unvarying, so that they are not sufficiently distinctive on their own.... I like to use the example of the roaring noise of the sea which impresses itself on us when we are standing on the shore. To hear this noise as we do, we must hear the parts which make up this whole, that is the noise of each wave, although each of these little noises makes itself known only when combined confusedly with all itself." *New Essays on Human Understanding*, trans. and ed. Peter Remnant and Jonathan Bennett (Cambridge, U.K.: Cambridge University Press, 1996), 54.

15. Valère Novarina: "Man has a pebble in the middle of thought, around which thought turns. It is the mind that it is the house of the body, and not the contrary, as we have been taught. Thought is not housed in a brain set in the skull; it is our skull that is in us like a stone, always at the center of thought." *The Theater of the Ears*, trans. and ed. Allen S. Weiss (Los Angeles: Sun and Moon Press, 1996), 66. Or again: "The actor speaks to pebbles and reminds matter that it exists at the very interior of words." *Theater of the Ears*, 146.

16. Nahum Tate, in his 1681 adaptation, *The History of King Lear*, makes a telling adjustment to this line, having mainly retained Shakespeare's words: "Lest my brain turn, and the

It is more than a fainting plummet. It is a directed flight, even an aim, as the eyes lead the head into their target. He wants to get closer to the evidence. He wants to count those pebbles that so defy measurement. He wants to be immersed in the elements and to "cast" himself into untrammeled possibility.

❧

The pebble is already there, exactly where the eyes are heading. Throughout this speech the speaker is toppling down headlong, doing exactly what at the speech's end he says he dare not do. This is more than a rehearsal of a death leap. This is the thing itself.

❧

The temptation is death: perhaps as distribution of excess; perhaps as a commitment to feeling; perhaps as knowledge of the last frontier; perhaps as defeat; perhaps as a body that cannot contain all that bursts within; perhaps as a return to the predicative condition of being; or perhaps, finally, as a release from, or release for, Tom.[17]

❧

And the blind man? He jumps.

---

disorder make me / Tumble down headlong" (4.4.22–23). As ever in such things, the revision points to the alarming strangeness, the physical derangement, and the metaphysical audacity of Shakespeare's original.

17. William C. Carroll: "The fall from top to bottom, 'so many fathom down' (4.4.50), is also a refraction of Edgar's fall, who as Poor Tom was 'fathom and half' down. For Edgar, the fall as Poor Tom is over, his life also a miracle. . . . This is what it felt like to be Poor Tom: to live in the body of a nightmare." "The Base Shall Top," 438. This is very sensitive and eloquent: but I think the past tense is mistaken.

Ƿ 19 Ƿ

INTERLUDE

The Binding

A story stirs in the background of the son and father's passage toward Dover, one famous in all three Semitic religions and a staple of medieval theatre: the Binding (Genesis 22) in which God commands Abraham to slaughter his son Isaac atop Mount Moriah. Abraham obeys the injunction, travels to the top of the mountain, and binds his son to the altar. He is about to deliver the fatal cut when an angel of God intervenes. Abraham is released from the task and a ram is sacrificed instead.

The basic story is consistent throughout its numerous retellings; the main difference is the amount of knowledge or acquiescence granted Isaac. The issues at stake are in many ways the same as in the Book of Job: the goodness or cruelty, alertness or absence, of God; the suffering of obedience, and its moral dubiety; the astonishment of mind and heart that faith demands; the scandal of an essentially unilateral contract, persisting amid functional blindness, in which you walk to the edge of a precipice with nothing to hold you back or keep you going other than whatever moves in your so-lonely mind—barring the intervention, providential or capricious, of some utterly unexpected agent of release.

Kierkegaard gives the ancient tale its most memorable gloss: the ethical response (to refuse God's demand to murder innocence, to stay faithful to the most primal duty of care) is the temptation, a fatal error that Abraham resists through his silent faith in the absurd. By the absurd, Kierkegaard means faith in the absolute: and what is more, faith that his particular individual case is exempt from ethical account—that it can suspend universal law and defy the state and society. As Kierkegaard puts it, with beautiful simplicity: "What if he had made a mistake, this lonely man who climbs Mount Moriah?"[1] The ethical is teleologically suspended, and Abraham enters a space of hallowed abeyance, where anything is possible, anything is permitted. This scene really does resemble the shocking liberties of *Lear*'s cliff-not-cliff.

And yet Kierkegaard wonders why Shakespeare never engaged with this particular terror: "Thanks to you, great Shakespeare, you who can say everything, everything, everything just as it is—and yet, why did you never articulate this torment?"[2] As he clarifies in his notebooks:

> He [Abraham] destroys his happiness in the world in order to have his happiness with God—and now if he has misunderstood God—where shall he turn?
> A eulogy on Shakespeare, regretting that he has never depicted this final torment.[3]

Now consider Edgar, the formal hero, who (like Abraham) will never elicit a tear. Does he not begin as a terrified escapee from becoming-Isaac and end up as a failed or abandoned Abraham? He does not take his father to the cliff-edge; he appeals falsely to divine intervention to explain the fact of release. He disobeys his father's injunction because he believes in no redeeming interruption. Recall Kierkegaard's closing words (or those of his pseudonymic Johannes de Silentio): "the single individual as the single individual stands in an absolute relation to the absolute," or he "is lost."[4] Perhaps Edgar becomes the paradigm case of

---

1. Søren Kierkegaard, *Fear and Trembling/Repetition: Kierkegaard's Writings*, Vol. 6, trans. and ed. Howard V. Hong and Edna H. Hong (Princeton, N.J.: Princeton University Press, 1983), 61.
2. Ibid.
3. Ibid., 248.
4. Ibid., 120.

Shakespeare's refusal of this ultimate torment: of a goodness that cannot trust to the absolute.[5]

Perhaps. But perhaps to conclude this is to forget the permeable ontologies of this playworld, the way the action twists upon torturous surrogacies. The gap between father and son and beggar disappears in a single shared vision-not-vision. All three are at the cliff-not-cliff; all three experience the only fall there possible, a fall of desire, a fall as a pledge to death, a fall that is only saved from being terminal by the framing conceit of art. We can call this art evasive, a comic miracle; we can call it rehearsive, practicing deaths to come; or we can call it dizzying brinkmanship, taking life to the verge, living the fall, knowing a knowledge that shall survive survival.

5. Stanley Stewart: "Shakespeare's tragic vision includes 'everything, everything, everything' that is in the 'immanent' aesthetic and ethical domains. But Shakespeare's 'everything,' while assimilable by society, includes 'everything' except the 'transcendent.'" "*Lear* in Kierkegaard," in *King Lear: New Critical Essays*, ed. Jeffrey Kahan (New York: Routledge, 2008), 295. Stewart makes no mention of Edgar or Tom in his essay.

20

SCENE 9

Fallen, or Not?

It could hardly be a bigger moment: for Gloucester, as he moves to jump to his death, and for Edgar, as he watches his father try to end his life, knowing that he has taken the most absolute responsibility for another's living. And so what actually happens? In some ways it may seem straightforward enough. First Gloucester gets Tom to take him (as he thinks) to the edge of the cliff; then he dismisses Tom; then he curses the world and the gods; then he speaks a tender apostrophe to his son; then he bids farewell to his guide; then he jumps:

> *Glou.* Set me where you stand.[1]
> *Edg.* Give me your hand:
> You are now within a foote of th'extreme Verge:
> For all beneath the Moone would I not leape upright.
> *Glou.* Let go my hand:
> Heere friend's another purse: in it, a Iewell
> Well worth a poore mans taking. Fayries, and Gods

---

1. Herbert Blau: "*But where exactly is that?* . . . What impressed me when we did it was the manic exactitude, which filtered down to the staging before the 'suicide' in *Lear*, not here, not there, but 'Set me where you stand,' the blinded father exactly in the footsteps of the dispossessed son." *The Dubious Spectacle: Extremities of Theater, 1976–2000* (Minneapolis: University of Minnesota Press, 2001), 300; italics in original.

> Prosper it with thee. Go thou further off,
> Bid me farewell, and let me heare thee going.
> *Edg.* Now fare ye well, good Sir.
> *Glou.* With all my heart.
> *Edg.* Why I do trifle thus with his dispaire
> Is done to cure it.
> *Glou.* O you mighty Gods!
> This world I do renounce, and in your sights
> Shake patiently my great affliction off:
> If I coulde beare it longer, and not fall
> To quarrel with your great opposelesse willes,
> My snuffe, and loathed part of Nature should
> Burne it selfe out. If *Edgar* live, O blesse him:
> Now fellow, fare thee well [Quarto: *He fals*].
> *Edg.* Gone Sir, farewell. (TLN 2460-81)

But is it so transparent? Remember: the scene's basic principle is one of semispectral, permeable identities, as persons and places ghost into one another. The claims of substantial and imaginary bodies, of truth and pretense, merge and morph unpredictably, exchange places in the blink of an eye. The effect is that every breath, every fidget, is at once rehearsal *and* the thing itself, terminal *and* redeemable. True to these principles, a prime purpose of the scripting here is clearly to bring the "Fellow" closely back into the blind man's ambit. He had been told to go "further off" (TLN 2467), with this command reinforced by two further instructions: to bid farewell, and to let the old man hear him going (TLN 2468). Gloucester seemed to want to speak his suicide speech alone; he seemed to want to die alone. But does he? And even if he did want to, could he? Gloucester falls somewhere, sometime, in the cue-space, one that is framed by two curiously rhyming phrases: the Gloucester-part's "fare thee well" and the Edgar-part's "Gone sir, farewell." The effect is a kind of aural speculum, a mirror in the air, as though the participants are somehow coordinate, their fates uncannily echoing. This is the space we must enter: a space into which Tom is invited (by Gloucester's cue) and which Tom in turn defines (by speaking the first line of Edgar's response). To recover the cue-space, then, may be to discover not only Gloucester's fall, but also its intimate attender, Tom.

Block 1

Gloucester is blind. The Gloucester-actor is blindfolded—his eyes covered by the cloth supplied by Cornwall's servants. The player cannot see. He must nervously assess and rehearse his every movement. He may be unsure where his fellow actor is, or unusually reliant upon him. In turn, the Edgar-actor is given a strange liberty: partly, because he cannot be seen, the improvisatory power to do anything imaginable; partly, because his fellow man cannot see, the superadded responsibility for another's safe passage. More than ever, things must be acted feelingly. The actors are the action's pioneers. Their choices, moment by moment, measure the event's probationary reach.[2]

Block 2

"Now fare ye well, good Sir", says the beggar (TLN 2469), appearing to accede to Gloucester's request that he go "further off," with the Edgar-actor moving away from Gloucester, closer to the verge of the stage, from where he can confide his rationalization, "Why I do trifle thus with his dispaire / Is done to cure it" (TLN 2471–72). But remember: Edgar is invisible. Perhaps he only pretends to accede; perhaps he says farewell and remains where he is; perhaps he starts to move away and as quickly

---

2. Steven Connor: "The world of sound is only ever there at the moment of our hearing it. The world of pure hearing would therefore be, so to speak, *unremittingly intermittent*.... To be reliant upon sound rather than sight is to be exposed to the sense of 'something going on, something active, a kind of evanescent effluvium which exists only as long as something or someone is actually producing it.'" Connor proceeds to quote the memoir of John Hull: "When you are blind, a hand suddenly grabs you. A voice suddenly addresses you. There is no anticipation or preparation. There is no hiding round the corner. There is no lying low. I *am* grasped. I *am* greeted. I am passive in the presence of that which accosts me.... For the blind person, people are in motion, they are temporal, they come and they go. They come out of nothing, they disappear." *Dumbstruck: A Cultural History of Ventriloquism* (Oxford: Oxford University Press, 2000), 17; italics in original.

returns. He can do what he likes, assay anything, traverse utterly forbidden spaces: because he is as invisible as a spirit, as a ghost.

Block 3

Edgar hears himself addressed—"If Edgar live"—and says nothing. It can seem like a shameful evasion. But perhaps there is nothing reprehensible about it at all. Imagine the difficulty, if the son were to reveal himself now, just as the father is about to leap, as though pulling a happy rabbit from his hat, like some gloating practical joker relishing the eleventh hour. It would be far more grotesque and sadistic than what the scene gives us: a man trapped in a fiction barely half of his own making, in a chain of fraudulence that is impossible to break without hateful indecorum.

Block 4

We hear the good son invoked and then blessed. We see the good son hearing himself receive his father's blessing. And then what do we see? Do we *see* him not answering to the benediction? Do we *see* him ignoring his father's implicit call for forgiveness, as though unable, even now, to remit his barely conscious need to punish? Or do we rather *hear* him not answering to the call, in words that can only evade it ("Gone Sir, farewell"), while we *see* him—face crumpled, eyes wet, knees buckling—precisely answering it, in the actions and gestures that protest the injustice of the scripting? For what can the good son do as he watches his father try to leave his life behind, having chosen one final thought, one final love, to acknowledge as a cue for suicide? Can we imagine the suffering of this? Emotion is ratcheted up, but will not be adequately expelled. Edgar can do nothing but *feel* in the black prevention of the cue-space.

Block 5

The base reality of this scene is theater. Edgar's cliff speech is pure scriptwriting, the scenario that of a playmaker; Gloucester's fall ends with the stage boards. But this very hypertheatricality makes it evident, perhaps paradoxically, that the actor here is not sufficient. Bodies in this world are layered and shared and hived. The actor cannot fall from a cliff; the character can, but he cannot do so on stage. Or he cannot, unless the fall happens to a body whose space is not identical to his actor's: that is, we might say, to Tom. After all, Gloucester gave him the instruction: "Bid me farewell, and let me hear thee going." "Gone Sir, farewell," says Tom a few moments later—and he goes, exactly as instructed. The spirit takes over where mimesis fails.

Block 6

Gloucester addresses Tom: "fare thee well." The words cue the Edgar-actor but are a prompt to multiple agents. They are a signal for the Gloucester-character, who will now leap into what he thinks is fathoms-down death. Before this, however, they are an action cue for the Gloucester-actor, who must in a moment fall onto the dusty boards of the stage. But even here it is not simple. The capitalized word *Now* (like the capitalized *So*), when it starts both a line and a locution, almost always signifies resumption after a particular action has finished; it alerts the actor to action that should happen immediately before he says "Now." In other words, it is a retrospective action cue, creating space and time for stage business.[3] But if this is the case, what action precedes the word *Now*? The action might be the Gloucester-actor's; it might be his fellow actor's. The mere fact of noticing a resumption cue—which Shakespeare's actors surely would—creates pressure and expectation. What should he do? What can he do, if he is preparing to jump, but has not yet jumped, because he still has a line to say?

Block 7

The resumption cue, generating expectations of just-finished action, makes every motion of the actor one of portent and overdetermined

---

3. The term *resumption cue* was coined by my graduate student Alessandro Simari. I am indebted to him for noticing the recurrent use in this way of *now, so,* and occasionally *thus*—further examples of a shared actorly code that crosses plays, playwrights, and companies.

thought. Perhaps Gloucester gets on his knees and prays, for himself or for his son. Perhaps he tries to leap, makes stuttering moves toward it, but cannot quite make it. Perhaps he stands stock still, frozen to the moment. And whatever the decision, the Edgar-actor must respond. Should he crouch, hide, console, sneak away? Has he heard himself addressed, and likewise frozen? Has he collapsed? Words are unavailing; words have lapsed: and so what is he to *do*?

Block 8

Edgar/Tom has crept back close to Gloucester, who hears his approach, or feels his breath upon him, or senses another body rustling next to his. And so the blind man speaks, part as confirmation of intent, part as comfort or even consolation—as the departing can sometimes do to the surviving, finding untenable strength because the moment of departure has come. The living (foolishly, fondly) would prevent the dying. But Gloucester knows there is a better way. His words are a concession to life's holy trembling in the face of extinction; they forgive the survivor's fear and turpitude. Even so, the beggar-man's presence is a clinging too far: "fare thee well," says the man resolved to death. Leave me to my dying.

Block 9

Gloucester is never more fatherly than now. Indeed it is only now, we might say, that he becomes a father. A father should go before his son. He should do so with courage, leaving the son free from guilt or resentment or shame, lighter for the old man's passing. It is the least a father can do: and the most.

Block 10

The strange emotional misprision of the moment—the fact that Gloucester cannot see the boy who tugs his sleeve, that he doesn't even know him, that this frightened thing hovers in his ambit for reasons that the old man can only misconstrue—generates a tremendous objectivity, as of allegory bared to the bone. For in one sense, this "fellow" is nobody's son, and certainly not the blind man's. He barely knows him from Adam. The blind man has simply paid the beggar to take him to the edge of life. The fellow, then, is a kind of existential prostitute, all the more appropriate for not being known, for having neither past nor future. He can fit the bill, furnish the fantasy, and then disappear without further claim.

Block 11

But then this unreachability, the affinity in strangeness, the attachment in irreducible severance, may exactly speak to the supercharged passion of love: how love always wants; how it subsists in substantial ignorance of the beloved. Edgar is never more the son than in not being truly seen, in not being able to express anything of his love — or in being able to express it to anyone in the world except his father.[4]

Block 12

The Edgar-actor has not crept closer to Gloucester. He is far away on a distant part of the stage. Gloucester is calling for him ("Now Fellow") across the air and the waters. He is bidding farewell and reaching for connection, as though for a trapeze wire that will carry him safely in his leap. As he falls he gets closer to earth; as he calls he gets closer to Tom. He meets the earth: he meets his "Fellow."

Block 13

Gloucester speaks the line — "Now Fellow, fare thee well" — and then he jumps.

---

4. James Kearney: "The play seems interested — in the Poor Tom scenes particularly — in dramatizing . . . the alterity, the sheer strangeness, of the other person . . . the *son* as stranger, the *daughter* or *father* as stranger, 'no less inaccessible, separate, and distant' than the divinity itself": "'This Is Above All Strangeness': *King Lear*, Ethics, and the Phenomenology of Recognition," *Criticism*, 54, no. 3 (2012): 465.

Block 14

Gloucester does not jump until Tom has spoken his line in reply: "Gone Sir, farewell."

Block 15

Gloucester speaks half the line—"Now Fellow"—and then leaps. "Fare thee well" is the cry that lifts him as he falls, as he delivers himself to the plummet and trusts that his body will be carried across the line by his exultant, fear-defying voice.

Block 16

Gloucester expected his words of parting to extend across air. He expected the "well" to become a long wail as he accelerated down toward the distant beach. Instead the words die on his lips, as inert as his actor's stranded body. He leaps with his cue phrase only just begun ("fare thee w—"). Before he knows it he has reached earth, slumped on the stage with a cue still to finish.

Block 17

The old man lies sprawled before Edgar, evidently unhurt. Edgar-Tom's line— "Gone Sir, farewell"—is not addressed to Gloucester at all, but to himself, or to some fold of himself. He is echoing his father, just to hear those deadening last words a second time, rehearsing the murderous resolution, replaying its horror in baleful, bitter delectation.

Block 18

Gloucester and Edgar twice speak doubled farewells: once before the suicide speech, once after. First Gloucester says, "Bid me farewell," and Edgar-Tom replies, "fare ye well" ("you well" in the Quarto). Then Gloucester says "fare thee well," to which Edgar-Tom responds, "Gone

Sir, farewell." Why the repeat? Perhaps the second pair of "farewells" turns the first into a rehearsal of them: Gloucester, wittingly or not, has instructed Tom how to cue his death-leap—"Now Fellow, fare thee well"—which at the requisite moment Tom repeats. Gloucester does not leap at his own cue, but at Tom's; not at the end of his own speech, but inside the speech of his guide. Tom is his fall, and his net.

Block 19

If Gloucester has not yet fallen then the voice that speaks ("Gone sir, farewell") is Tom's. If he has already fallen then the voice is Edgar's. And if he is falling? What then? What if Gloucester, in hallucinatory delirium, is dilating the vowel, imagining a plummet that will end only when the power of speech does, when the sound is stopped, when the pebbles, as they must surely do any moment, crash through his brain, shred his tongue, and complete his cue? And so the old man is huddled in a heap, his voice roaring. The cry goes on and on. For as long as it is sustained, Edgar cannot speak. He is held in the cue-space, just as we are.

_____*fare thee weeeeeeeeeeeeeeeeeeeeeeeeeeeeeee*—

Eventually, when voice fails or realization of failure dawns, the cry will end. It will end, and there will be silence: a silence that remembers the scream; a silence that may last as long as the crying had. And only then, when this silence ebbs, can Edgar finally speak his line: "Gone sir, farewell."

Block 20

What then has gone? Perhaps death has gone. Good riddance to death. Or if Edgar speaks the words then perhaps Tom has gone. This is Edgar's fond wish, inextricable from his father's wish to suicide. Remember, Tom was called back to bring Gloucester to the cliff. This Tom, the second or third Tom of the play, is a moving vector of despair, acedia, life as a "great affliction," the very fact of it a burden too far, a thing to offload. For as long as Tom lives, so does death as a live temptation. The fiction of the cliff fools Gloucester, and saves Edgar, and kills Tom.

Block 21

The fiction doesn't kill Tom. Nothing can. It moves him into death. Who knows how wide or long that is? Who can see it to tell? All we know is that death survives us.

21

INTERLUDE

Everyman

The morality play *Everyman* is a sustained persuasion to be ready for death, which comes suddenly, and in the face of which all of our virtues, of mind and of body, are as nothing. Life is only ever a preparatory to death. Everyman's climactic fall into the waiting grave is a happy surcease, a release into the divine comedy. Shakespeare appears to recollect this with Gloucester's fall—recollect it, and multiply subvert its predeceasing teleology.[1] First, by insisting that life is for life's sake, and death a protest on behalf of life's potential; second, by turning Everyman's fall into the grave, so single and cushioned, so terminally happy, into the scandalous irresolution of a trick that makes life and death a thing of theatre; third, by making the grave a bed only in the sense that it is a site of insomniac alertness, cursed sentience, and unappeased rising.

But subversion of clear teleology does not mean an evasion of ends: quite the contrary. Living here is liminal: life teeters on the verge, and then moves into it. In this world, life is happening *at* the end.

---

1. Harold Fisch: "Gloucester's question precisely defines the structural irony of the whole play: 'Have I fall'n or no?' In one sense he must fall; this is the hellenic myth pattern. But in another sense such a tragic fall is denied him, for his 'life's a miracle.' As well as having a part in the tragedy of *King Lear*, he is indeed also in something more like a miracle play." *The Biblical Presence in Shakespeare, Milton, and Blake: A Comparative Study* (Oxford: Oxford University Press, 1999), 130.

The scene asks the biggest questions. What is there beyond the limit point? Is it even possible to arrive there? Do we think we have only to find that the verge continues, the edge extends, for as long as life does? We cannot trip beyond it, and yet stay to know the details. Shakespeare is moving here to the very limit of mortal experience and imaginative speculation. The fact that life is at all, an arrival from nothing, a possibility in the midst of impossible odds; the fact that we love; the fact of mind in body, or body in mind; the epiphenomenal weirdness of consciousness; the fact that bodies pass into death, and the mystery of mind and soul in the wake of this blank fact. Can it—*life*—really be hostage to this paltry web of cells? Can the miracle of body, all of those magically coordinate energies, really end in a crumpled heap, no better than the remnants of a meal? How can it not?

22

SCENE 10

Alive, or Dead?

I

This is a moment of true suspension for Edgar: after the fall, before the rise, when he has to pick up the pieces, if possible, and continue. But the very possibility of continuance or resumption is in abeyance. At this moment nothing can be taken for granted. Hence the probity of Edgar's thinking, as though he is nervous even about expressing what hangs in his mind:

> And yet I know not how conceit may rob
> The Treasury of life, when life it selfe
> Yeelds to the Theft. Had he bin where he thought,
> By this had thought bin past. (TLN 2482-85)

Is he excusing the guilt of his "conceit" (his fiction of the cliff), as though to say, How can it be wrong to trick him as I have, to steal possibility as I have, when life cannot protect itself, when it will give itself away?

Is there an elliptical double negative? Edgar doesn't understand how conceit may indeed rob from life, as it has done, right here before his eyes, with his father willing to end his life on the strength of the merest fancy.

Is he recognizing the sheer existential power of a thought? The old man believes he can kill himself, believes he has made the terminal move. Does this alone make it so? Hence the queasy literalism of Edgar's words: "Had he bin where he thought." A conceit is more than whimsy. Thought itself is a pioneer, traveling into unmapped spaces. Even the terrified projections into the death-state of Hamlet, or of Claudio in *Measure for Measure*, imagine that consciousness will survive the sacred barrier. But Edgar sees through to the end of all thought. Death promises no terrors, any more than it promises a life among the angels. It is oblivion, annihilation, utter nothing.[1]

Is he puzzling over a very particular scandal: not only that a life may be taken in the first place, but that a man might give away his life and yet do so as though something remains in reserve—as though some power inheres in the giving, some absurd assurance that the mere fact of choice promises survival? After all, how can something so owned as a mind possibly be extinguished with a body? The thought is unthinkable. Hence the midline break: it is the terminal abyss where neither speech nor mediation can linger. The only release is to shake the head free and dive into immediacies: "Alive, or dead? Hoa, you Sir."

Edgar's aside, for all its baffled diffidence, enters the territory of the deepest religiosity. We might understand it in terms of sublime astonishment: that point where the senses fail, the mind's conceptual furniture breaks, and all securities are voided. In Kant's formulation of the sublime, this is an event little short of revelation: in our diminishment or disabling, as we are filled to bursting with objects or ideas beyond measurement, in the paralyzing immensity of our passivity, we apprehend the necessary transcendent, which is God.

But what about here? Does anything allay the vertigo of nothingness?

It is usually assumed that Edgar, however much in pain or doubt, however mixed his motives, really is the playmaker. He has foreseen

---

1. Jan Kott: "It is only a somersault on an empty stage.... Gloster did fall, and he got up again.... Nothing has changed. Edgar's comment is ironical.... If there are no gods, suicide is impossible. There is only death.... It is a surrender." *Shakespeare Our Contemporary*, trans. Boleslaw Taborski (London: Methuen, 1964), 120-22.

it all: the fanciful description, the mistaken leap, the saved life, the swift passing into a new simulation, the extravagant fiction to rationalize it all and reconcile his father to survival. But surely this is to miss the moment-by-moment surprise of the scene: how Edgar continually comes upon unexpected possibilities; how he is at every instant himself at the verge; and how thought, or conceit, really may rob the treasury of life. These are visions to induce a swoon and a faint. We should not hear them as completed formulations, to be enunciated and pocketed away, like little ex cathedra savings. He has entered the space of the thought, a space of blank loss and panic. And so let's imagine we are in the moment, as Edgar is; not after it, as he wishes to be, but at it, as he is. Let's stop assuming that his words to the prostrate Gloucester are some preconceived pantomime. Instead, let's hear the panic that comes when comforts slide away, when you don't know what has happened, or where you are, or whether you can row back to safety.

Let's assume, then, that Edgar's question is real:

Alive, or dead?

The simple question generates others: whether the difference between life and death is always evident; whether to be in one condition precludes being in the other; whether it is possible to pass from either into the other; and how to tell either way? We might think that it is all too possible to move from life into death, and all too impossible to move back the other way. But this, I repeat, is the theme, and we should know by now, if we really want to feel this play, not to rest so casually in commonsense assumptions.

Gloucester has as yet said nothing. Edgar continues, now clearly addressing the prone blind man:

> Hoa
>
> you
>
> Sir
>
> Friend
>
> heare
>
> you
>
> Sir
>
> speake

The single line includes perhaps eight distinct illocutions. Each one is potentially succeeded by a pause as Edgar searches the inert body of his father or waits for it to move or to speak. Shakespeare often finds vast spaces in the arc of a single line, and indeed the rising terror, perhaps disbelief here recalls a still more awful line from earlier:

> Give me some helpe.———O cruell! O you Gods. (TLN 2142)

This is the line in which Gloucester succeeds, by graduated revelation, to fear, see, suffer, and survive the unthinkable fact that his eye will be torn from its socket. As the cliff speech exemplifies, a single line is a lifeline.[2] And so what to make of Edgar's line before his father rises, when the act of the falling, the attempted suicide, *is still happening*, its destination in limbo? Perhaps we are watching the possibility that the play might actually issue in death. Perhaps this is the horror that Edgar suddenly faces: the dawning thought that his father, slumped on the ground, is dead. Perhaps a play can truly end a life; perhaps the scripted player shall not always rise; perhaps some acts will have no repeat. Edgar's wordplay makes the point: "Thus might he passe *indeed*" (TLN 2487).

As usually understood, theater has an existential get-out clause. The actors will rise from any falls, survive any derogations required by the fiction, just as we spectators can all leave the arena, essentially unaltered. It isn't so much that the play isn't real, as that its reality is comic or romantic. This is the insurance that Edgar relies upon. He hasn't really taken his father to a cliff. It is a play-cliff, no more true than the words that evoke it. It is impossible, literally impossible, to move in this world from living to death. Theater is a hallowed place, where death shall not enter.

Or theater was such a place, and now it has changed.

The question is not left in peace:

> *Edg.*   Alive, or dead?
> Hoa, you Sir: Friend, heare you Sir, speake:

---

2. In a moment Edgar has another single pentameter that encompasses extensive time and numerous movements: "Up, so: How is't? Feele you your Legges? You stand."

> Thus might he passe indeed: yet he revives.
> What are you Sir?
> *Glou.*   Away, and let me die. (TLN 2486-89)

Gloucester's brief line of despair—"Away, and let me die"—is cued three times. This is a struggle *for* death as much as against it. Edgar is not getting his way easily. Unlike the repeated cues of Tom in the storm scene, these cues are directly addressed: "Hoa," "heare," "are you Sir." The Gloucester-actor has to *hear* the cue, or the nearly cue. He will necessarily rehearse in his mind the scripted answer: "Away, and let me die." It is not essential that the cued line be spoken more than once. The experience might be the more intense for not being enunciated out loud:

> Away, and let me dye—
>   Away, and let me dye—
>   Away, and let me dye—

The words might garner the compulsive charm of a mantra, all the more implacable, perhaps, for not quite being heard, for not quite being fully spoken: worded but revoked, or spoken sotto voce, or dying in some liminal interim, neither in the scene nor out of it, a pure potential that is in the actor's safekeeping. The phrase might purchase the bitter grace of prophecy: known, resisted, but implacably scripted. After all, its truths are sure to arrive, come hell or high water. Others shall go away; he shall be allowed to die.[3]

This is to suggest that the thrice-cued line—"Away, and let me die"—does more than remove itself from punctual lineation; more even than that it creates for itself a promissory space, a kind of proleptic eventuality, in which the terminal scene is acknowledged and deferred. I think that Shakespeare was imagining something still more spectral than this. The words might be silently rehearsed, in preparation for their

---

3. Exactly the same technique is repeated a moment later: "Looke up a height, the shrill-gorg'd larke so farre / Cannot be seene, or heard: Do but looke up. *Gloucester.* Alacke, I have no eyes" (TLN 2500-501). The repeated cue, "Looke up," allows the Gloucester-actor to commune intently with the fact of his blindness: he can shout it, whisper it, rehearse it mutely. It is notable that "Alacke, I have no eyes" shares rhythm exactly with "Away, and let me die."

single articulation; they might be started and stopped; they might be whispered or spoken over; or they might be shouted in the interstices of Edgar's speech, heard where they should not be heard, an intervallic refrain that, for all that we hear it coming from the body of Gloucester, cannot quite be attributed to his bounded role. The line, that is, becomes a refrain: it speaks of haunting. It is speech as disembodied presence, speech as ghost, speech that detaches from a named subject and begins to echo of coterminous presences.[4] The blind Gloucester is Everyman, of course, and his claim for death is every human's. But far more specifically, the haunting voice is Tom's. He is the figure who is drifting from view, lost from body—and now, precisely at this speech of Edgar, cut from the part.

But if he is cut off, where is he now? Floating, sinking, adrift? Whatever his motility, Tom is now a ghost: but a ghost, paradoxically, that longs to die.

What can this mean? We might say that of course Tom cannot die. How on earth could he when he never had his own body in the first place? Like his first host, he is condemned to survive. And so this phantom refrain, calling to be left in peace and allowed to die, is also adumbrating, with the utmost metaphysical delicacy, the fact that Tom has once more become a figure for potential: awaiting a new host, condemned to the life sentence—or perhaps better, the lifeline. He is in death, but death promises not so much an end as a suspension, and a painful one at that.

Or we might say that Tom is here some kind of angel, made of voice alone. From his first appearance he has had an aura of divinity, perhaps cloven or caducean, harboring some spiritualized nascence that neither

---

4. Jacques Derrida: "If it—learning to live—remains to be done—it can happen only between life and death. Neither in life nor in death *alone*. What happens between two, and between all the 'two's' one likes, such as between life and death, can only *maintain itself* with some ghost, can only *talk with or about* some ghost. So it would be necessary to learn spirits. Even and especially if this, the spectral, *is not*. Even and especially if this which is neither substance, nor essence, nor existence, *is never present as such*." *Specters of Marx: The State of the Debt, the Work of Mourning, and the New International*, trans. Peggy Kamuf (New York: Routledge, 1994), xvii; italics in original. I think Shakespeare's dramaturgy and his layered scripting produces more felt historical and spiritual possibilities than countenanced in Derrida's atheistic, messianic deferral.

Tom's bodies nor narrations can quite accommodate. Of course this has almost always been unrecognized (though Lear intuits in Tom some such privilege) because it comes from deep in past or future, or some incommensurable dispensation, hardly to be reckoned with now. But here, as the issue of the cliff scene, Tom appears to reclaim something similar. As we have seen, Gloucester's leap is attended or anticipated by Tom's. The spirit does his falling for him; the fall is double: not just the Gloucester-actor's collapse to the floor, but Tom's skein-like unraveling into air, correspondent to the lines flung out and down, like fishing wires, in the cliff speech.

The action can be pictured one way on stage, and another way in the scenographic mind. At some level it is clear that the visible scene, manufactured by Edgar, is a charade. But far from reducing the scene's significance, its manufactured nature makes it all the more prone to allegory. The true event is invisible, a transliteration of spoken words into subjunctive achievement. This in turn proposes a graded metaphysic, by which the scene is at once the present materialized world and the mesh of spiritual purpose that attends it. These purposes hang in the air, like subvisible webs of uncertain origin, tenuously present, attesting to finer constitutional principles and more delicate morphologies than daily agreements ever know.[5]

II

It is just such intimations of extramundane substance that feed into Edgar's memorable next speech, cued by the reverberant "let me dye":

---

5. Emmanuel Levinas: "[For] the totalisation of history to not be the ultimate schema of history, it is necessary that there be in dying another direction than that which leads to the end as to a point of impact in the duration of survivors. Separation designates the possibility of an *existent* being set up and having its own destiny to itself, that is, being born and dying without the place of this birth and this death in the time of universal history being the measure of its reality. Interiority is the very possibility of a birth and a death that do not derive their meaning from history. Interiority institutes an order different from historical time in which totality is constituted, an order where everything is *pending*, where what is no longer possible historically remains always possible." *Totality and Infinity: An Essay on Exteriority*, trans. Alphonso Lingis (Pittsburgh, Penn.: Duquesne University Press, 1999), 56; italics in original.

> Had'st thou beene ought
> But Gozemore, Feathers, Ayre,
> (So many fathome downe precipitating)
> Thou'dst shiver'd like an Egge. (TLN 2490-93)

The words purport to report a counterfactual, leading to the claim of miracle: were you not made of unearthly lightness, you would have been smashed to pieces; but look at you, you have "heavy substance," and yet still you "bleed'st not, speak'st, art sound"—thy life's a miracle![6] (TLN 2494-97). Edgar's conceit can seem at best unlikely, perhaps absurd, and certainly exploitative of his father's fractured vulnerability. But criticism and performance has tended to accept this false appeal to supernaturalism as the conceit's only explanation. Surely this is inadequate. The words have an alarming precision—the sensuous exactitude of some kind of truth, even as the illocution is a lie.

Edgar's miracle, for all its flagrant mendacity, typifies Shakespeare's extravagant, catachretic, metaleptic compositions, by which violently juxtaposed metonyms, severed from the things they are normally contiguous to, claim their own novel adjacency. In this case, the logic is transformed by peculiar intratrope silences that help give to each part of the sentence a supercharge of alteration. There are two bodies: one light as air, the other heavy with substance. They are absolutely different, but they are also the same body. The body of air can turn, in the twinkling of a conceit, into heaviness. Likewise, the heavy body, again through the magic of language, can obtain the properties of air. The speech thus apostrophizes exactly the processes that go into the composition of Tom: the merest thought is a meme; fancy begets bodies.

The effect is that these weightless things have precipitated—they have magically accumulated the mass required for a plummet. Gossamer is at once as light as a web and weighted as a stone. Feathers fly and they fall. The physics are both metamorphic and perdurable. So: you could not have fallen and survived unless you were gossamer, which you are;

---

6. Alan Dessen sees the true miracle of the moment as Edgar's assertion of loving sonship. "Two Falls and a Trap: Shakespeare and the Spectacle of Realism," *English Literary Renaissance* 5 (1975): 291-307.

the gossamer couldn't have fallen without the magic addition of weight, which it has; you have hit the ground and remained intact because you have no more substance than air or feather; you have hit the ground and shattered because you are corporeal. The shatter has happened because it has been spoken; but the shatter presages continuance. Here in miniature are the scene's great principles. Precipitation is not a fatal fall. It is alteration, crystallization, resolution into a new form. The chemistry, and thereby ontology and identity, is alchemical: at once a trick, a metaphor, and a possibility that mysterious transformation might come true.

Once again the genius of such transpositions is Tom. For the words exactly describe the only type of material that he can by now partake in: things invisible to the eye, that cannot tip a scale, but that can plummet, as he always has, deep into the elements and rise again; whose precipitation invokes equally a sudden fall and alchemical recomposition, as the violence of process leaves a new solid behind; and whose substance, as ever, is akin to a shivered egg: an ovum of potential, caught at the moment of cracking, shattered dizzyingly into shards—a shattering that might equally presage self-annihilation, the aborting of the sole and singular one, and the multiplying survival of self-fractals, as the tiniest shaving generates untold replicants or variants, like some slip of plant on the wind.

But the intimacy of the images is still more. It obtains particularly in their tactile delicacy, as of things ineffably fine and durable, sustaining or resisting radical change. To be shivered evokes more than fragmented dissipation. It evokes the tremble of life, its vulnerable innocence, hurt by cold or fluttered from an excess of feeling. It suggests the quivering of sentience, even the "shudder of the idea" that for Kierkegaard is the childlike apprehension of an absolute beyond rational explanation.[7] Above all, it is the tremor of alertness to possibility. The egg shivers from exposure to intimated futures as much as present assaults. It is the shiver of surviving flesh, quite as much as the cracked particles of a too-fragile shell. The imagined egg thus suggests perilous bodily abidance, stripped clean of shell and asked to bear the elements.

---

7. Kierkegaard, Søren, *Fear and Trembling/Repetition: Kierkegaard's Writings*, Vol. 6, trans. and ed., Howard V. Hong and Edna H. Hong (Princeton, N.J.: Princeton University Press, Princeton, 1983), 9.

But just as when the germens spilled in the storm, cracking open the seeds of man, primal violence need not signal the end. The egg shivers to pieces—and then what? Perhaps it survives as multiple chipped fragments, each one severed from its source, lamed and apparently helpless; perhaps the rocks are wet with egg-gunk, as the waste of albumen laces the pebbles, and the exposed embryo, fertilized or not, waits for further mutation; perhaps the egg is boiled in the enraged waters, transformed from liquid to a wobbling, bulbous sphere of pale flesh, as though brain or breast exposed.

Whatever its shapes, the surviving remnants are Tom.

III

Edgar tries to bid farewell to Tom.[8] He figures him as an angel of death, recommending despair, taking into himself the entire vista, sky and sea and mind-dragons, an insatiate monster of the last days:

> Upon the crowne o'th'Cliffe. What thing was that
> Which parted from you? . . .
> As I stood here below, me thought his eyes
> Were two full moones: he had a thousand Noses,
> Hornes wealk'd, and waved like the enraged Sea:
> It was some Fiend. Therefore thou happy father,
> Thinke that the cleerest Gods, who make them Honors
> Of mens Impossibilities, have preserved thee. (TLN 2495–519)

Edgar's "fiend" engrosses the scene and all of its agents, seen and unseen, human and nonhuman.[9] He resembles Job's Leviathan, whose

---

8. Many have thought the attempt successful: for example, Meredith Skura, who identifies a process of exorcism in which Edgar "makes his ghosts his ancestors." "Dragon Fathers and Unnatural Children: Warring Generations in *King Lear* and Its Sources." *Comparative Drama* 42, no. 2 (2008): 141. This is a striking and apposite phrase, mainly because it works against the notion of a clean exorcism. Ghosts haunt.

9. For Christopher Pye the cliff scene's "strangely composite and theatrical demon" anticipates the "multiform figure that looms up over the horizon of the frontispiece to *Leviathan*, Hobbes's political treatise that belatedly attempts to reclaim for the king's body a power more

"scales are his pride," from whose mouth "go burning lamps," and who "maketh the deep to boil like a pot."[10] We might almost hear in the vision Job's otherwise silent God, answering from the whirlwind, with Tom a figure of both unregenerate creatureliness and divine power.[11] Certainly Edgar's vision draws upon deepest myth—topographies that are in fact disguised gods, or cliffs and waters whose apparent geographies are a holographic illusion. Edgar seems amazed at his own creation, both the scene of the cliff and the beggar-man who spoke it. Perhaps at the level of positivistic actuality, the sublime event has not happened. But the sublime transport certainly has. The cliff is not here. But what is here is something Kant might have identified as truly sublime: the apprehension of one's own sensory and conceptual limits, the intuition of truths beyond the subjective event-horizon, and so a paradoxical conviction that the truths that transcend are nonetheless one's own.

At face value it appears that Edgar wants Gloucester to believe in an impossibility that we all know has not happened ("Thinke that the cleerest Gods, who make them Honors / Of men Impossibilities, have preserved thee"; TLN 2518–19). Gloucester, it seems, just about accepts this ("I do remember now"; TLN 2520). We, presumably, do not. Nevertheless, there is a counterresistant beauty in the idea: if it were true. If it were true that his body had turned to air, that he had been parachuted to safety, that the gods had intervened, then his life indeed is a miracle.

---

phantasmatic and apparitional than it ever had." In turn, the splitting off of fantasy, which emerges as the "demonic beyond of the perspectival subject," can be understood as "an index of the appearance of the modern political subject, the subject possessed amounting to the other face of the modern possessive individual." *The Vanishing: Shakespeare, the Subject, and Early Modern Culture* (Durham, N.C.: Duke University Press, 2000), 103.

10. Job 41:15, 19, 31 (King James Version).

11. Ewan Fernie identifies this scene with the Gospels' episode "where Jesus casts the demons of a possessed man into swine which in turn cast themselves over the bluff and into the sea.... But what really links him with Edgar is his 'unclean spirit' (Mark 5.2) and multiple personalities. 'My name is Legion: for we are many' (Mark 5:9).... And yet Shakespeare radically departs from the biblical story.... The swine are rolled up into Gloucester and saved," a remission that Fernie identifies as strung between repairing sympathy and diabolic cruelty, because it saves Gloucester for further pain. Likewise, he sees a portion of the "preserved swine" surviving in Edgar's image of the "horns whelked and waved like the enraged sea," a demonism incorporated into Edgar's "grotesquely unsettled being." *The Demonic: Literature and Experience* (London: Routledge, 2013), 229–31.

But if it were true, it could only be because the agency of Tom was actually efficacious: Tom, Gloucester's guardian angel, cushioning his fall, turning a plummet into a float. And here is the paradox upon which the whole scene twists. As we have seen, *Tom does do this*. He does it, but no one will recognize the fact. The miracle has happened, truly happened, but no one knows it. Call Tom whatever you like—the present angel or the fallen god, the idea of sacrifice or of absolute charity—Tom is its tragically unacknowledged emissary. This is the shadowing pathos of these scenes.

Even if a savior were here, nobody would realize.

Tom's vanishing returns to the foundational kenosis of the Edgar-part, the emptying into nothing with which it began. And the question, as ever, is the substance in nothing. Tom's distinctive prestige is that he lives as and into apparent nothing. He cannot quite be construed in apophatic terms, as some divine figure conceivable only as sublime negativity. But nor is he reducible to ancient associations of nonbeing with evil, or with bare matter, cast out from form, unregenerate and godless. The more Tom retreats into shadow, not seen, denied, deposited, the more he is the hanging man: a loneliness like El Greco's homonculus, neither Christ nor not-Christ, but any way presently incompossible, harnessed to no story, to no stage, and to nobody else. For whatever Edgar's efforts to cleanse the slate, Tom is still there, occupying a folded experiential envelope all his own, not quite in the moment, not quite out of it, at once a memory and a promise. Shakespeare is creating a uniquely staggered departure: death by graduated kenosis; or by a thousand and one cuts, with always one more to go.[12]

---

12. Tom's continuance is, among other things, the continuance intrinsic to Shakespeare's interlacing, telepathic forms. His passion continually fissions and folds into others. So, among other mutations, his extravagance and pain, his multitudinous voices, his loneliness and exile, his bodily introjection of a wind-blasted antipastoral commonalty, as of despised weeds or agitated sea, the sense of a single life as a collocation of numberless severed others—all pass, as though by sympathetic magic, into the king himself: "Alacke, 'tis he: why he was met even now / As mad as the vext Sea, singing alowd, / Crown'd with ranke Fenitar, and furrow weeds, / With Hardokes, Henlocke, Nettles, Cuckoo flowres, / Darnell, and all the idle weedes that grow / In our sustaining Corne" (TLN 2350–56). The mad king takes up where one of Tom's floating song cues left off: singing wild, the mock-crown of weeds and nettles on his old head, closer to his land than ever before, and gone for all money.

IV

The scene could be straight out of Edmund Spenser's *Faerie Queene*. Two pilgrims, alone in the desiccated nowhere land; one the battered nobleman, blind with intemperance and despair, the other his faithful palmer, moralizing him into perseverance. And then from nowhere arises the diabolic adversary. He appears out of thin air, an automated monster on the featureless plain, a figure of the baldest venality:

> A proclaim'd prize: most happie
> That eyeless head of thine, was first fram'd flesh
> To raise my fortunes. (TLN 2677-79)

Oswald the Steward is a pure agent of opportunity, without hinterland, morally infantilized, acting upon the rote-remembered cues of his mistresses. Luckily the palmer has his staff, which morphs into a weapon as he turns by magic into Justice's henchman, kin to Spenser's ironman Talus, and splits the monster's head like the softest round fruit ("Costard"). It then becomes apparent that this monster, once opened up, is the agent of others whose motives and missives he contains. He is the vehicle of his employers' lechery: but also its host. So the slain villain literally carries the vices which the pilgrim—now mutating into the "fair unknown," the repairing chevalier—can extract and moralize upon:

> I know thee well. A serviceable Villaine,
> As duteous to the vices of thy Mistris,
> As badness would desire. (TLN 2704-706)

His mistress is an Acrasia, a sex-witch, employing men to service her insatiable appetites. Swine like this—again, in true Spenser style—deserve no proper burial: "heere, in the sands / Thee Ile rake up, the poste unsanctified / Of murtherous Letchers" (TLN 2727-28). Edgar taps into the scene's almost pure allegorism: nothing is but what it can be said to mean; and what things mean depends on their position in decisive moral binaries.

But even to think so decisively might well give us pause. What is more, there is something almost obscene in Edgar's vow, or in its curious expression. He seems to mean that he will give this man a rough and ready burial, raking a bit of sand over his corpse with a stick, because he was the dirty conduit of Goneril and Edmund's (and Regan's, as it happens) murderous lechery. But can Edgar really only refer to the fact that Oswald delivers their post? He seems very specifically disgusted by Oswald: "in the sands / Thee Ile rake up" suggests that he will desecrate the corpse, mash it to pieces like the wild raptor mob does to Ben Jonson's *Sejanus*. It is as though to be lechery's "post" is to have lascivious desire delivered physically into him, a foul embodiment of the foul ménage that sticks in Edgar's craw. He has to be raked up to destroy all trace of the seedy evidence. Hence, perhaps, the tumid discharge of wordplay: the "poste unsanctified" describes not only the corrupt servant, but his burial ground, the "sands" into which he has now been mixed. Place and person once again merge: the "poste" is the stump of Edgar's, stuck in the sands to mark the burial "ground"; the earth is "unsanctified" because far beyond holy precincts.

The portrait of viciousness is unremitting. But it is also oddly supererogatory. Who cares about the Steward?[13] Why is Edgar so bothered? Certainly it adds to the rising tide of sexual disgust. But next to Lear the recoil here feels programmatic. For all Lear's twisted paranoia,

---

13. There is much to be said for Nick Davis's reclamation of Oswald the Steward against the interpretive arrogations of Kent and Edgar: "The project of his existence clearly stands as the polar antithesis of Lear's or Edmund's: he embraces a courtly rationality of a kind, in accepting a life arbitrated in all significant respects by letters, where willing is made the business of other people. There are several hints that he sees to the satisfaction of Goneril's sexual needs, as bawd and/or more directly.... Oswald... fulfils the role with dedication and even a touch of heroism: as scribe, bearer and deliverer of letters, he is responsible for quite a lot of the play's busy postal activity; he risks his life, at least according to Regan, in order to deliver a letter, ... and his dying words are an attempt to make sure this letter reaches its correct destination.... Oswald in this last scene has attempted to kill Gloucester because a proclamation puts a price on his head, ... on which Edgar has rather neatly settled his hash by miming the counter-role of an illiterate peasant who has no use for written proclamations, and who therefore resists Gloucester's legal assassin." *Stories of Chaos: Reason and Its Displacement in Early Modern English Narrative* (Aldershot, U.K.: Ashgate, 1999), 146. Compare Harley Granville-Barker: "As a tailor made him, he must be tailored right." *Prefaces to Shakespeare*, Vol. 1 (London: B. T. Batsford Ltd., 1930), 325.

there is both cause and mollification to plead on his behalf: he has been destroyed, as he sees it, by his own daughters; he is demented, and his visions partially diseased ("good Apothecary sweeten my immagination"; TLN 2572). This gives him a fool's acid license, by which his horror at women's "sulphurous pit" (TLN 2570) contributes to a savage indictment of all creation, understood as a chaos of appetite that renders all forms and laws and authority, including his own, the most disgusting hypocrisy. But what cause has Edgar either for his abiding misogyny or his fastidious dwelling upon the sexual peccadilloes of his class? Of course it might be that Edgar is simply being good, or perhaps Pauline, in his feeling for the dangers of desire and the sanctity of marriage and the folly of female government. It is wrong to make your servants have sex with you, no doubt, and wrong to be happy to do the deed so very duteously. But still: the reflexive denunciation of women ("O indistinguisht space of womans will [Quarto: wit]" (TLN 2724), in which mind is swallowed and engrossed by essentially vaginal desire, seems ugly, puerile, infantile, and what is more, strangely *interested*.

Placed in one frame, Edgar-the-yokel's actions have their own swift decorum. The old man once again demands protection. Murder is not an exquisite epistemological puzzle, as it is for Hamlet; death in Lear's Britain doesn't stand on ceremony. And so Edgar swiftly effects what is necessary:

> *Edg*. Nay, come not neere th'old man: keepe out che vor'ye, or ice try whether your Costard, or my Ballow [Quarto: bat] be the harder; chill be plaine with you.
> *Stew*. Out Dunghill.
> *Edg*. Chill picke your teeth Zir: come, no matter vor your foynes.
> *Stew*. Slave thou hast slaine me (TLN 2692–99)

And yet the yokel accent is also troubling, as though killing is no more than a child's game, permitted by the adrenalin of pretence, hidden by frankly ridiculous gusto. The death once achieved, Edgar emerges out of disguise, seeming to regret that someone else couldn't have done the necessary dirty deed: "hee's dead: I am onely sorry / He had no other Deathsman" (TLN 2710-11). But then of course he did have another "Deathsman": his own serviceable yokel.

Edgar feels here the queasiness of his impostures, his ambivalent complicity in the possibilities they touch. His shifty sentiment is understandable enough if we once take him as a discrete human. But of course he isn't just this. As Edgar he has to speak Christian orthodoxy; as Tom he has to search out the boundaries of living and not; as yokel he has to smash a head in with a stick, without hesitation. We may feel one possibility to be more refined than another, perhaps more civilized. But the play knows that there is no progress here that cannot be abrogated in an instant. Just think of Gloucester, who even now, after all of Edgar's efforts to save him, greets the Steward's drawn sword with deathlonging gratitude ("Now let thy friendly hand / Put strength enough too't"; TLN 2681-82). Certainly this potential for revocation, for regression to former conditions, includes the much-vaunted acquisition of moral fineness, or delicate probing at what it might be to die. Edgar lives such superpositions. This is history in action, a house in which the levels might at any moment exchange.

It is the intensity of Edgar here that is remarkable: the sense of enormously overdetermined violence producing extravagant diversions and overcompensations, like the Mummerset accent and the furious burial. That he sees his devilishly attractive brother in the Steward's aspect is one explanation. But this hints at a still more intimate recognition. Edmund is always Edgar's potential double as well as opposite, and so too is Oswald.[14] As we find time and again in Spenser's epic romance, the hateful opposer is also a kind of mirror. In facing Oswald, Edgar is faced by himself, or by a perverted fragment or memory of self: more particularly, by an aspect of self that previously found expression only in Tom. The explanation for the frankly unnecessary information about Oswald, then, is an uncanny return of the explosive biography of Tom.

Here again is Edgar's account of Oswald:

---

14. William C. Carroll suggests that in slaying Oswald he slays "yet another parodic alterego of Edmund." "'The Base Shall Top th'Legitimate': The Bedlam Beggar and the Role of Edgar in *King Lear*," *Shakespeare Quarterly* 38, no. 4 (1987): 439.

> A serviceable Villaine,
> As duteous to the vices of thy Mistris,
> As badnesse would desire. (TLN 2704-706)

And here Edgar's account of Tom:

> A Servingman? Proud in heart, and minde; that
> curl'd my haire, wore Gloves in my cap; serv'd the Lust
> of my Mistris heart, and did the acte of darkenesse with
> her. (TLN 1865-68)

Evidently the meeting with Steward is another meeting with Tom, the mashing and burying another attempt to render Tom extinct. But of course it cannot succeed. Oswald may refract a part of Tom, but it is a part that cannot stand for the whole. Not for the first time, Tom will survive this suicide.

23

INTERLUDE

The Pending World

The world of *Lear* is without the revelation of Christ: perhaps before, perhaps after, perhaps simply beyond. Equally, this is a world without the single God.[1] It is instead a world where there are too many gods, as many gods as there are changes in the weather or in fortune. Perhaps this world is in the interim, the lapsed time between resurrection and return. Perhaps it evokes the time before any savior, rife with the kind of contagious demonology skeptically reported by Hobbes: "The souls of men were substances distinct from their bodies, and therefore... when the body was dead, the soul of every man, whether godly or wicked, must subsist somewhere by virtue of its own nature, without acknowledging therein any supernatural gift of God."[2]

Tom, lacking his own body, is perhaps such a floating undead soul, epitome of a world in eschatological limbo. But even if such demonic associations are more shadow than fact, the effect is an experience of living in the half-light, of dawn or dusk it is unclear, whether before true birth (waiting unborn) or after false death (waiting undead). To

---

[1]. G. Wilson Knight identifies a development in the play from ubiquitous "nature worship," in which the gods are essentially human-made, figments of the human mind speaking the stresses of circumstance, to Lear's vision of himself and Cordelia being "God's spies," a single God of a religion "born of disillusionment, suffering, and sympathy": *The Wheel of Fire* (1930; reprint, London: Routledge, 2001), 216.

[2]. Thomas Hobbes, *Leviathan*, XLIV.

exist is to live in this pending condition, suffering its consequences, working toward a time when the dispensation might alter.

The ensuing questions are foundational: What comes to the human, in the wake of this vacuum, as responsibility or possibility? Can we imagine living precisely in this place: in the place of the removed savior; in the place where he would be, were he; or where he will be, when he? Or perhaps in the place of his departure, exactly where he has departed to, wondering unrecognized.

It is not that Edgar is a Christ allegory, on a pilgrimage like Piers Plowman. Any such associations are glimpsed and then gone, shadowy and contingent, their modality barely even optative. It is more like an option—a hermeneutic choice that needn't be taken. A good example of this is the "shivered" egg: a symbol of various possibilities, including rebirth and fertility, and as such potentially an allegory of Christian resurrection (the eggshell equals the cave or tomb of Christ). In truth this specific association doesn't add much to what the image and context already give. Nonetheless an aureole of Christian historicity clearly hedges the Edgar-part's experience, as it does more obviously the symbiotic enduring of Cordelia: a trace of righteous struggle, perhaps the suffering gift of unacknowledged grace or chosenness, perhaps the wretched experience of exile from the same.

In Tom's "mortified" (TLN 1266) bareness there are shadowy suggestions of Christ's deposition, when he is removed from the cross but not yet returned. Likewise his fury and vexation in the hovel might suggest the harrowing of hell, when Christ descended to the prison of condemned souls and released them from limbo.[3] But if Edgar-Tom adumbrates Christ, it is more like a waking effigy than a disguised messiah—a pseudomorphosis, a look alike that is not alike, and yet whose formal resemblance may generate scandalous, historically impossible connections.[4]

---

3. Compare David K. Anderson: "*King Lear* is an Easterless tragedy, which never moves beyond Golgotha" and the "image of that horror," its violence "unsanctified and unsanctifying," Cordelia's death "terrible because it is not extraordinary but mundane." "The Tragedy of Good Friday: Sacrificial Violence in *King Lear*," *English Literary History* 78, no. 2 (2011): 279.

4. Amy Knight Powell: "The emergence of a form A, morphologically analogous to, or even identical with, a form B, yet entirely unrelated to it from a genetic point of view." *Depositions:*

Or perhaps it is no scandal at all. Insofar as the Edgar-part imitates Christ's passion, this makes it less a figure for Christ than for everyman. Even the moment where the fabric threatens to tear open directly onto Christian allegory, suddenly exposed and irrefutable—"O thou side-piercing sight!" as Edgar sees the lunatic king (TLN 2532)—works most forcibly as a confession of renewed human sympathy, and of the impossibility of processing suffering into ethical theology (as Edgar has just attempted with Gloucester). The wound that is renewed is the stigmata of shared humanity: "I would not take this from report, / It is, and my heart breaks at it" (2586-67). Indeed we might go even further: if there is a divinity here, a feeler-out of truths, then it is the hypersensory layers of theater, typified in scenes like this, where stunning immediacy interweaves with mediated witness, where immersion in emotion can be interrupted by sudden calls to judgment, where serene intellectual detachment can at any moment be blown onto the rocks and shattered.[5]

At moments such as Lear's entrance, shafting all peace and security, it can seem as though the only providence in this world, the only dependable care, is accident, or some exhausting commitment to sleeplessness and interruption. We might conclude that accidents, in this world, *are* providence. There is nothing but the instant, with its terrible capacity for suddenness. But there can be inaccuracy in this, too: the inaccuracy of embracing pure contingency; the approximateness of chaos, as though it truly does describe things, when in fact the creation is also miraculously patterned; the turning away from the evidence, even a paradoxical kind of squeamishness, in embracing haphazard

---

Scenes from the Late Medieval Church and the Modern Museum (New York: Zone Books, 2012), 10-11. Powell notes how the term is generally used in art history as one of abuse, quoting Donald Judd, "A lot of things look alike, but they're not necessarily very much alike" (11). But she follows Georges Bataille in redeeming the term, because it reveals formal liaisons across distant times and places, transgressing linear conceptions of history.

5. Maynard Mack observes the thrice-repeated pattern where "a formula summarizing Edgar's present stage of learning is presented . . . only to be followed at once with an experience that explodes it." *King Lear in Our Time* (London: Methuen and Company, 1966), 62. Compare Stephen Booth: "In Edgar's desperate efforts to classify and file human experiences, Shakespeare tantalizes us with the comfort to be had from ideologically Procrustean beds to which he refuses to tailor his matter." *King Lear, Macbeth, Indefinition, and Tragedy* (New Haven: Yale University Press, 1983), 47-48.

nihilism as life's only routine. It isn't. For a start, the suddenness is scripted. What is more, it is typological, which means it is always likely to be or to cue a recurrence: to look forward to its own future recollection, and potentially its transformation. As much as each note and shiver has its own integrity, hardly a moment in this play is simply for itself—arising from a blank, exhausted in commission. And it is just such compositional principles that ensure the continuance of Tom.

❊ 24 ❊

SCENE 11

Dark Places

When Lear awakes from restorative sleep, he speaks not of where he is but of where he was, assuming himself still in the nightmare world of storm and cliff, a scene beyond this daily world, beyond this life. He has never been more serious. "You do me wrong to take me out o'th'grave" (TLN 2794).

I have spoken of Lear's horizontal cosmos, in which all things, men and monsters and cheese and gods, are equally present to hand. And we have seen how Tom, again very literally, is the coming-true of just this vision. Hence Lear's first question to Cordelia. Resistant to consciousness he may be, but he isn't at all surprised to be seeing what he sees:

> *Cordelia.* Sir, do you know me?
> *Lear.* You are a spirit I know, where did you dye? (TLN 2798-99)

Cordelia has been long awaited. But there have also been sleepless preparations for her return. She is in part Edgar-Tom's double, her experience *now* earned by his in the world of nightmare. Earned, and also foreshadowed. Lear simply assumes that this "spirit," hovering over his grave, shares a world with the "spirit" whose first irruption clinched Lear's descent into the drowned world ("Did'st thou give all to thy Daughters? And art thou come to this?" 1820-31). We might of course aver that Lear is mistaken. This lady is not a spirit, but his child,

Cordelia. He is not in a grave, but in a bed. Both of them are alive, which will become clear when he fully awakes.

But the delicacy of the moment depends upon the emotional reality of the things being spoken, things that cannot be gently dismissed as the final disbandaging of lunacy. Lear is indeed returning from the dead—as she is. And that world—of graves, bliss, wheels, fire, oblivion—is *here*, parallel or immanent, a drawn curtain away from our knowledge. We cling to this world, our world, as no scene in drama more exquisitely realizes than this one, as the father, in hesitant self-wondering steps, is returned to the face of his child. We cling to this world, but the other one is here. And these places, like Lear's words—"out of the grave," "soul in bliss," "bound upon a wheel," "you are a spirit," "where did you die?"—are also Tom's. For this too is the scene's delicate pain. It could not move as it does were it not implicitly *known* that remittance—from death, oblivion, terminal account—is short and only for the few. These two are the privileged exceptions, living the dream. Tom is the waiting reality, shared by all who are not here now, or not now here.

※

In a context such as this, Edgar's manufactured duel with his brother can seem banal and redundant. It seems to belong to some other world, one where a knightly fight might indeed resolve something. This is no such world.[1] The whole burden of the cliff scene, with its shuttling between presence and absence, departure and return, was to take the play into shadowlands where evidence lacks and visible victory is little more than a holographic tableau of deeper causes, themselves tussling in shadows. The figure for this is Tom, as he slowly fades from palpable presence into echo and shadow. But when Edgar reappears as the knight, he has nothing of Tom about him. Indeed the knightly guise might seem the most absolute denial of the very possibility of a Tom. And this, surely, is the basic problem. Edgar-the-knight is as second-

---

1. The redundancy of this sort of win-or-lose mathematics is evident throughout the final movements. As A. C. Bradley says, "There is something almost ludicrous in the insignificance of this battle." *Shakespearean Tragedy: Lectures on Hamlet, Othello, King Lear, Macbeth* (1904; reprint, Basingstoke, U.K.: Macmillan, 1985), 209.

hand and callow as Spenser's Redcrosse knight, really believing that a flailing sword can finish off Error.

It isn't that chivalry simply belongs to yesterday, or that the ersatz medieval duel inaugurates the playworld's final reentrance into an unwritten present: there is nothing left but modernity, whatever that may herald. Chivalric nostalgia was hardly unknown to the Jacobean court or its satellites; as militant disappointment with James grew, hopes turned more and more to the fledgling Protestant knight errant, Prince Henry.[2] Nonetheless our antennae are sure to be alerted by Edgar-the-knight's opening speech—prolix, clichéd, labored, programmatic, and tendentious. First comes a throat-clearing repetition, as though establishing the right to speak, or perhaps simply a nervous stutter, followed by three barely distinguishable abstract nouns:

> Behold it is my priviledge,
> The priviledge of mine Honour,
> My oath, and my profession (3083-35)

Having shielded himself in feudal tautologies, Edgar moves onto the accusation: that his opponent is "a Traitor." But not before an extended subclause, featuring three more such abstract sets:

> Maugre thy strength, place, youth, and eminence,
> Despite thy victor-Sword, and fire-new Fortune,
> Thy valor, and thy heart, thou art a Traitor:
> False to thy Gods, thy Brother, and thy Father (3086-89)

The speech is easily open to parody, but it can be played most naturally, perhaps, as simple nervousness: Edgar, playing yet another role, struggling for a persuasive register, clumsy and maladroit because he is so close to the end, so close to revelation. The invective with which he

---

2. Henry was eleven in 1605, a student at Magdalen College, Oxford. A 1605 painting by Robert Peake of the prince with drawn sword over a dead stag attests to the dauntless image already in circulation.

closes is almost endearingly childlike as it pieces together appropriate terms of superlative disdain:

> And from th'extremest upward of thy head,
> To the discent and dust below thy foote,
> A most Toad-spotted Traitor. (TLN 3091-93)

"Say thou no"—if Edmund denies the allegation—then "Thou lyest"! (3093-96) He is back in the Gloucester playground, complaining to Daddy of another wrong done him by his naughty bastard brother.

There are of course options here for the actor. But what seems clear is that any attempt to play it straight, as noble indignation, is likely to come across as orotund and shrill and somehow out of time. Edmund's urbane response—"In wisdom I should aske thy name" (TLN 3097)—speaks a very different register: wry, ironic, tired with ceremony. He quickly gives this over, as though consciously agreeing to descend to the level of his guest ("By rule of Knight-hood, I disdaine and spurne: / Backe do I tosse these Treasons to thy head"; TLN 3101-102). Shakespeare gives deliberate attention to this discursive gear shift—downward, backward—into pseudochivalrous simulacra. Boys will be boys. No less than the bedtime song with which Edgar-Tom departed the hovel ("Childe Rowland to the darke Tower came, / His word was still, fie foh, and fumme"; TLN 1966-67), Edgar is back where he grew up, in the infantile nursery. Of course there are other mythic traces—Abel returned to take vengeance on Cain; Esau on Jacob. But either way, the world-historical is diminished to, dependent on, these brotherly pathologies.

The problem isn't that romance (the mode of the duel scene) is false to the play. It is that the duel scene is false to Shakespeare's emerging idea of romance. This certainly seeks reconciliation. But it also searches for genuine political repair, going well beyond the locked horns of bovine knightly combat.[3] A palimpsest of morality play is discernible in Tom from the start. Edgar's probationary path might well be under-

---

3. For extended analysis of the politics of Shakespeare's late plays see my *Late Shakespeare: A New World of Words* (Oxford: Oxford University Press, 1997).

stood as a kind of purification by fire, as he hives off the vicious parts of himself, experiencing and eschewing vice, working toward an achieved magnificence.[4] But as the cliff scene shows, staging a mini-morality is beset with difficulties. There is no simple progress through temptation into virtue, nor clear demarcation between one's self and one's opposers.

Indeed Edgar's "interlude," if such it is, seems stuck between two narratives, confounding both. Traditionally the hero can either meet with adversaries he is supposed to dispel or meet with partners whose virtues he absorbs. Edgar appears to think that the first path describes his own: he goes into exile, copes with the demons of Tom, manages Gloucester's despair, quells Oswald's luxury and pride, and finally kills Edmund, the bad brother. But in fact his path seems more to resemble one of Spenser's knightly quests, in which supposedly defeated enemies continually reappear, in one or another guise; in which death seems no more final than a postcoital slumber; in which the knights continually encounter what they have already countered, or believed they had; in which demonic simulations, or Terminator-style resurrections, or pass-the-parcel ontologies, or the simple eternalism of vice (jealousy, despair, even hope) chain the sufferer to miserable unkillable life; in which passion and pain fester, and love is a wound that will not heal; in which the claims of moral instruction or temperate behavior are repeatedly superseded by violence; and so in which the good man's means and methods become barely distinguishable from those they would proscribe.

Consider the duel's outcome. Edgar wins; Edmund starts bleeding to death; it is time to unveil. But when Edgar starts talking, it is not about what one might expect: himself, his own miseries since Edmund ushered him into exile. He instead purports to explain, with forethought precision, exactly why his father lost his eyes:

---

4. Sarah Beckwith suggests that Edgar employs various Christian medieval genres of reparative play: Morality, Miracle, and the "fair unknown," staging himself as the "hero of romance," the "un-named redeemer" in whom virtue and force can be reconciled. *Shakespeare and the Grammar of Forgiveness* (Ithaca, N.Y.: Cornell University Press, 2011). 86–87. Drawing on Stanley Cavell, Beckwith sees Edgar's stratagems as "avoidance": "Such forms will no longer answer to the paths of unknownness in *King Lear*" (88).

Edmond. I do forgive thee.
Edgar. Let's exchange charity:
I am no lesse in blood then thou art *Edmond*,
If more, the more th' hast wrong'd me.
My name is *Edgar* and thy Fathers Sonne,
The Gods are iust, and of our pleasant vices [Quarto: virtues]
Make instruments to plague [Quarto: scourge] vs:
The darke and vitious place where thee he got,
Cost him his eyes. (TLN 3126-34)

Remember: we don't yet know that Gloucester is dead. The last we saw of him he was with Edgar, being moralized out of despair—and yet still, in the scope and injustice of his suffering, far removed from the goatish chuckler of the opening scene. And here is the good son, dwelling upon this father's peccadilloes, identifying in them the cause of his torture, and declaring the contract of "got" and "cost" satisfactorily "just."

Edgar's jurisprudential mathematics is sometimes thought to have a choric finality, as the chivalrous knight sets the whole thing straight: you reap what you sow, you suffer for your sins, you get away with nothing.[5] Punishment is the better for its aesthetic concordance with the crime; pleasure's tools produce the instruments of vengeance. But surely we—and indeed the play—must rebel against this summary. It is original sin with bells on, an egregious coalition of sub-Augustinian sex revulsion with pornographic relish.[6] Edgar effectively legitimizes the vicious act of blinding, with Regan and Cornwall roped in as agents of godly justice, their invasive "instrument" handed to them by Gloucester's original trespass. He moves from cosmic teleology (the gods see

---

5. Stephen Booth's identification of Edgar's insufficiency and triviality is closer to the mark, even as he recognizes how "Edgar's desperate efforts to classify and file human experience" tantalize an audience with some kind of flat and soggy "comfort." *King Lear, Macbeth, Indefinition, and Tragedy* (New Haven. Conn.: Yale University Press, 1983), 47-48.

6. There is a considerable critical literature on the way Edgar shares in the play's abiding misogyny, often taking this statement as proof of Edgar's disgust at the woman's part. See Janet Adelman, *Suffocating Mothers: Fantasies of Maternal Origin in Shakespeare's Plays, Hamlet to The Tempest* (London: Routledge, 1992), 119-20; Peter L. Rudnytsky, "The Darke and Vicious Place": The Dread of the Vagina in *King Lear*," *Modern Philology* 96, no. 3 (1999): 291-311.

and determine all), to preemptive storytelling (the script says what we do even though we don't know it), to murderous sibling rivalry (the motive behind both his statement and the wider tragedy). Just as Edmund is obsessed with his conditions of conception and uses them as the justification for everything that follows, so too does Edgar. And, according to his summary, so too does the play. This is why the "Wheele is come full circle." They are all back where they began, in a "darke and vitious place" of conception and damnation.

This imaginative telescoping pretends to capture the hidden narrative principle of the whole play, as the "darke and vitious place" collects metonymic referents in one unholy site: the adulterous bed, the mistress, the mother's womb; Gloucester's lecherous state of mind in commission; his blinded eyes, all "dark and comfortless"; and of course Edmund, the "vicious" thing made and released as agent of this "place." Edgar's mininarrative performs a hideous catachresis, as events, ethics, and agents brutally superimpose. History becomes a single action, played over and over again.

The "dark and vitious place" transforms gynecology into scenic and narrative embryology. It conflates vagina with uterus with parturition, pleasure with conception and gestation—all secret, all maleficent. It therefore expects future births from this first one. The "germaines" have been spilled, and out comes not only the "ingratefull Man," Edmund, but the entire Gloucester plot. Edgar has suffered, and now he has come out the other end. He frames himself as the playworld's spectral imp—perhaps Tom's dark cousin, perhaps his catechizing fiend—haunting the play's atrocities and avidly tabulating the cost.[7] Suddenly, as though for the first time, Edgar seems to know exactly what he is for: all this time he has been the exemplary victim and invisible agent of moral surveillance. Hence the palpable sense in which Edgar becomes recharged, literally and symbolically reborn, through the annihilation of his father and brother. In their passing is his emerging: a Hegelian

---

7. Cavell: "Edgar's avoidance of Gloucester's recognition precisely deprives Gloucester of his eyes again. This links him, as Lear was and will be linked, to Cornwall and the sphere of evil." "The Avoidance of Love," 55.

passage into consciousness, the fight to the death with the mirroring other that confers his identity.[8]

Surely all of this must give us pause. Edgar seems to announce some sort of religious coming to account, baldly reprising the "wisdom" of Job's comforters ("they that plow iniquity, and sow wickedness, reap the same"; Job 4:8). But he is too early, or too late, and either way it is not quite his duty to perform.[9] What is more, he argues for a punitive moral network that ignores the tempered gradations of feeling that the action everywhere dramatizes, preferring instead a severely formal regulatory poetic justice: one that this very scene will in a moment flout (or perversely observe) as never before. Edgar-the-knight appears in hock to ideology: to false consciousness, and to a protofascist mix of hieratic martialism, eye-for-an-eye ethics, and genetic ascendance.

The truly demoralizing thing is the type of attention that Edgar seems to recommend: not attending to feeling, but to rhymes and symmetries, a kind of geometry of guilt. But this is also the terrifying thing: What if he is right? What if this is how things happen in this world? After all, no one in the play (excepting the deluded dupe Albany) ever seems to think that divine justice is remotely fair. And is it not exactly the case that such unforgetting, unforgiving geometry is part of the play's logic? It goes something like this: words come true; small things are magnified; a laser shines on hiddenness; nothing is forgotten; actions escalate into necessary consequences. Myth demands it. Poetic justice is cruel; it lets no one off the hook. And what is worse, in the Shakespeare-world this telepathic consequentiality does not obey daylight logic. Anything

---

8. Maurice Blanchot: "The horror—the honor—of the name, which always threatens to become a title. In vain the movement of anonymity remonstrates with this supernumerary appellation—this fact of being identified, unified, fixed, arrested in the present. The commentator says (be it to criticize or praise): *this is what you are, what you think*; and thus the thought of writing—the ever-dissuaded thought which disaster awaits—is made explicit in the name; it receives a title and is ennobled thereby; indeed, it is as if saved—and yet, given up. It is surrendered to praise or to criticism (these amount to the same): it is, in other words, promised to a life surpassing death, survival. Boneyard of names, heads never empty." *The Writing of the Disaster*, trans. Ann Smock (Lincoln: University of Nebraska Press, 1995), 7; italics in original.

9. G. Wilson Knight; "Edgar's trumpet is as the universal judgment summoning vicious man to account." *The Wheel of Fire* (1930; reprint, London: Routledge, 2001), 203.

might connect to anything, as mercurially as words. Apparently disparate events or agents—a mistress's vagina, an old man's eye, the stabbing of either—collocate with the merciless logic of sin.[10]

The effect can be chilling. Once we start translating metalepsis and catachresis into moral orders, into moral cause and effect, it is the end of mens rea, jurisprudence, and the rest. The only law becomes formal or physical sympathy, or whatever kind of connection the fertile imagination might venture. The mad Lear's logic—"None do's offend, none, I say none" (TLN 2610-11)—becomes hideously, hysterically, handily-dandily indicative of the playworld. Perhaps Edgar is rarely so faithful a creature of the playworld as he is here: discovering connections, but only formally (catachrestically); refusing imaginative sympathy; or being overcome by interestedness and losing the capacity to feel anything but his own pain. Perhaps this is what it means to *live* this playworld. Or perhaps this is why Edgar so needs Tom.

---

10. Maynard Mack: "To exclaim with Mr. Empson (and a number of other critics who should know better) that 'even the resentful Edgar, and the sex-resenting Shakespeare cannot have believed all through the play that Gloucester deserved to have his eyes put out,' is to miss the point. The punishment is exemplary like the act, the blindness is not what will follow from adultery, but what is implied in it. Darkness speaks to darkness." *King Lear in Our Time* (London: Methuen and Company, 1966), 70.

25

INTERLUDE

Jacob and Esau

The biblical tale of Esau and Jacob is a tantalizing precursor of the story of *Lear*'s brothers. As in *Lear*, the future of Esau and Jacob is predicted in the drama of the womb, with the woman's "place" one of allegory and prophecy:

> Two nations are in thy womb, and two manner of people shall be separated from thy bowels. (Genesis 25:23)

> And when her days to be delivered were fulfilled, behold, there were twins in her womb. And the first came out red, all over like an hairy garment; and they called his name Esau. And after that came his brother out, and his hand took hold on Esau's heel; and his name was called Jacob: and Isaac was threescore years old when she bare them. (Genesis 25:24–26)

Esau is the elder and, initially, the father's favored child. Jacob, the more domesticated brother, persuades the virile hunter Esau to sell his birthright as the firstborn in exchange for a little food. The almost comic facileness of this transaction is then reprised, made still more symbolically fratricidal, when Jacob steals the paternal blessing promised his twin. He does this, at the suggestion of his doting mother Rebekah, by preempting the gift of savory meat their father requests of Esau. Isaac is blind, and the "smooth" Jacob is able to pretend to be the "hairy" Esau by dressing in goat's fur. It is thus he rather than Esau who is blessed with power and preeminence, and he who will become the father of the patriarchs. Esau is wild with anger and vows revenge; once his father is dead, he will murder his scheming brother. Hearing this, Rebekah hurries her favorite son away. The sons marry and propagate, and when eventually the twins meet they are reconciled, aided by Jacob's magnificently opulent propitiations. The brothers then go their separate ways, founding different tribes in different lands.[1]

Clearly it was mainly the framework and opening episodes that attracted Shakespeare: the birth, the boys' basic qualitative difference, the blind father; the emulation via trickery and disguise; the brooding vengefulness and itinerance. But it is precarious trying to identify who corresponds to whom. Esau is the elder, and so he suggests Edgar. He is cajoled by his brother into losing his inheritance, again suggesting that Esau is Edgar and Jacob is Edmund. But then Jacob never relinquishes his illegitimate blessing: he has to grow up to deserve it. This he does principally through a succession of revelatory dreams, speaking face to face with God, wrestling with an angel, eventually founding a nation. Such a pilgrimage obviously suggests Edgar; encounters such as the one between Jacob and the angel correspond in broad terms to Edgar's battle to come upon charity and discover a clear sense of mission. But when Tom courses his own shadow for a traitor, the correspondence

---

1. Harold Fisch sees the father's blessing as the heart of both Shakespeare's interest in Genesis 27 and the whole Edgar/Gloucester tale, the teleology of which is "clearly in accordance with the letter and spirit of Genesis 27 in which the disguised Jacob presents himself to his father with the sole purpose of winning his blessing, appropriating it by stealth from his more favoured brother, Esau. That blessing included material benefits—'the dew of heaven, and the fatness of the earth, and plenty of wheat and wine' (verse 28)—but also moral and spiritual gifts—'blessed be he that blesseth thee' (verse 29). These are momentous blessings and their power will shape the subsequent history of Jacob and his offspring. We are here in the realm of salvation-history and something of this quality attaches itself to the subplot of *King Lear*. Like Jacob, Edgar is a survivor. Lear and his daughters are doomed by the laws of tragedy, but Edgar will carry a blessing from his father into the future. Here the biblical notion of history ruled by covenant promises enters into the play." *The Biblical Presence in Shakespeare, Milton, and Blake: A Comparative Study* (Oxford: Oxford University Press, 1999), 129-30. But Fisch also notes that the kneeling and blessing motif was ubiquitous in the earlier *Leir* play (140).

once more becomes dizzyingly ambiguous, priority and teleology all hurly-burly.

Furthermore, it is Edmund who broods, like Esau, with sullen and turbulent menace, going into exile and cogitating revenge; it is Edmund who is defined as the disenfranchised. And it is Edgar who dresses in a pelt and so reprises the mixture of savagery and disguise used by Jacob to fool *his* blind father. Esau and Jacob swap places: each lives out the life meant for the other. And Jacob does so by stealing not only the manner, but the youth of his brother. By dressing in goat's fur, he purports to be his brother, and thereby steals the father's love for his brother. The fur stands for the past, for the childhood and young manhood that made Esau in Isaac's eyes. Identity is frangible. To the extent that Shakespeare is inspired by this tale, it might produce a part just like Edgar's.

26

SCENE 12

Departures

Edgar's final attempt at exorcising Tom comes a few minutes before the duel with his brother. We don't see it on stage; we only hear about it after it happens. It is when he reveals himself to his father:

> Never (O fault) reveal'd my selfe unto him,
> Untill some halfe houre past when I was arm'd,
> Not sure, though hoping of this good successe,
> I ask'd his blessing, and from first to last
> Told him our pilgrimage. But his flaw'd heart
> (Alacke too weake the conflict to support)
> Twixt two extremes of passion, joy and greefe,
> Burst smilingly. (TLN 3159-62)

In announcing himself Edgar presumably hopes to mark the irrevocable passing of Tom. The beggar-man no longer exists; more than that, he never existed. Gloucester is told that he was fooled; that his guide and nurse and savior was not poor mad Tom, but his own son. And the report kills him.

What to make of this? We might say that the return of the son is lethal to the father. Alternatively, that the erasure of Tom generates the death of the father. Certainly Shakespeare is orchestrating strange exchanges. It is a basic method of the play, and the principle of this tortuous final scene (Edgar's "Let's exchange charity," TLN 3127; Edmund's "all three / Now marry in an instant," TLN 3179-80). Edgar's life for Tom's; Tom's life for Gloucester's: so it seems to go. We get near-parodic versions of this in a moment. We fear for Cordelia's life, we hear of offstage slaughter, and we then find brief relief when the unlamented corpses of Regan and Goneril are brought out. Bad sisters for good, a fair exchange; we'll shake on that if we're allowed—which of course we are not.

A crucial effect of this technique is a sort of graded existential reality: some things are closer, more real, more felt than others. Death is not always a dumb, hideous, morally impossible scandal. It may come as light relief, a counter in a plot, the merest cipher. Likewise, reconciliation between parent and child need not be the moment (as it is for Lear) that sanctifies one's very existing. It may be a belated report, tying up knots and dubiously revisionist. Lear and Cordelia get the best and the worst; Edgar and Gloucester—not so much. They are sacrificed to scenic technology.

But what does this mean? That they are relegated to some penultimate tier of apprentice intensity and suspended recognition, such that we are not asked fully to allow the suffering that they must assuredly feel? Or is it that they are *substantially* denied: actually sacrificed in the play's economies of exchange? The provocation isn't so much that a life or a death is waylaid. Rather, that it isn't quite seen; that it happens just over the lip of evident eventuality; that it is somehow not quite here. The structure of playlife—of lives in scenes, as sacrifices to stories or symmetries—has its evident cruelty. And if this is an existential allegory of living in scenes, it is an existential reality of living for Tom.

Nevertheless, such life—and such death—is there to recover. Let's look closer at the report of Gloucester's death, and see whether it does indeed mark the passing of Tom:

> But his flaw'd heart
> (Alacke too weake the conflict to support)
> Twixt two extremes of passion, joy and greefe,
> Burst smilingly. (TLN 3159-62)

The image train is double. First, a flaw is a detached piece of something, whether a flake of snow or spark of flame or shard of pot; it is only via metonymic transference from this more primary meaning that *flaw* means defect. Shakespeare's "flaw'd" is the first record of the noun turned to an adjective—always a sure sign that the words are working with precisely directed energy. So, a flawed heart doesn't just mean a weak heart or a cracked heart, or still less a morally soiled heart. It means a heart made up of flaws: of flaws that gather together to constitute the pumping organ of life. Typical of the play, the putative unity is a concatenation of conative fragments, working as a perilous, barely sustainable assemblage.

Second, a flaw is a sudden burst, as of wind or rain or passion. And so when Edgar says that the old man's heart burst, he means that its flaws in a basic sense came true. They did what a flaw does, which is explode into the atmosphere. And so the two connotations of *flaw* meet in a single wondrous image: fragments of heart swirling into air, shot into the weather. Each flaw is a suffering, a small shard collecting a particular hurt of living; each flaw is detonated personal history, moving with the past into futurity.

But in this world, the personal often exceeds discrete human personality—it isn't that Edgar/Tom is some mercurial, protean silverfish and all the rest are ontologically enclosed. Rather, Shakespeare gives frangible potential to all of his bodies and body parts, generating all kinds of compounding and cross-fertilizing: not just between one character and another, but between characters and environment, and between characters and sweeping moral, social, and spiritual allegories. Accordingly, Gloucester's "flaw'd heart" clearly picks up—picks up like a burden, or an infection—Lear's desperate vow, made the very moment he left Cornwall's castle to enter the storm:

> No, Ile not weepe, I have full cause of weeping.
> *Storme and Tempest.*
> But this heart shal break into a hundred thousand flawes
> Or ere Ile weepe: O Foole, I shall go mad. (TLN 1583-86)

Shakespeare is here specifically imagining Lear's rage and grief erupting into storm. In a sense the "flawes" of his heart *are* the storm, the very "spits" of fire and "spouts" of rain that he suffers (TLN 1669). And Gloucester at his end is returned to just such a pass. This is Gloucester's very own private storm, endured in darkness, beyond the loving shelter and attendance provided Lear. Beyond all palliation, cruelly belated, lost from view—he "burst smilingly."

I find it hard to get pass the weirdness, even the affront, of this phrase. The suffix, "-ly," turns the action of smiling into an adverb, modifying the imputed smile as well as the verb. The thing like a smile isn't him, but his burst. The burst is a smile, and the burst is of smiles. There are hints of self-exculpation and euphemism, as Edgar tries to give his pilgrim's tale a heart-warming end. But the same impulse also produces the phrase's catachretic violence, compacting numerous agents into a single ecstatic pay-off. The burst is inward, hidden in his heart, but then it is magnetically transferred to a smile. The smile is Gloucester's, but it is also clearly the grimace of gripping cardiac arrest. And so the smile is also Edgar's, his secondary revision of the trauma, construing the event as tragi-happy. In turn the smile is bursting, shattering into crescent-shaped fragments. The air is filled with subvisible cherub's wings, or a hundred thousand Cheshire cats, grinning from a goodman's heaven, each smile a piece of his heart.

As such mercurial metaleptic travel suggests, Edgar's control of the phrase is strictly limited. What is more, the image is only partly for Gloucester. The image comes more fully true later in the scene, in and for Lear: when the old king, cynosure of all eyes and ears, bursts smilingly into death, apparently rapturous with the delusion that his child breathes again: "looke there, looke there" (TLN 3283). The echoes are simple but patent. Lear's child has returned, just like Gloucester's; neither father sees much, as Lear's "eyes are not o'th'best" (TLN 3244) and Gloucester's are out; each child is glimpsed amid pain; a second later the father is gone.

Of course, we might say that there is one decisive difference: the son returns to life; the daughter stays dead. But it is not quite so simple. For if the son returns to life, his life is in exchange for Tom's passing. Gloucester dies, then, split like Lear between two extremes: the life of Edgar, the death of Tom. If he has joy for one, he may have grief for the other. And notice what Edgar is given to say: the old man's flawed heart is "too weake the conflict to support." The conflict does not disappear. It crashes down between the twin poles of joy and grief, living and dead; or else it bursts into the attendant air. Either way, it perseveres: down into the depths of impending grief; out into the promise of the play's end.

Because Tom is not dead at all. He is not dead because Edgar lives; he is not dead because Edgar cannot kill him; he is not dead because Gloucester dies for him; he is not dead because Tom, the grief for him, the memory of him, the coincidence of his extinction with Gloucester's, means that he is sustained and active in the bursts that Gloucester's death vents into the atmosphere. The futurity of Tom is both at Edgar's beck and call—as though his semiaccidental consequence or expression—and moving quite independently of him. What is more, it directly consummates the wish with which the very same speech began:

> *Alb.* How have you known the miseries of your Father?
> *Edg.* By nursing them my Lord. List a breefe tale,
> And when 'tis told, O that my heart would burst. (TLN 3145)

The tale is told, and Gloucester's heart bursts: the bursts carry Edgar's longing.

What is Shakespeare up to? Principally, these dizzying substitutions allow the Edgar-figure to experience death: to suffer it in his doppelgangers—brother, father, Tom—and so to survive:

> O our lives sweetnesse,
> That we the paine of death would hourely dye,
> Rather then die at once. (TLN 3147-49)

The statement's purpose is elusive. The immediate context is his brother's "paine of death," as Edmund bleeds away before Edgar's eyes. Perhaps Edgar exults in the fact that it is not he that is dying ("rather than die at once"); perhaps he intuits their shared condition, his brother's pain a cut to his own being, his brother's death a rehearsal and forestalling of his own, as one Ed does the dying for the other. But even so, we might think such a statement impossible to speak aloud at this moment (after a deadly joust, to the nation's rulers, in wartime). Impossible to speak aloud, and directed to something—or someone— still more intimate than the treacherous Edmund. Surely the sentiment is too exposing, too confidential, in its strange equipoise of savagery and rapture, in the tribute it makes to pain, in its dizzy thanks that every endured moment is a kind of sweet assay of a death that its tasting delays. This surely invokes a relationship of the fiercest inwardness: it invokes the torture that was—that *is*—being-Tom. This is where we find the multiple contingent deaths that Edgar here apostrophises, proxy or rehearsal deaths, hourly down payments that extend possession of life by cutting it inexorably away. So it is to suffer Tom; just so Tom suffers. The "we" is Tom and he, dying for each other, dying so that the other might abide.

❦

To the extent that things are coming to a head, and for all that Edgar wants to reclaim his own personal distinctiveness, the principle is one of remorseless experiential merging. In the Quarto Edgar has still more to report:

> Whil'st I was big in clamor, came there in a man,
> Who having seene me in my worst estate,
> Shund my abhord society, but then finding
> Who twas that so indur'd with his strong armes
> He fastened on my necke and bellowed out,
> As hee'd burst heaven, threw me on my father,
> Told the most piteous tale of *Lear* and him,
> That ever eare received, which in recounting
> His griefe grew puissant and the strings of life,
> Began to cracke twice, then the trumpets sounded.
> And there I left him traunst. (V. iii. 207-17)

The usual assumption is that Edgar speaks in awed respect for a fellow sufferer and servant. But what he actually says invites a different interpretation. First he seems to remember (how bitterly it is difficult to assess) that Kent had disdained him—not the bedlam beggar, but *him*—at his lowest point ("seene *me* in *my* worst estate"; my italics). Then when Kent finally realized who the beggar-man was—that is, the disguised Edgar—he fastened on Edgar's neck with his strong arms, bellowed to the heavens, and threw Edgar upon the still-warm corpse of his father. This sounds like an action of rage and revenge; of an older man disgusted at the younger; of a loyal servant indignant that a son would evade his father's recognition for so long, effectively murdering him with misery. Kent throws him on the corpse to make Edgar *feel* what he has done. No doubt Edgar intends a quite different construction. But the words are not his to own; the telepathies go far beyond his volition.

In this reading, Kent merges with vicarious ferocity into Gloucester. To drum the message home, he tells Edgar the tale of Lear—which Kent knows Edgar already knows. It becomes a kind of pleonastic lesson, reiterating the selflessness of service, the vulnerability of age, life's cruelty. And as he tells the tale, his heartstrings crack. He is thus still more firmly one with Gloucester, as he was with his bellow that might "burst heaven," the echoing verb returning once more to the final moments together of father and son. The scenic rhymes are drummed home. "And there I left him traunst," says Edgar-the-lethal: left him for dead, just like he left his father, "burst" under some tree, because the trumpet sounded and Edgar had a plot to execute.

The repetitions accumulate; the recursive playing of the terminal moment. It is something like the layering of future memory: the seeds of a son's deep guilt; the recollection of negligence or of absence. It is the same kind of thing that the Quarto text does in allowing Edgar/Tom to witness Gloucester's blinding. Once again the memory of horror is actualized. Remember: this is once more Edgar's story; once more the return to the scene of trauma. And what is he recording? It is no neutral act, no everyday carelessness of an egoistic son. He is recording the act of killing his father.

And it doesn't stop there. For consider Kent's next movement. Once upon a time Edgar had risen into Tom from the sleep of the stocked Kent; now the ghostly somnambulism is reversed, as Kent rises from trance into his own final mutations: into himself and "Caius" (his disguised persona), the lifelong servants of Lear; but also, and once again, into a ghostly counterversion of Edgar, replaying his past, projecting into futures. So, Kent comes on stage and repeats exactly what Edgar has just recorded himself doing with his father: he finds his master, and at the eleventh hour purposes to reveal himself and share the story of their pilgrimage:

> *Kent.* O my good Master.
> *Lear.* Prythee away.
> *Edg.* Tis Noble *Kent* your Friend.
> *Lear.* A plague upon you Murderors, Traitors all,
> I might have sav'd her, now she's gone for ever:
> *Cordelia, Cordelia,* stay a little. (TLN 3230-35)

Imagine Edgar with *his* father. Did he too reveal himself only to be cursed as a traitor?

> *Lear.* I am old now,
> And these same crosses spoile me. Who are you?
> Mine eyes are not o'th'best, Ile tell you straight. Who are you?
> *Kent.* If Fortune brag of two, she lov'd and hated,
> One of them we behold.
> *Lear.* This is a dull sight, are you not *Kent*?
> *Kent.* The same: your servant *Kent*,
> Where is your servant *Caius*?
> *Lear.* He's a good fellow, I can tell you that (TLN 3242-50)

Lear no more sees Kent, perhaps, than Gloucester saw Edgar. They see some passing shadow, as of the disappearing past. The son or servant becomes a cipher of past failures, of regrets that come flooding home, a bursting wish that life had been different, or could be different, if only death were not approaching in the mist.

❧

But of course death is already here, isn't it?

> *Enter Lear with Cordelia in his armes.*
> *Lear.* Howle, howle, howle: O you are men of stones,

> Had I your tongue and eyes, Il'd use them so,
> That Heavens vault should crack: she's gone for ever.
> I know when one is dead, and when one lives,
> She's dead as earth: Lend me a Looking-glasse,
> If that her breath will mist or staine the stone,
> Why then she lives.
> *Kent.* Is this the promis'd end?
> *Edg.* Or image of that horror.
> *Alb.* Fall and cease. (TLN 3216-26)

Edgar speaks of what they see before them as an "image" of the promised end, an allegory of irredeemable teleology. And so what does he behold in his mirror? Not just a dead child or a grieving father, but this:

> She's dead as earth: Lend me a Looking-glasse,
> If that her breath will mist or staine the stone,
> Why then she lives.

How to know that life has passed, or that death is final? How to know that death will not issue in life, or whether death is a shaded process, a thing of degrees? How to know but through images, art, play, and the hopeful inferences they elicit? As we saw at the cliff scene, there is little possibility of evidence with such things. Empiricism lacks authority; the senses cannot get close enough: and even if they could, how to know the meaning of a mist? To breathe on the glass would instantly occlude any image. The mist or stain suggests the impossibility of clearly visible mimesis. The image is left to imagination.

It is a unique moment. Lear asks for a mirror, not to see a reflection, but *to hide one*, hoping to witness the evidence of breath. If the "looking-glass" is an allegory of art, then the inference is remarkable: art becomes not so much a mirror of life—of life that exists primarily in the face that looks into it—as it is a proof of life, and indeed a generator of it. For what else can this misting mirror be? It is a supremely wistful projection of life returning from the blank opacity of a surface, renewing from abatement, emerging as though from a burying pond. This life will be witnessed precisely as a stain, which might then transfer, by magical telepathy, to the lips and throat before it. Art is the origin of life; theater is the image of otherwise unwitnessed possibility.

Presumably there is no such glass in the scene, or at least it would seem extraordinary if one of the miserable bystanders had one in his pocket to produce. But this is the point. The glass is projective, projected. Hence the way it seems once again to pick up memories of the cliff scene—a "mist" of life emerging from the "stone" like furry condensation from waves on the pebbled shore. Cordelia's rising would be another such miracle. Perhaps she doesn't rise; but once again the counterfactual is countenanced.

This is the moment's strange audacity. The horror is not just death: it is a looking-glass onto renewed life. The "promised end" imagined by Edgar does not offer closure. Rather, it opens onto recessive ghosts of a thought beyond proof, or a life beyond sight, continuing like imagination to the crack of doom. For consider the vision's elusiveness: *an image of an absent glass*. In one sense, we might understand this as mimesis receding impossibly out of sight into the sheerest chimerical dreamland. And yet: if life is possibility, if futurity has possibility, then it will be founded precisely in such a not-yet origin, in the kind of imaginative intensity that might bring forth a Tom, and a playworld such as this one, where words uncannily or sublimely project beyond the bodies they address. Tom gives the key here, in particular his ambiguous lapse from simple empirical presence. For if he cannot die, then where is he now? He hasn't so much vanished as entered into some virtual life-exchange, where he haunts, substitutes, or impends. The world appealed to by Edgar, and inhabited by Tom, is moving beyond the materialized and verifiable. It is a world like El Greco's, but an El Greco in which at one moment the tumid skies are suffocating with cherubs and skulls and angels and ash, and the next—wiped clean!

※

This sense of multipresent figures suggests some sort of typology coming to a head, as earlier climactic scenes hover or superimpose over the one visible on stage:

> *Lear.* This feather stirs, she lives: if it be so,
> It is a chance which do's redeeme all sorrowes
> That ever I have felt...
> *Alb.* ... O see, see.
> *Lear.* And my poore Foole is hang'd: no, no, no life?
> Why should a Dog, a Horse, a Rat have life,
> And thou no breath at all? Thou'lt come no more,
> Never, never, never, never, never.
> Pray you undo this Button. Thanke you Sir,
> Do you see this? Looke on her? Looke her lips,
> Looke there, looke there.   *He dies.*
> *Edg.* He faints, my Lord, my Lord.
> *Kent.* Breake heart, I prythee breake.
> *Edg.* Looke up my Lord. (TLN 3227-86)

Finally, it seems, the play breaks the spell of reported or suspended death, of living in the time of dying: here is true extinction, first the daughter, and then the father. To deliver it Shakespeare violates his source, violates his own play and the hard-won satisfactions it allows. He well-nigh murders his actor in the act of doing it, insisting that Cordelia not move, not breathe, all the time Lear is looking harder than ever a human has for the smallest sign of life, even as he holds a feather to the actor's lips and dares it not to stir. Cordelia devastatingly trumps the ambiguous departures of Fool and Tom. She has gone. "I know when one is dead, and when one lives, / She's dead as earth" (TLN 3220-21).

And yet still, for all this torture, for all this insistence that the fiction of survival is a wistful lie, perhaps Shakespeare cannot do it. Perhaps this is why he returns to his play and revises it as he does. It is all for one addition, one repair to the killing scene: "looke there, looke there." The Folio is a second "looke"; a second "image"; a second go at the same action. Shake your head, blink, look again—and might the facts have altered? For this is what Shakespeare writes back in, the foundational impossibility of his theatre: the impossibility of death. *Look there, look there!* We must do as Lear bids. We must look and look again at the corpse of his child. All around there is wailing and horror. But "looke there" is a repeated cue: the cries of Edgar and Kent inter-penetrate as much as answer Lear's words.[1] "Looke there" transcends the on-stage situation, ranging beyond the knowledge or interpretation of Lear's closest immediate witnesses. It can appeal directly to the present audience, an appeal to see things that the others on stage cannot. And so what happens if we "looke on her," and the actor's young chest is heaving? If we look on Cordelia's lips and see a furtive tongue licking? What does it mean if the feather moves, or the glass, if there is one, mists? Is this the possibility that is scripted, risked, dared *not* to come true? *Look there, look there!* Perhaps theater is truer than the story it appears to tell?

꙳

The thought is possible. But it leads less to visions of Christian resurrection, I think, than to a reminder that in this play all life is somehow played on the same string. One figure is plucked, and another trembles. If Cordelia promises something, then there is only one figure that can bear the debt: her deepest abiding double, Edgar/Tom. But that too is for the moment deferred, as futures wait upon Lear's tortuous "passe"-ing.

Shakespeare is intently thinking about the travel of living into dying into death. As Gloucester found out at the cliff, and again beneath his tree, it is the hardest passage of all.

> *Kent.* Vex not his ghost, O let him passe, he hates him,
> That would upon the wracke of this tough world
> Stretch him out longer. (TLN 3287-89)

There is more in Kent's terrible exhortations than empathy and pity. The curtain has torn between mundane and spirit realms, if indeed it was ever there. Everyone present is submerged in the physics and metaphysics of dying. Kent wills his heartstrings to crack, tuned as they are to his master's. But as much as Kent seems to be sinking like Beckett's Winnie into earth, his thoughts, like Lear's and Edgar's, are spiritualized. We need to take seriously the fact of death-rapture. And the only

---

1. See Simon Palfrey and Tiffany Stern, *Shakespeare in Parts* (Oxford: Oxford University Press, 2007), 261-65.

passage to the "blast," it seems, is as a "flaw." Kent too is speaking with his new familiars. He is battling with the gods, exquisite torturers that they are. Kent's modality is partly optative, wishing for pain to relent; partly imperative, demanding the justice of release; and partly a modality beyond modalities, where subjunctive melts into indicative, *is* into *if*, *if* into *is*, because the fences are down, the fields are leveled, and the incompossible is here. For look closely at the scripting. Kent's address is at least partially contingent on Edgar's. But who is Edgar addressing?

> *Edg*. He faints, my Lord, my Lord.
> *Kent*. Breake heart, I prythee breake.
> *Edg*. Looke up my Lord.
> *Kent*. Vex not his ghost. (TLN 3284-87)

The obvious inference is that Edgar is pleading with Lear, trying to reboot his stopped heart, perhaps slapping his face, vainly pleading for resuscitation or attention. But there are two other Lords present—Kent and Albany—and potentially a third who may or may not be present: I mean, of course, God. It may seem unlikely that Edgar offers a prayer to this third Lord, the otherwise absent God of the Christians. But is it? His king and godfather is about to die, and dying demands prayers.

"He faints, my Lord, my Lord."

The Edgar-actor hears Lear ask a second time for his button to be undone:

"Pray you undo this Button. Thanke you Sir."

How can he not recall Lear's earlier instinct to unbutton, happening at a moment of barely less exquisite tension and sadness?

> Thou art the thing it selfe; unaccommodated man, is no more but such a poore, bare, forked Animal as thou art. Off, off, you lendings: Come, unbutton here. (TLN 1881-89)

Edgar is once again face-to-face with the undressing king. Once again, Edgar is anyone, everyone, no one, a human helper at a time of distress, with no thought of a more particular recognition: "Thanke you Sir." And once again the specter of Tom begins rising from his grave.

The two scenes draw together. Edgar draws toward Lear; Lear draws Edgar toward him; Edgar draws close, yet again, to Tom. A shiver of Tom passes through, like a wind across the pond, his voice in the storm, his fearful loneliness and longing for blessing:

"My Lord, my Lord."

Perhaps he looks up to the sky, fearful of annunciation, in case it is the "promised" horror; perhaps he hunches his body to a fetal ball and whisperingly calls for comfort; perhaps he recognizes, in the king's ecstatic paroxysms, his own father, dying between joy and grief, and sees in Lear's passing the consummation of a heart bursting smilingly; perhaps he feels the upsurge of this burst, as the flaws of a long life shatter into the air; perhaps his life collapses into all the lives in his mind's eye, every one of them his torturing or tortured double—Lear, Gloucester, Fool, Tom, Oswald, Edmund, Cordelia—and for this one moment of blissful sharing, perhaps he too enters the blast and delivers himself to ecstatic disembodying, exultant and annihilating: look there, look there, *look up!*

Who knows what spirits might be shaped in the blast?

If Edgar's words appeal to God as well as to Lear, then the eschatological implications of Kent's words likewise explode. Kent now speaks partly in answer to Edgar's call for him to "looke up," joining the younger man in heaven-blasting appeal: "Breake heart, I prythee breake." Both are rapturous, seeing through the veil where the body becomes ghost and the undead specter struggles for peace. Kent means what he says. He isn't just telling Edgar to shut up. He is speaking direct to the gods:

> Vex not his ghost, O let him passe, he hates him,
> That would upon the wracke of this tough world
> Stretch him out longer.

Together they watch the king's ghost travel into distance:

> He is gone indeed. (TLN 3290)

Kent continues in this vein, going beyond metaphor into the sheerest literalism, directly beckoned by the dead:

> I have a journey Sir, shortly to go,
> My master calls me, I must not say no. (TLN 3296-97)

It is like something from Wagner, the spirits calling across wasted vistas, calling it would seem for death. Kent, it seems, gladly follows, content with whatever negative revelation is at hand. The living is left to Edgar.

❖

The play's last words are spoken by Albany in the Quarto and by Edgar in the Folio.

> The waight of this sad time we must obey,
> Speake what we feele, not what we ought to say:
> The oldest hath borne most, we that are yong,
> Shall never see so much, nor live so long. (TLN 3298-301)

The change of speaker can seem fairly meaningless—one or other decent survivor, struggling to say something plausible. The easiest thing is to accept the Folio version as better, more final. Edgar has gone through more than Albany, and been closer to us; he is a slightly more persuasive aphorist and a lot more competent politician. Perhaps that will do. What is more, the contingent displacement of Albany by Edgar shows the Edgar-part persevering in its manners—we might say its sentence—to the very end. This is what Edgar does: he acts for others. Part surrogate, part parasite, part scapegoat, part healer, and always, in some inescapable way, the cursed primogenitor, born to inherit the land.

But I think the fact of a switch matters as much as its possible rationalizations. For a start, it shows the playworld's shuttered take on events persisting to the end: Albany says it, Edgar says it; one says it first, the other says it second; one auditions, the other gets the part; they say it together, they speak over each other; one voice speaks in the other's interstices, one voice haunts the other; they compete, defer, harmonize—and retreat mutually into silence. This last fact in particular should not be forgotten: that Edgar is possibly silent. In the Quarto he says nothing after his blank notice of Lear's death—"O he is gone indeed" (V. iii. 315)—not responding to Albany's request to rule with Kent. We can make what we like of this. It is invariably assumed that he takes up the mantle, perhaps through gritted teeth. But this is no more than implied (if that). Even in the Folio he answers at an oblique angle to Albany's summons ("The waight of this sad time we must obey"; TLN 3298), and may as easily be rebuking the recalcitrant Kent as expressing his own reluctant obedience. The "sad time" he means to obey may be history's runes, which Edgar will study for himself, in his own sweet time.

The only sure thing is that he hasn't become King Edgar. He has been offered something without institutional definition, without clear narrative teleology. The part-text is finished, and the actor may mime what he chooses: stand mutely still, weep over death, nod sturdily in assent as the Duke hands him power, collapse into a catatonic shiver. But these choices reinforce the active principle: a single action, multiple rehearsals; a single cue, multiple actions. History is unfinished, but so too is the past, as the endlessly uncertain invitations of the doubled-text testify, inviting repeated differential revisiting. Single things occur in simultaneously divergent fashion: they are constitutionally unstable. Any achievement, any authority or possession, might at any moment be whisked from one's grasp.

The uncertainty of the speaker informs the sentiment too. It hovers close to vacuous banality, but also to a shocking indifference to consequences.[2] Must we really speak what we feel? Edmund's candor, to us if to no one else, opened the floodgates to confusion. The more Regan and Goneril spoke as they felt, the worse for everyone else. Lear would have been better to stick to decorum and curse his daughters less. But then they are all the creatures of institutionalized hypocrisy, of flattery

---

2. Franco Moretti: "It should not seem strange that the extraordinary dramatic efficacy of these lines consists in their chilling stupidity, in the drastic banalization they impose on the play. In the very work that has unhinged our trust in the meaning of words, there reappears the obtuse assurance of sing-song proverb and of dead metaphor.... The close of *King Lear* makes clear that no one is any longer capable of giving meaning to the tragic process; no speech is equal to it, and there precisely lies the tragedy." *Signs Taken For Wonders: Essays in the Sociology of Literary Forms*, rev. ed., trans. Susan Fischer, David Forgacs, and David Miller (London: Verso, 1988), 52–53.

and bitten tongues, and the desire unleashed so enviously and jealously may be no less than the explosive consequence of too much *ought*. And so perhaps these closing words are good enough. They denounce false precedents and destructive obedience. They recommend feeling as the guide to speech, and thus to observable law. They advocate attending closely to the passions of a sentient body, and so to get closer to the vision that great experience confers. That, we might think, will do as a moral amid the slaughter.

But still there are curious tensions. The speech seeks liberation from models, presumably because there is no one left to tell anyone what to do. But it also longs for them, appealing to "the oldest" as authority. This in turn links to the speaker's ambiguous relation to his own wisdom. If it is Albany who speaks, we may well wonder what he is doing talking on behalf of the young. He may not be old like Lear—but he has never been young. Perhaps this is why he is so curiously shuffled out of the speech, silently removed to the superannuation to which his wife from the start condemns him. Edgar is young enough, but in speaking the speech he must assume something of the Duke's exhausted accent. What is more, if Edgar has earned the right to speak of terrible endurance, it is partly because he has endured terribly. But can he then also be the unpracticed youth, new to the wearying sights of pain?

The answer, I think, is in the abiding doubleness of the Edgar-part. In some sense Edgar has hidden away for the duration of the play. He only reappeared a few moments ago, having discarded his helmet after the duel. At the same time, Edgar has been present throughout. He has seen perhaps more than anyone, and borne hardly less. To the extent that he speaks simultaneously for unfledged youth and exhausted endurance, it is the Edgar-part and not the Edgar-persona that speaks. Once again, Edgar is host to more experience than a single youth can bear.

It is just this ambiguity that informs the four-times repeated "we" of this final speech. The "we" is both addressor and addressed, but who or what it actually signifies is unclear: "we must obey" suggests service, perhaps deference, certainly duty; "speake what we feele" suggest long-borne oppression and burgeoning passion (as suffering and vehemence); "we that are young" suggests anyone except the others on the stage, who are dead, dying, or departing.[3] Clearly *we* speaks to the people, as symbolized by the present and listening audience. But how then can this *we* also signify Edgar? How can the polity survive if it does? To the extent that *we* is Edgar, it suggests a collective without the numbers to let it make sense. *We* then signifies its own ruin, with Edgar the last man, surviving to a life defined only by being shorter than the father's.[4] The closing speech beckons to the future only to revoke it.

Of course Edgar, as the putative inheritor of sovereignty, may be tentatively experimenting with the royal *we*: as king he would be more than a single individual, responsible for all, and so the site of both a natural and a sublime body. But what faith can be placed in this? Even before he dies it is ambiguous whether Lear remained king. And the king's second body, the sublime idea of sovereignty, is at best in cold storage from the play's very first scene. Monarchy becomes little more than a shadow (an idea) tracing a shadow (Lear's disappearing authority, retinue, body), as sovereignty passes into fractions and appetite. Cordelia is the main repository for hopes of restoration. But she is slaughtered, denied the reign that the chronicles tell us she had. Shakespeare's violations serve prophecy more than history. *Lear* looks ahead to a day when monarchy will wither into merely formal investiture, whether from its own excesses or from its inadequacy in the face of the rivals it breeds. But the proleptic gaze is equally turned upon the play's present moment. What place can there be here and now for any such royal *we*?[5]

---

3. Kent is already dead in later Folio versions, in which he dies immediately after his final couplet.

4. Giorgio Agamben: "The scene that interests us in particular here is the last in every sense, since it concludes the codex as well as the history of humanity. It represents the messianic banquet of the righteous on the last day.... The miniaturist has represented the righteous not with human faces, but with unmistakably animal heads.... According to the rabbinic tradition . . . the righteous in question are not dead at all; they are, on the contrary, the representatives of the remnant (*resto*; also "rest," "remainder") of Israel, that is, of the righteous who are still alive at the moment of the Messiah's coming." *The Open: Man and Animal*, trans. Kevin Attell (Stanford, Calif.: Stanford University Press, 2004), 1–2.

5. Moretti: "Fully realized tragedy is the parable of the degeneration of the sovereign inserted in a context that *can no longer understand it*.... The political dimension of tragedy does not consist in illuminating the displacements of power, as happens in the long procession of sovereigns in the histories and even in *Julius Caesar*; it lies rather in posing the question of whether a *cultural foundation* of power is still possible, and in answering it in the negative." *Signs*, 55, 64; italics in original.

Dramaturgy suggests half an answer; a kind of hopeless answer. Albany, with his final command before abdication (the shortest reign in recorded history, as the play comes full circle with a closing renunciation) orders the bodies to be borne from hence. Clearly they must be picked up. The nameless Messenger may still be on stage; and sundry men may come in from the shadows to perform the carriage. But this is a play that thinks about such matters: recall the uncertain departures into the hovel, after the first storm scene, with Kent and Gloucester worrying about courtesies, the king insisting that he be attended by his philosopher; recall the servants in Cornwall's castle, again defying house procedure, patching the maimed Gloucester and delivering him to the Bedlam. In both cases a more attentive decorum, in the face of disaster, issues in the notice of Tom.

And so what of this final exit? The survivors must pick up the dead. Necessarily, Kent picks up Lear ("My master calls me, I must not say no"). Edgar therefore picks up the body of Cordelia, cueing the mordant jokes in his departing words:

> The waight of this sad time we must obey,
> Speake what we feele, not what we ought to say:
> The oldest hath borne most, we that are yong,
> Shall never see so much, nor live so long. (TLN 3298-301)

Cordelia is the weight that Edgar now must bear.[6] She is in his arms as he speaks. She is what he feels, in touch and sentiment, in spoken and spiritual imperative. And so the very final couplet embraces this shared burden and curse: "we that are young" means both Edgar and Cordelia. Her closed eyes and attenuated life threaten his. Her promise—lapsed or deracinated, political or spiritual—is his.

This is half an answer. The end of this play allows nothing else: various halves that cannot add up to a whole. Clearly Shakespeare is resist-

---

6. There is a possibility that Cordelia in this final scene is a mannequin—easier to carry, and with no chance that a breathing chest will mock the stony fact of death. If so, then she is more like Tom than ever, because she is not quite human, waiting to be sparked into animation or allegory. More pertinently, it means that Cordelia and Edgar can be played by the same actor.

ing the conventional decisiveness of tragic closure. Partly this is because he is adumbrating some sort of return to the play's beginning, to quasi-abdication, tetchy competitiveness, and the improvised division of the kingdom into two. After all, Cordelia is here again, silent once more, still impotent to take up her third. It is difficult to measure these recollections, or to take their temperature: perhaps they are mordant, or sarcastic, or coyly anxious; perhaps they are thunderously pessimistic. Either way it is Edgar who must sublate any possible repetitions, mediate them in his continuance.

Consequently, if he is indeed left alone with the succession—left alone with survival—it is a desolate inheritance, marked not only by the death of fathers and fraternity and women, but by these ambiguous cosharers, neither present nor departed, but rather *departing*, moving into shadow or nullity, like resigned or retired doubles. The effect is a kind of grey corona around Edgar's tiny, overburdened persona—a corona of fading. The responsibility passed on to him is almost literally an experience of deficit: of living as constitutional departure, burdening him by drawing from his stock, like some half-human egg timer. As the retiring doubles die from life or from view, Edgar remains to embody the withdrawal. He is not-king and nearly-king; not-subject and nearly-subject. He is not dead, but he is assuredly dying, the only kind of living that is left. Reality has become penumbral, coronal, curiously recessive.

❦

And what this means is that Edgar, at play's end, also shades into a kind of Tom-ness. Not into the Poor Tom–role; there is no need to imagine Edgar starting to spasm or scratch, Tom-style, as the action ebbs into nothingness. But he shades into the existential condition, the pending, crepuscular half-life of being-Tom. Of course it is perfectly possible to have forgotten Tom by now: if we have, he need not return to mind. But Shakespeare has not forgotten, and he drops little reminders throughout the scene, brief hints or echoes of Tom, which help give the closing moments their transversal, sempiternal, dusk-descending, going-not-gone aura. I have noted some of these: Lear's request to "undo this Button," recalling his recognition of "unaccommodated man" in the storm; the "stone" that Lear wishes might "mist or staine," recalling the "Pebble" chafed by the "Surge" on the beach; Edgar's cry to "look up," recalling the same cry made to suicidal Gloucester, asking him to bid good riddance to the "Fiend" at the top of the cliff. And there is Lear's infamous cry: "And my poore Foole is hang'd: no, no, no life?" (TLN 3277). If his lament potentially evokes Cordelia and the Fool, then it evokes Tom as well: after all, Tom pretty much takes over as Lear's interlocutive "Fool" in his first scene; and the word "poore" is overwhelmingly Tom's word. Thoughts of his extinction are suddenly possible; perhaps Lear's philosopher has gone the way of all flesh, another victim of war or law. This triple reference in turn informs Lear's three climactic negatives ("no, no, no"), which nod at each of them by turn—Fool, Cordelia, Tom—and ask the most basic question: life, or not? Is the Fool forgotten? Not any more: his life returns, once again unfinished in the act of being recalled. Is Tom?

The half-answers multiply, true to a world in which ghosts have as much presence as any living flesh, and in which the only interlocutor has become oneself. For this is what Edgar arrives at and departs to; this is the burden of the "dead March" with which the playworld passes from view: a half-life in which the only hopes for completion are in the surrogates one carries off-stage: the dead Cordelia; the undead Tom. For Tom too is immanent in the play's final couplet:

> The oldest hath borne most, we that are yong,
> Shall never see so much, nor live so long.

The obvious referent of "oldest" is Lear. But it is also Tom: the figure whose every jerk and cry seemed to speak untold places and times; who suffered over and over the prescriptive strictures of *ought*; who had to take on, repeatedly reborn, remorselessly overborne, the mutations of history; the figure of nascence and futurity, condemned to survive. Tom is the final necessary partner of Edgar's *we*, moving between the agents like an undead spirit, touching each word with painful responsibility:

> oldest   born
> we   young

see	much
live	long

At the last, Edgar's survival becomes strangely epiphenomenal. The more primary reality abides in what Frank Kermode, after Aquinas, has called the *aevum*: the third place, where the angels abide, one of "deathlessness" and "perpetual succession."[7] This is the habitat of Tom's ghostly continuance. But this *aevum* is less some transcendent angelic abode and more a durative abidance, latched ineradicably to daily human suffering. It isn't out of time, but nor is it stuck to clock time; it doesn't transcend earth, but nor is it placed.

Such a presence necessarily defies conventional stage-representation: hence Tom's murmuring, floating, ghostly immanence in Edgar's closing movements. The Edgar-part thus doubly takes on the strange curse of second bodies and deathlessness. "Tom" is the figure for lapsed subjecthood; "Edgar" for lapsed authority.[8] As we have seen, Edgar as he departs is at once not-king and king-elect. But kingship is itself mainly an allegory of a more fundamental subject-condition, of a life that is never identical to its vehicles, never quite grounded or institutionalized, never quite in the hand. It is appropriate, then, that this should remain a world without a functioning monarch, just as it is without a functioning God. *King Lear* is a play that in a profound sense happens at the deposition, in the lapsed space between one covenant and the next: between death and life, extinction and recovery, participation and eradication. And as ever, the ultimate figure for this tantalized condition is Tom. He and Edgar pass into one another, each the other's ghost and augur. They depart together, unrepealable.

---

7. Rather than the "being-for-ever of the higher forms" (or God): Frank Kermode, *The Sense of an Ending: Studies in the Theory of Fiction* (Oxford: Oxford University Press, 1967), 76.

8. Kermode: "The end is now a matter of immanence; tragedy assumes the figurations of apocalypse, of death and judgment, heaven and hell; but the world goes forward in the hands of exhausted survivors. Edgar haplessly assumes the dignity; only the king's natural body is at rest. This is the tragedy of sempiternity; apocalypse is translated out of time into the *aevum*." *Sense of an Ending*, 82.

27

CONCLUSION

Shakespeare's Radical

Imagine choosing to send the Edgar-part to another galaxy, as a representative of our world's most celebrated dramatist. What possible forms could such a missive take? What would it look like, or sound like? Would it even resemble a human body, or would a small army of Edgar-avatars be needed to begin to do the thing justice?

No doubt the part passes many of us by, just as the post-Dover Tom does, barely registered amid the play's stunning immediacy. No doubt actors struggle madly with it, defying as it often does clear motive for its teeming and discontinuous particularities: you choose one persona (a concerned son, a schizophrenic, a Christian moralist, an opportunistic pretender) and immediately stunt others.

The part's relation to theatrical precedent is an intensification of its relation to history, indeed to any other context. The part cannot be sized-up via a single referent or context: any context we care to name must be instantly supplemented, a supplementary context that makes the others only tenuously recognizable. One body cannot be all these things; or if it is, these things cannot remain as they are ostensibly were. The part becomes a kind of motley screen, or an echo-trap, whose motions concentrate, extend, mimic or foreshadow numerous worlds, past, present, and possible.

Edgar is probably the most violent part in Shakespeare, in the sense that it stretches a single life over farther distances, physically felt distances, than any other, stretches that have to be borne in the tissue of a single body and played by a single actor. Sam Goldberg, arrestingly but accurately, called Edgar the "most lethal" character in the play: meaning that if you cross him, perhaps even *touch* him, you die.[1] I would modify and extend this: the role is the most lethal because it is the closest to death; the closest to death, because for him it is impossible. Death cannot be passed beyond, and so he is always, to borrow from Augustine, living the dying life.

The Edgar-role bears the burden of the play. Edgar is the one (the two, three, four, or more) who has seen so much and lived so long. He alone is forced to try to understand. He becomes each character, plus his own, plus all the lives he recalls or narrates. He merges in and out of untold animal and vegetable and even geologic forms. He is the spectator or reader, alone of all the characters forced to look at the play, sometimes from deep inside its wounds, sometimes as though from another space in time entirely. He has to look back at it as though it has all already happened, and yet he repeatedly experiences life as an occurrence of and from the past—as though living, distilled to its bones, is when something that has already happened happens *again* to us, when we face the fact of it, and we are left with the superadded burden of trying to catch up to the fact that we were not there, or that we were inadequately there, unable either to prevent it or even really to experience it. And the corollary of this is that Shakespeare never leaves the Edgar-role in peace. He harries it until the play ends, when still it is left without a get-out, without an excuse for anything but continuance. Edgar alone truly *lives King Lear*.

Hamlet is most often thought of as Shakespeare's truest model of the human—resisting the types or models that he is supposed to imitate, thereby implying inwardness—and his on-stage and off-stage attenders go casting after reasons why he is as he is. But in a curious way the Edgar-role takes this much farther. His part calls the bluff on a privately possessed self, upon the very notion of self-originality—almost blows its lid off by insisting that even in our hiding places we are *taken*,

---

1. S. L. Goldberg, *An Essay on King Lear* (Cambridge, U.K.: Cambridge University Press, 1974), 121.

or issued, or repeating, shadowed by past and imminent occurrence. And perhaps in this the Edgar-role is the true paragon of what it is to be—in a play, in life—stripped of all sentimental accommodation and preempting, post facto coherence. Perhaps we too are only intermittently or fugitively at the center of our own lives, experiencing life as the residue of allegories, translations of the real into formal simulacra: used or employed by others; taken hostage by irresistible aspects of our own condition, all of which we can never quite know or even acknowledge. Civic function and family are witnessed through a screen, experienced as an alien and assaulting shadow play. Our ostensibly self-collecting consciousness is too slow for the moment, a belated nostalgia: as Schlegel said of this playworld, "the auxiliatory virtues are every where too late."[2]

And love? At its happiest it is barely thought, barely spoken, anterior even to intuition. And then, once known and felt, once observed as *something*, it is externalized only in networks of pain, scripted by others, horribly institutionalized, and possessed, again, only as allegory: as a disguise that strips to the bone, or hides inside armor, or gets channeled into silly voices or secondhand moralizing or substitutions that never quite return home to the one substituted. In a life such as Edgar's or Tom's, love is no more secure than a home, or warmth, or trust, all so easily blown away on the wind. This is the knowledge that Edgar-Tom lives: that we are foundationally alone, hunkered in our minds, dying in our bodies, twitching in our dark, doomed to experience love only as its loss, after or just before its severance, as one by one the loved ones disappear, as we miss the moment or flail our hands in impotent anguish.

That wasn't life, and now it is almost gone.

Unless in precisely this abjection there is some curious privilege. The Edgar-part is never at liberty, and always coerced. And yet from the moment of escape into the "happy hollow," Edgar steps out of social continuities, into an exile and destitution that is also a kind of freedom. Freedom because every moment, every itch and fidget, has to be thought and felt, has to find its own indigenous language. Freedom be-

---

2. August Wilhelm von Schlegel, *A Course of Lectures on Dramatic Art and Literature*, Vol. 2, trans. J. Black (London: Baldwin, Cradock, and Joy, 1815), 208.

cause living in this way requires unsleeping attention. Freedom here is nothing at all to do with warm beds or shimmering sands; nothing to do with choices about how to spend your day or use your talents. It is to do with finding out the basic contract, and actually experiencing the question of what it is to be alive.

This isn't the freedom, if freedom it is, of "unaccommodated man" (TLN 1886-87). It is the freedom of experiencing the depth-charge in an instant, such that an entire life is active in a single moment; of life as churning repetition, but with every turn of the wheel different, making change as possible as constraint; of being many-in-one, bound in networks of obligation, such that communities of others are remembered or implicated at each motion; of existence as a dying for life, dying every moment, death which at every instant is imminent and remitted. This freedom is the astonishment of life—of a life, your life, any life. The astonishment that it really might not be and might not have been: and yet, once here, that it opens onto endless magical connectivity, inevitable and obligatory, and as necessary for others as for oneself. Substance, it appears, truly is accidental. The only thing for it, we might say, is to pay attention; to take care; to feel it as it happens and, where possible, to take the chance of passion.

Only Edgar survives to experience these imperatives—and not least the awful struggle to keep up with it all, to bring the assaults and astonishment into some kind of livable order. That the character never quite achieves such perspective is no surprise. To do so is our challenge. But perhaps we too still await an aesthetic, and an apperceiving framework, that might catch up with Shakespeare's audacity.

But of course it is here already: here, that is, in Shakespeare's play, which everywhere embodies the necessary ways of feeling and understanding; as Michael Goldman nicely puts it, "we share the experience of discovering new precisions of feeling."[3] Such an experience is not reducible to representational description, or visible models, or detached

---

3. "*King Lear*: Acting and Feeling," in *On King Lear*, ed. Lawrence Danson (Princeton, N.J.: Princeton University Press, 1981), 28. Goldman is talking specifically of "the action of the principal actor" (28), in particular "a demand placed on the actor—and a concomitant opportunity given him—to apprehend concrete, sharply defined foci of pain" (39). But this applies just as much to the Edgar-actor.

superintendence, or positivistic laws. Theater is sometimes associated with cloistered enclosure and representational object-observance, as though a 3D-model of Cartesian epistemology. Try to capture Edgar/Tom in such a frame, and we will immediately recognize how hopeless it is for Shakespeare. His worlds work very differently. They animate, and require of us, multiple subject-positions at once: a condition of which Edgar/Tom is an instance, allegory, and projection. To feel this we need to think far more finely than we are often accustomed to doing; far more attentively to the gradations and striations in a single movement or voice. At every moment—not just before Tom first arrives (whenever this is) or after Tom finally departs (whenever that is), but at every instant and interval of his motions—we should remember the essential questions: *Where does it come from*—this word, this action, this being—*and where does it go?* And what can be asked of Tom can be asked of anything. He is the personification of Shakespeare's restless, species-traversing craft.

In order to apprehend the part of Edgar-Tom—without which we cannot really apprehend the play of *King Lear*—we have to recognize just how radical and estranging Shakespeare's methods can be. The decisive thing is that theater's in-the-moment satisfactions, its sensory continuity, its assumption of shared pleasures, should begin to give way: not simply to text, or to the satisfactions of reading over other forms of attendance, but rather to embedded technical resources, specific to theater, that defy communication. Instead of moving spontaneously from medium to receiver, the meaning and emotions remain wrapped up in the medium: a medium always in motion, alive with change, but not to be simply downloaded or delivered.

This is true whatever the technical medium. It might be the latent networks of metaphor and metonym; the latent networks of a cue-space; the latent networks of an actor's momentary apperceptions. All these techniques are characterized by the need to communicate: to reach others, present or not, human or not. But they are equally characterized by the shortfalls in such connection. A measure of secrecy and latency is the necessary result. It isn't that truth is simply private. Rather, we get layered minds and anachronous eventualities, in which the event at issue always exceeds visible or articulable occasion. Very often the event confuses the boundaries between now and not yet, being and nonbeing, living and death. One effect is to reach closer to grasping ineffable possibilities, as though finding a medium capable of life's spiritual enigmas. Another is to consign experience, at its deepest, to a barely communicable *sub-subjectivity*.

> Hearke, do you heare the Sea? (TLN 2435)

Questions such as this herald the limitations of theater as it is habitually practiced, the inadequacy to experience of its evidentiary appeal. Habitual theater is the most basic instance and allegory of all normative institutions, those warders of abstraction and approximation. This is what so many of the great modern theatrical innovators know and fight against—Sergei Eisenstein, Antonin Artaud, Vsevolod Meyerhold, Peter Brook, Valère Novarina—often appealing to *Lear* as ultimate proof of the inadequacy of regulated theater and regulating criticism.

The terms in which we experience the play are those that must sustain any future. Theater is the model of human and social contracts. And this means a specifically Shakespearean theater: not a courtly theater, or a Cartesian one, or a proscenium-arched spectacle; not any kind of theater that envisages a centered cynosure, a detached spectatorship, a clear order of proceedings and punctual description of events. Instead, a theater of echoes and intervals and overlays; of hauntings and telepathy, suddenness and irruptions; and of a persistent knowledge that the senses are never adequate. It can't be summarized, digested, observed from a distance. Instead, the truth of this theater will be found in the experience of *attention*. This attendance implies a deep-lying abidance, one that depends as much upon suprasensory notice as open passivity to the immediacies of action and emotion. These latter remain essential: but we need to attend more closely to what it is that makes them, and to what it is they actually are.

However, Shakespeare also pushes theater close to collapse. Not because theatre is inadequate, but because the singular event, the monovoice, the classical body, is inadequate to theatrical possibility. This is where Shakespeare remains ahead of even his most adventurous animators. And Tom is the crucial vector of this. He epitomizes the play's becoming-beings, its telepathies and digitized bodies. He is a figure for all of Shakespeare's deepest latent networks, of metaphor and metalepsis, cue and cue-space, actorly craft and apperception—blessed with shattered and eventually vanishing manifestation in him. In a very basic sense Tom cannot be played; he waits for some future medium, or a technology able to sustain and communicate the play's unleashed presences.[4]

To think like this is to begin to feel how inadequate our customary measurements are for understanding Shakespeare's creation. Let's not dismiss strangeness as irrelevance, or obscurity as nonsensical. Let's beware the instinct to avoid offense or obscenity, or to turn away from any suffering that we cannot allay. Equally, let us acknowledge the possibility that such suffering may be our own. This will entail the difficulty of intimacy, and not just its civilized comforts. We must see as well as look, but also realize that eyes are never enough. Nor is hearing sufficient. We must listen even when the sound appears to have ceased. It is axiomatic for Shakespearean drama, I take it, that articulated sentences are inadequate—inadequate to passion, history, thinking—and that sentience carries on where the senses leave off. This is why we have plays, and an art form of unpredictably collocating fragments such as Shakespeare's: one in which nothing exists only in its moment; in which each utterance is a quarry of many others; in which no gap, however dark, is without action, and no ruin, however mute, is truly finished.

---

4. Valère Novarina: "The actor who truly acts, who acts forcefully, who acts from the core . . . shows his face white, disfigured, bearing his own death. The actor who acts knows very well that this truly modifies his body, that it kills him each and every time. And the history of the theater—if we really wanted to write it, finally, from the actor's point of view—would not be the history of an art, of a spectacle, but rather the history of a long, deaf, obstinate, ever beginning, never ending protest against the human body." *The Theater of the Ears*, trans. and ed. Allen S. Weiss (Los Angeles: Sun and Moon Press, 1996), 59.

28

AFTERWORD

This book has a twin sister, called *Shakespeare's Possible Worlds*, published by Cambridge University Press, bigger and better-mannered than *Poor Tom*. The two works are the outcome of a single process, and it is in this other book that I express my thanks to the many people who have helped me over the years of gestation. Here I'd like very specifically to thank the two readers appointed by University of Chicago Press, whose reports were enormously intelligent, scrupulous, sensitive, and helpful. I'm likewise grateful to Alan G. Thomas for his swift encouragement, and to Meg Murphy-Sweeney for her very lucid and attentive copyediting.

The true sources of *Poor Tom* are not really scholarly or theatrical. The book has grown from somewhere inside, from fears and fascinations that I still don't fully understand. Perhaps this has to do with the fact that *Lear* was the first Shakespeare play I read, when I was sixteen, in a state school in Hobart, Tasmania, and just about ready to explode with desire for things I knew were near but I had never quite touched. *Lear* wasn't the most important discovery of that year. But it seems to have lasted longer than some of the others.

At the time I was struck by the play's immediacy. Partly this immediacy was comic. Two lines especially I remember repeating with friends, as though from the first true comedy I had ever witnessed.

> Let me wipe it first, it smells of mortality.
> Out vile jelly.

They were endlessly adaptable. During morning recess: "Pass that spoon." "Let me wipe it first, it smells of mortality." Layering a gristle-thick National Pie with tomato sauce: "Out vile jelly." Heedlessness was the thing. In the gap between football and cricket seasons we'd drink in the bush on Saturday afternoons, the uncut stuff on the hill where the cul-de-sacs hadn't yet reached. We'd get quickly plastered, then reenter the silent empty streets, and I'd feel sort of amazed that they were still there, these houses and streets, so peaceful and pointless and as though eternal. A friend called Adrian, a very fast runner, aboriginal, would start trying to set fire to the manicured nature strips. Of course they were far too trimmed to burn, but still, should the grass briefly catch, with that gassy singeing smolder, it would cue the cry as we hot-footed it, "It smells of mortality!"

But in more private moments, the play's immediacy was differently stirring. It seemed simply to say what was needful, about unfairness, or about the shocking cruelty of accidents. For all that I was a normal heedless sporty dickhead, I was also highly wired, partly from love for a girl, partly from long-brewed anticipatory grief for my mum, who every day suffered the jerks and spasms of multiple sclerosis, as her motor functions started slowly dying. *Lear* wasn't raw enough for this, but it was more raw than anything else I'd come across, except perhaps the hoarse screams of Lennon or McCartney. Anyway, *Lear* was there during these seasons, as almost-consciously I felt myself enter into life.

As it happens, a weird number of the blokes I went to school with were killed within a few years, all from accidents. A sawn tree crushed one, another fell from the pier, two drowned, a few smashed into trees or ditches in their cars. Why should we realize that the words in *King Lear* will come true? Or that they have already come true, and that we play our games, like we build our buildings, on the ashes of the fact.

I think that when I was sixteen or seventeen, the phrases that struck me in *Lear* did so because they glamorized, even exalted, the primitive discovery that the most vital thing in life had nothing to do with anything I had ever been taught, by parents or school or friends or books.

It was found in secret, through touch and trust. It was indifferent to deserving, it mocked mind and talent, and it was very astonishing. I found something similar a few years ago, when I had children. Again, the simple astonishment; again, the knowledge that such things are given, or taken, and we are made and unmade by accidents with the gift of duration.

Lear still has the power to kill. It seems both more cruel and more compassionate than ever. But the play is here differently for me these days. I feel less its immediacy of statement, and more the preventions that lurk just behind what is spoken, or in the gaps where words lapse. All I now demand is that my kids not die before I do.

❦

Oxford, October 2013.

Bibliography

Adelman, Janet. *Suffocating Mothers: Fantasies of Maternal Origin in Shakespeare's Plays, Hamlet to The Tempest* London: Routledge, 1992.
Agamben, Giorgio. *Homo Sacer: Sovereign Power and Bare Life*, trans. Daniel Heller-Roazen. Stanford, Calif.: Stanford University Press, 1998.
———. *The Open: Man and Animal*, trans. Kevin Attell. Stanford, Calif.: Stanford University Press, 2004.
———. *Profanations*, trans. Jeff Fort. New York: Zone Books, 2007.
Anderson, David K. "The Tragedy of Good Friday: Sacrificial Violence in *King Lear*," *English Literary History* 78, no. 2 (2011).
Artaud, Antonin. *The Theatre and Its Double*, trans. Victor Corti. Richmond, U.K.: Oneworld Classics, 2010.
Augustine. *The City of God against the Pagans*, ed. and trans. R. W. Dyson. Cambridge, U.K.: Cambridge University Press, 1998.
———. *Confessions*, 2nd ed., trans. F. J. Sheed, ed. Michael P. Foley. Indianapolis: Hackett, 2006.
Baker, Timothy C. "Praying to an Absent God: The Poetic Revealing of Simone Weil," *Culture, Theory and Critique* 47, no. 2 (2006): 133–47.
Beckwith, Sarah. *Shakespeare and the Grammar of Forgiveness*. Ithaca, N.Y.: Cornell University Press, 2011.
Benjamin, Walter. *Illuminations*, trans. Harry Zohn. London: Fontana, 1992.
———. *The Origin of German Tragic Drama*, trans. John Osborne. London: Verso, 1998.
———. *Selected Writings, Vol. 2: 1931–1934*, trans. Rodney Livingstone et al., ed. Michael W. Jennings, Howard Eiland, and Gary Smith. Cambridge, Mass.: Harvard University Press, 2005.
Berger, Harry, Jr. *Making Trifles of Terrors: Redistributing Complicities in Shakespeare*. Stanford, Calif.: Stanford University Press, 1997.

Blanchot, Maurice. *The Infinite Conversation*, trans. Susan Hanson. Minneapolis: University of Minnesota Press, 1993.

———. *The Space of Literature*, trans. Ann Smock. Lincoln: University of Nebraska Press, 1982.

———. *The Writing of the Disaster*, trans. Ann Smock. Lincoln: University of Nebraska Press, 1995.

Blau, Herbert, *The Dubious Spectacle: Extremities of Theater, 1976–2000*. Minneapolis: University of Minnesota Press, 2001.

Bloom, Harold. *Shakespeare and the Invention of the Human*. London: Fourth Estate, 1999.

———. *William Shakespeare's* King Lear. New Haven, Conn.: Yale University Press, 1987.

Booth, Stephen. *King Lear, Macbeth, Indefinition, and Tragedy*. New Haven, Conn.: Yale University Press, 1983.

Bradley, A. C. *Shakespearean Tragedy: Lectures on Hamlet, Othello, King Lear, Macbeth*. 1904. Reprint, Basingstoke, U.K.: Macmillan, 1985.

Bratton, J. S., ed. *Plays in Performance: King Lear*. Bristol, U.K.: Bristol Classical Press, 1987.

Calvin, John. *Sermons of Master Iohn Calvin, Vpon the Booke of IOB*, trans. Arthur Golding. London: Lucas Harison and George Byshop, 1574.

Carroll, William C. "'The Base Shall Top th'Legitimate': The Bedlam Beggar and the Role of Edgar in *King Lear*," *Shakespeare Quarterly* 38, no. 4 (1987).

———. "Songs of Madness: The Lyric Afterlife of Shakespeare's Poor Tom," *Shakespeare Survey* 55 (2002).

Carson, Anne. *Decreation: Poetry, Essays, Opera*. New York: Knopf, 2005.

Cavell, Stanley. *Disowning Knowledge in Seven Plays of Shakespeare*, updated ed. Cambridge, U.K.: Cambridge University Press, 2003.

———, *Must We Mean What We Say?* New York: Scribner's, 1969.

Colie, Rosalie, and F. T. Flahiff, eds., *Some Facets of* King Lear: *Essays in Prismatic Criticism*. London: University of Toronto Press, 1974.

Connor, Steven. *Dumbstruck: A Cultural History of Ventriloquism*. Oxford: Oxford University Press, 2000.

Cressy, David. *Birth, Marriage, and Death: Ritual, Religion, and the Life-Cycle in Tudor and Stuart England*. Oxford: Oxford University Press, 1997.

Davis, Nick. *Stories of Chaos: Reason and Its Displacement in Early Modern English Narrative*. Aldershot, U.K.: Ashgate, 1999.

Dekker, Thomas. *Belman of London; Bringing to Light the Most Notorious Villanies*. London: N. Butter, 1608.

———. *The Guls Hornbook and the Belman of London in Two Parts*. London: J. M. Dent, 1905.

Derrida, Jacques. *Specters of Marx: The State of the Debt, the Work of Mourning, and the New International*, trans. Peggy Kamuf. New York: Routledge, 1994.

Dessen, Alan. "Two Falls and a Trap: Shakespeare and the Spectacle of Realism," *English Literary Renaissance* 5 (1975).

Donne, John. *The Sermons of John Donne*, Vol. 9, ed. Evelyn M. Simpson and George R. Potter. Berkeley: University of California Press, 1958.

Dostoevsky, Fyodor, *Memoirs from the House of the Dead*, trans. Jessie Coulson. 1861–1862. Reprint, Oxford: Oxford University Press, 1956.

Empson, William. *The Structure of Complex Words*. London: Hogarth, 1985.

Enright, D. J. *Shakespeare and the Students*. London: Chatto and Windus, 1970.

Fensham, Rachel. *To Watch Theatre: Essays on Genre and Corporeality*. Brussels: Peter Lang, 2009.

Ferguson, Margaret W., Maureen Quilligan, and Nancy Vickers, eds. *Rewriting the Renaissance: The Discourses of Sexual Difference in Early Modern Europe*. Chicago: University of Chicago Press, 1986.

Fernie, Ewan. *The Demonic: Literature and Experience*. London: Routledge, 2013.

Fisch, Harold. *The Biblical Presence in Shakespeare, Milton, and Blake: A Comparative Study*. Oxford: Oxford University Press, 1999.

Flahiff, F. T. "Edgar: Once and Future King," in *Some Facets of "King Lear": Essays in Prismatic Criticism*, ed. Rosalie Colie and F. T. Flahiff. London: University of Toronto Press, 1974.

Fletcher, Angus. *Allegory: The Theory of a Symbolic Mode*. Ithaca, N.Y.: Cornell University Press, 1964.

Girard, René. *Violence and the Sacred*, trans. Patrick Gregory. Baltimore, Md.: Johns Hopkins University Press, 1977.

Goldberg, Jonathan. *Shakespeare's Hand*. Minneapolis: University of Minnesota Press, 2003.

Goldberg, S. L. *An Essay on King Lear*. Cambridge, U.K..: Cambridge University Press, 1974.

Goldman, Michael. "*King Lear*: Acting and Feeling." In *On King Lear*, ed. Lawrence Danson. Princeton, N.J.: Princeton University Press, 1981.

Goodall, Jane. *Artaud and the Gnostic Drama*. Oxford, U.K.: Oxford University Press, 1994.

Granville-Barker, Harley. *Prefaces to Shakespeare*, Vol. 1. London: B. T. Batsford Ltd., 1930.

Graves, Robert. *The Common Asphodel: Collected Essays on Poetry, 1922–1949*. New York: Haskell House, 1949.

Greenblatt, Stephen. *Shakespearean Negotiations: The Circulation of Social Energy in Renaissance England*. Oxford: Oxford University Press, 1988.

Gross, Kenneth. *Shakespeare's Noise*. Chicago: University of Chicago Press, 2001.

———. *Shylock Is Shakespeare*. Chicago: University of Chicago Press, 2006.

Halperin, Richard. *The Poetics of Primitive Accumulation*. Ithaca, N.Y.: Cornell University Press, 1991.

Harraway, Donna. *When Species Meet*. Minneapolis: University of Minnesota Press, 2008.

Harsnett, Samuel. *A Declaration of Egregious Popish Impostures*. London: James Roberts, 1603.

Hart, Kevin. *The Dark Gaze: Maurice Blanchot and the Sacred*. Chicago: University of Chicago Press, 2004.

Hegel, G. W. F. *The Phenomenology of Spirit*, trans. A. V. Miller. Oxford: Oxford University Press, 1977.

Heidegger, Martin. *The Fundamental Concepts of Metaphysics: World, Finitude, Solitude*, trans. William McNeill and Nicholas Walker. Bloomington: Indiana University Press, 1995.

Hiscock, Andrew, and Lisa Hopkins, eds. *King Lear: A Critical Guide*. London: Continuum, 2011.

Holinshed, Raphael. *The Firste Volume of the Chronicles of England, Scotlande, and Irelande*. London: John Harrison, 1577.

Husserl, Edmund. *Experience and Judgment*. trans. J. S. Churchill and K. Ameriks. Evanston, Ill.: Northwestern University Press, 1973.

Kahan, Jeffrey, ed. *King Lear: New Critical Essays*. New York: Routledge, 2008.

Kantorowicz, Ernst. *The King's Two Bodies: A Study in Medieval Political Theology*. Princeton, N.J.: Princeton University Press, 1981.

Kearney, James. "'This Is Above All Strangeness': *King Lear*, Ethics, and the Phenomenology of Recognition," *Criticism* 54, no. 3 (2012).

Kermode, Frank. *The Sense of an Ending: Studies in the Theory of Fiction*. Oxford: Oxford University Press, 1967.

Kermode, Frank, ed. *Shakespeare: King Lear, a Casebook*, rev. ed. London: Macmillan, 1992.

Kierkegaard, Søren. *Fear and Trembling/Repetition: Kierkegaard's Writings*, Vol. 6, trans. and ed., Howard V. Hong and Edna H. Hong. Princeton, N.J.: Princeton University Press, Princeton, 1983.

Knight, G. Wilson. *The Wheel of Fire*. 1930. Reprint, London: Routledge, 2001.

Kott, Jan. *Shakespeare Our Contemporary*, trans. Boleslaw Taborski. London: Methuen, 1964.

Kozintsev, Grigori. *King Lear, the Space of Tragedy: The Diary of a Film Director*, trans. Mary Mackintosh. London: Heinemann Educational Publishers, 1977.

Lamb, Jonathan. *The Rhetoric of Suffering: Reading the Book of Job in the Eighteenth Century*. Oxford: Oxford University Press, 1995.

Leibniz, Gottfried. *New Essays on Human Understanding*, trans. and ed. Peter Remnant and Jonathan Bennett. Cambridge, U.K.: Cambridge University Press, 1996.

Levi, Primo. *The Drowned and the Saved*, trans. Raymond Rosenthal. New York: Vintage, 1989.

———. *If This Is a Man*, trans. Stuart Woolf. London: Abacus, 1987.

———. *The Search for Roots: A Personal Anthology*, trans. Peter Forbes. Chicago: Ivan R. Dee, 2002.

Levinas, Emmanuel. *Totality and Infinity: An Essay on Exteriority*, trans. Alphonso Lingis. Pittsburgh, Penn.: Duquesne University Press, 1999.

Lupton, Julia Reinhard. *Thinking with Shakespeare: Essays on Politics and Life*. Chicago: University of Chicago Press, 2011.

Mack, Maynard. *King Lear in Our Time*. London: Methuen and Company, 1966.

Margulis, Lynn, and Dorion Sagan. *Acquiring Genomes: A Theory of the Origins of Species*. New York: Basic Books, 2002.

Marx, Steven. *Shakespeare and the Bible*. Oxford: Oxford University Press, 2000.

Mason, Peter. *Infelicities: Representations of the Exotic*. Baltimore: Johns Hopkins University Press, 1998.

Mentz, Steven. *At the Bottom of Shakespeare's Ocean*. London: Continuum, 2009.

Mohanty, J. N. *Edmund Husserl's Freiburg Years: 1916-1938*. New Haven, Conn.: Yale University Press, 2011.

Mooney, Michael E. "'Edgar I Nothing Am': Figurenposition in *King Lear*," *Shakespeare Survey* 38 (1985).

Moretti, Franco. *Signs Taken For Wonders: Essays in the Sociology of Literary Forms*, rev. ed., trans. Susan Fischer, David Forgacs, and David Miller. London: Verso, 1988.

Morton, Timothy. *The Ecological Thought*. Cambridge, Mass.: Harvard University Press, 2010.

Muir, Kenneth. "Samuel Harsnett and *King Lear*." *Review of English Studies* 2, no. 5 (1951).

Nagel, Alexander, and Christopher S. Wood. *Anachronic Renaissance*. New York: Zone Books, 2010.

Newsom, Carol A. *The Book of Job: A Contest of Moral Imaginations*. Oxford: Oxford University Press, 2003.

Novarina, Valère. *The Theater of the Ears*, trans. and ed. Allen S. Weiss. Los Angeles: Sun and Moon Press, 1996.

Palfrey, Simon. *Late Shakespeare: A New World of Words*. Oxford: Oxford University Press, 1997.

———. *Shakespeare's Possible Worlds*. Cambridge: Cambridge University Press, 2014.

Palfrey, Simon, and Tiffany Stern. *Shakespeare in Parts*. Oxford: Oxford University Press, 2007.

Panofsky, Erwin. *Studies in Iconology: Humanistic Themes in the Art of the Renaissance*. New York: Harper and Row, 1972.

Percy, Thomas. *Reliques of Ancient English Poetry*. London: J. Dodsley, 1765.

Plotinus. *Enneads*. Vols. 1-7, trans. A. H. Armstrong. Cambridge, Mass.: Harvard University Press, 1966-1988.

Powell, Amy Knight. *Depositions: Scenes from the Late Medieval Church and the Modern Museum*. New York: Zone Books, 2012.

Pye, Christopher. *The Vanishing: Shakespeare, the Subject, and Early Modern Culture*. Durham, N. C.: Duke University Press, 2000.

Rabkin, Norman. *Shakespeare and the Problem of Meaning*. London: University of Chicago Press, 1982.

Ricoeur, Paul. *The Symbolism of Evil*, trans. Emerson Buchanan. Boston: Beacon, 1969.

Rosenberg, Marvin D. *The Masks of King Lear*. Berkeley: University of California Press, 1972.

Rudnytsky, Peter L. "'The Darke and Vicious Place': The Dread of the Vagina in *King Lear.*" *Modern Philology* 96, no. 3 (1999).

Santner, Eric L. *On Creaturely Life: Rilke, Benjamin, Sebald.* Chicago: University of Chicago Press, 2006.

———. *The Royal Remains: The People's Two Bodies and the Endgames of Sovereignty.* Chicago: University of Chicago Press, 2011.

Scarry, Elaine. *The Body in Pain: The Making and Unmaking of the World.* Oxford, U.K.: Oxford University Press, 1985.

Schlegel, August Wilhelm von. *A Course of Lectures on Dramatic Art and Literature*, Vol. 2, trans. J. Black. London: Baldwin, Cradock, and Joy, 1815.

Shuger, Deborah. *The Renaissance Bible: Scholarship, Sacrifice, and Subjectivity.* Stanford, Calif.: Stanford University Press, 1997.Skura, Meredith. "Dragon Fathers and Unnatural Children: Warring Generations in *King Lear* and Its Sources." *Comparative Drama* 42, no. 2 (2008).

Smith, Bruce. *Phenomenal Shakespeare.* Chichester: Wiley-Blackwell, 2010.

Spivack, Bernard. *Shakespeare and the Allegory of Evil: The History of a Metaphor in Relation to His Villains.* New York: Columbia University Press, 1958.

Spurgeon, Caroline. *Shakespeare's Imagery and What It Tells Us.* Cambridge, U.K.: Cambridge University Press, 1935.

Streete, Adrian. *Protestantism and Drama in Early Modern England.* Cambridge, U.K.: Cambridge University Press, 2009.

Tate, Nahum. *The History of King Lear*, ed. James Black. London: Edward Arnold Press, 1976.

Turner, Henry S. *The English Renaissance Stage: Geometry, Poetics, and the Practical Spatial Arts, 1580–1630.* Oxford: Oxford University Press, 2006.

Warlock, Peter, ed. *Giles Earle His Booke.* London: Houghton, 1932.

Weil, Simone. *An Anthology*, ed. Sian Miles. London: Penguin, 2005.

———. *Gravity and Grace*, trans. Emma Crawford and Mario von der Ruhr. London: Routledge, 2002.

———. *Simone Weil: Seventy Letters*, trans. and arranged by Richard Rees. Oxford: Oxford University Press, 1965.

Wells, Stanley. "Tom O'Bedlam's Song and *King Lear*," *Shakespeare Quarterly* 12, no. 3 (1961): 311–15.

Whitehead, Alfred North. *Modes of Thought.* New York: Free Press, 1938.

Witmore, Michael. *Shakespearean Metaphysics.* London: Continuum 2008.

Womack, Peter. "Secularizing *King Lear*: Shakespeare, Tate, and the Sacred," *Shakespeare Survey* 55 (2002): 98–104.

Zuckerman, Bruce. *Job The Silent: A Study in Historical Counterpoint.* Oxford: Oxford University Press, 1991.

Index

Abraham (*Genesis*), 180-81
accident: as existential condition, 4, 100, 117, 130, 214, 253; as providence, 214
actor: choices, 75, 118-19, 185-91, 254-55; distinct from character, 52, 53; Edgar, part history of, 22-24; living the part, 10, 171
aevum, 249
Agamben, Giorgio, 29, 107-8, 116n34, 159n4, 174n8, 245n4
Albany, 18, 45, 137, 139, 223, 240, 242-44, 246
allegory: of art, 236-37; character's susceptibility to, 29, 78-82, 112; cliff scene, 167, 188-89; and ethical-political typology, 135-36, 138-39, 207, 214, 236; living as, 81-82, 117; multiplying, 54, 87; violence of, 22. *See also* Tom
Anderson, David K., 213n3
Angelo (*Measure for Measure*), 22
animal life. *See* creatureliness
apocalypse, 15-16, 26, 59, 259
Ariel (*The Tempest*), 31, 53, 76
arrivals. *See* entrances
Artaud, Antonin, 63n1, 255

attention: as ethical act, 122, 134-35, 149-50, 223, 253, 255
audience: surrogates of, 130-31, 134-35
Augustine, 65n4, 96, 251
Autolycus (*Winter's Tale*), 75

Bacon, Francis, 12
ballads, 13-16, 71, 75
bare life, 94, 107-8, 113
Beckwith, Sarah, 220n4
becoming: as horror, 96
beggars, 31, 93, 114
Benjamin, Walter, 80n7, 112, 116n34
Berger, Harry, Jr., 87n2, 119n2, 170n4
Blanchot, Maurice, 65n3, 148n15, 223n8
Blau, Herbert, 174n10, 183n1
Booth, Stephen, 9, 18n16, 175n11, 221n5
Bradley, A. C., 16n11, 17, 20, 42, 217n1
Brook, Peter, 255

Cain and Abel, 219
Caliban (*The Tempest*), 47, 53
Calvin, John, 33n11, 36n5, 37, 38, 40, 41
Carroll, William, 75, 76, 126, 173n7, 179n17, 210
catharsis: and superflux, 54, 56

Cavell, Stanley, 22n21, 24n25, 132, 170n3, 220n4, 222n7
character: definition of, 9–10; embodying theatrical forms, 21; exceeding singular life, 14–15, 18, 20–21, 60, 79, 87–88; existing in sets, 60, 230; experiential exchanges, 110, 126, 184, 225, 228–31, 237, 233, 239; new ontology, 60, 124–26; suffering a playworld, 130–31. *See also individual characters*
Christ, 1–2, 31–33, 59, 206, 212–14
Christianity, 11, 104, 132, 144, 239; historicity, 213–14; millenarianism, 59; original sin, 104; privation, 96; resurrection, 239; suicide, 169
Clerke, Richard, 36n5
Connor, Steven, 55, 57n11, 185n2
Cordelia, 17, 39, 34, 44–45, 51, 54, 60, 93, 97, 133, 139, 212, 213; death, 19, 97, 229, 235–41, 246–8; Lear's awakening to, 216–17; mirror of Edgar/Tom, 114, 151, 216, 246; and resurrected sovereignty, 106, 245, 247
Coriolanus (*Coriolanus*), 22
Cornwall (*Lear*), 132, 134–35, 139, 221
creatureliness, 89, 90, 107
cues, 27, 73, 156, 160, 161, 184–86, 190, 243, 256; and non-appearance, 56–57; repeated, 70–72, 84, 85, 98, 100, 126–29, 199–200, 238–39; resumption, 187–88; uncertain, 118–19, 191; waiting for, 52–53
cue-space, 21, 184–86, 191, 254, 256

Davis, Nick, 208n13
death, 2–3; of children, 97–98; grades of, 229, 236; between living and dying, 1, 3, 8–9, 11, 65–66, 98, 141, 167–68, 176, 193–94, 212–13, 231–33, 239, 247, 249, 255; in motion, 112–13, 251; overcome, 191; possibility on stage, 198, 238–39; proximity of, 148, 194–96, 217, 235–36; rehearsed, 32–33, 181–82, 184, 232–33; returning from, 216–17, 237; as temptation, 84, 141, 175–76, 179, 189–92, 199
decreation, 113, 143–49
Dee, John, 12
Dekker, Thomas, 13n7
demonic possession, 55, 59, 71–72, 91–92, 114, 126, 212
Derrida, Jacques, 111n27, 200n4
Dessen, Alan, 202n6
disguise, 28–29, 61
Donne, John, 34, 58
Dostoevsky, Fyodr, 112–13n29
Dover scene: cliff, 167–79; Edgar's response, 195–206; Gloucester's jump, 183–92

Earle, Giles, 13
ecology: as dreaming, 57–8; and humoral thinking, 58; and interconnectedness, 159, 169; metamorphic, 202–3; personified in Tom, 83–90
Edgar: body, 24, 30–33, 125, 250; burdened by play, 251; cipher, 26–27, 244–45; connecting play's networks, 6; counterfactuals, 140, 202–3, 205; critical reputation, 16–17, 21–22; disguise, 28–29, 41, 171, 209; disgust, 207–8, 221–23; duality, 156–57, 210, 244; elusiveness, 17–22, 250; ending Tom, 122, 151–56, 204–6, 210–11, 228, 232; experiential pioneer, 5–6, 160–62, 181–82, 197–98, 231–33, 240–42, 251–54; experimental, 27; fiction-maker, 197, 204–6; final words, 242–45, 248–49; "happy hollow," 28–32, 37; identity with Shakespeare, 10–11; inheritor, 21, 27, 242–43, 245, 247; inside Tom, 62–63, 119–21, 123–25, 146–48, 159–60, 252; as instrument, 18–19, 21; intimacy with Cordelia, 114, 151, 216, 246; intimacy with Tom, 142, 155–56, 224, 240–41, 247; invisible, 155, 185–86; and Job,

34–44; knight, 217–20, 223; living theatrical forms, 21, 224; masks, 27; memories/past, 120–21, 128–29, 219, 234; moral agent, 222–23, 243–44; multiplicity, 20, 250–51; mutations, 128, 160, 251; name, 10–11; object, 43, 173–74; one body insufficient, 24, 250, 256; parricide, 128–29, 170–71, 234; part as distinct from character, 125; phantom presence, 128–29; philosophizing, 17, 195–96, 207–9, 221–23; political/spiritual promise, 246–47; re-emergence from Tom, 122; site of invasion, 100–101; son, 121, 123, 156–58, 171, 186, 188–89, 228–31, 234–35; sources, 11–13, 226–27; stage history, 22–24; subjective evacuation, 155–56, 159; surrogacies, 18, 135, 137, 159, 173–74, 210, 220, 222, 234–35, 239, 242, 244, 248; survivor, 15, 22, 130–31, 182, 232, 242, 245, 247, 249, 253; witness, 115, 127–29, 130; yokel, 207–10. *See also* Tom

Edgar, King, 12–13

Edmund, 18, 49, 60, 97, 113, 121, 133, 135, 156, 208, 243; duel, 217–20, 229, 232; homologies with Edgar-Tom, 93, 114, 124, 128, 210, 222, 233, 241; and Jacob and Esau, 226–27; view of Edgar, 22, 26–27

Eisenstein, Sergei, 255

El Greco, 1–4, 97, 206, 237

Elyot, Thomas, 12

empiricism, 236, 255–56

Empson, William, 157n2, 161

Enright, D. J., 16n11

entrances, 127–28; stage directions, 121; staggered, 52–53, 56, 56, 63

Esau. *See* Jacob and Esau

exception, state of, 29, 45, 116

Faerie Queene, The (Spenser), 79, 99, 207, 210, 218, 220

Fensham, Rachel, 157n3

Fernie, Ewan, 205n11
Ferrell, Lori Anne, 106n17
Fisch, Harold, 38–39n11, 193n1, 226n1
Fletcher, Angus, 78–79, 81
Folio and Quarto texts: relation between two versions, 6–7; variant examples, 26, 36, 46, 56, 68, 69, 71, 73, 121, 122–25, 128, 137–39, 149, 156–57, 160, 184, 233–34, 238–39, 242–43
France (*Lear*) 18, 151
futurity, 5, 31, 111–12, 117, 136, 230, 232, 237, 238

Gloucester: attempted suicide, 168–69, 179, 183–92, 198–200; attitude to Tom, 118–19, 121, 154, 167; blinding, 123–24, 134–36, 139, 198, 221; blindness, 152–53, 158; death of, 228–32, 239; as father, 124, 186–87
gods: Christian God, 240–41; cruelty, 40–42, 221–22, 240; kenosis, 143; man's intimacy with, 58, 160–61; too many, 212; withdrawal, 40, 95–96, 180–81, 212
Goldberg, Jonathan, 176n12
Goldberg, S. L., 50n4, 251
Goldman, Michael, 253
Goneril, 18, 19, 36, 208, 229, 243
Granville-Barker, Harley, 22n21, 26, 120, 208n13
Greer, Germaine, 23–24
Gross, Kenneth, 92n4, 141n8

Halperin, Richard, 56n10, 107n20
Hamlet, 22, 113, 251
Hamlet, 133
Harraway, Donna, 88n4
Harsnett, Samuel, 16n10, 91–92
hearing: distinct from seeing, 52, 56, 176, 185; failure of, 149; feeling beyond, 176–77, 255–56; life-bringing, 52
Hegel, G. W. F., 42–44, 222–23
Heidegger, Martin, 90
Henry (Prince), 218

history, 5, 14-15; anachronic, 89, 111-12; embodied in Tom, 88-89, 90, 92-94, 99-103; lapsed, 212, 246, 249; progress, or not, 99-100, 110-11, 134-36, 221-22; and prophecy, 245; simultaneity of, 98-99, 134; unwritten, 45
Hobbes, Thomas, 100-101, 103, 204n9, 212
Holinshed, Raphael, 12-13
Holocaust, 108, 112-17
hovel, 48-49
Husserl, Edmund, 5

incompossibility, 2, 65, 95, 206, 240
irreality, 5-6

Jacob and Esau, 219, 225-26
James I (King), 218
Job: cannot die, 36; cursing, 35-38; foul body, 39; and justice, 223; Leviathan, 204-205; model for Edgar, 34-44; silence, 34-35; typology, 41-43
Johnson, Samuel, 174n9
Jonson, Ben, 9, 76, 97, 208

Kant, Immanuel, 196, 205
Kearney, James, 59n16
Kent (*Lear*), 119, 121, 122, 133, 145, 208; attitude to Tom, 46, 48, 67, 74, 81, 118, 149; departure, 233, 239-41, 245, 246; identity exchanges, 93, 118, 234
Kermode, Frank, 249
Kierkegaard, Søren, 180-81, 203
king's two bodies, 105-7, 245. *See also* sovereignty
Knight, G. Wilson, 17, 133n3, 212n1, 223n9
Kott, Jan, 40n14, 72n10, 171n5, 196n1
Kozintsev, Grigori, 3n2, 30n7, 112-13n29, 139n6

Lamb, Jonathan, 41n16
law: beyond, 29-30; creation of, 100, 136; of formal telepathy, 135, 223-24; as hypocrisy, 209; moral, 92, 244, 248; as origin, 103-4; and sovereignty, 45; in storm, 230-31; suspension of, 45-6, 181
Lear, 99, 100, 107, 114, 120, 122, 123, 214, 224, 244; address to Tom, 61, 71, 73-74, 110-11, 118, 149-50, 201; curses, 39, 97-98, 243; degradation, 149; final scene, 231, 234, 235, 238-41; love test, 51; "poor naked wretches" speech, 49-56, 136; possession of power, 45, 245; sexual disgust, 208-9; in storm, 59, 98, 109, 230; waking, 216-17; way of speaking, 46-47
Leibniz, G. W., 2, 178n14
Levi, Primo, 34, 114-16
Levinas, Emmanuel, 21n20, 59n16, 80-81, 101-3, 126, 170n2, 201n5
Locrine, 19
love, 52, 54, 92, 121, 123, 142-43, 186, 189, 194, 220, 252
Lupton, Julia Reinhard, 40n15
Lyons, Bridget Gellert, 76n14

Macbeth, 113
Macduff (*Macbeth*), 97
Mack, Maynard, 20, 136n4, 214n5, 224n10
McKellen, Ian, 23
Mentz, Steven, 57
messianic promise, 16, 102, 147, 206
metalepsis, 21, 136, 202-3, 223-24, 231
metaphor, 2, 46-47, 254; turning into metonym, 87, 173-74
Meyerhold, Vsevolod, 255
millenarianism *See* apocalypse
mime, 70, 71, 76, 108-10, 116, 171n5, 186-87, 243
Mooney, Michael E., 19n17, 126n6
morality play: *Everyman*, 193-4; indebtedness to, 20, 219-20
Moretti, Franco, 243n2, 245n5
Morton, Timothy, 46n1
Mucedorus, 19

nature *See* ecology; place
Nietzsche, Friedrich, 32n10
nonhuman, 5, 15, 21, 51, 159, 194; in

between human and other, 29, 46, 61-62, 169; objects as potential subjects, 50, 173-74
nothing: existential condition, 27-28, 94-96; as promise, 31. *See also* Tom
Novarina, Valère, 47n3, 63n2, 70n6, 151, 178n15, 255, 256n4

Old Man, 152-54
original sin, 104, 110; as Tom, 63-64
Oswald (*Lear*), 18n16, 19, 93, 133, 137, 207, 208, 210-11, 220, 250

pain, 28
Panofsky, Erwin, 32
particularities: own conatus, 172-73, 177-78
perspective shifts, 172-75
place: alive, 58, 83-84; as body and mind, 87, 168, 172-74, 177-78; produced by language, 47, 57; of stage, 57-58, 128. *See also* Dover scene; hovel
Plotinus, 94-96
Plowden, Edmund, 106
Poor Tom. *See* Tom
possibility: of alteration, 50, 102-3, 135-36, 138-39, 179; resistant, 89, 246-47; tragic, 54, 117
primitivism, 132-33
privation, 38, 57, 70, 77, 94-95, 144
prosody, 69-72, 75, 76, 158
pseudomorphosis, 32, 213
puns, 98-99, 198, 208
Pye, Christopher, 177n13, 204n9

Quarto passages. *See* Folio and Quarto texts

Rabkin, Norman, 18n15
Regan, 18, 45, 123, 132, 135, 208, 221, 229, 243
repeated cues. *See* cues
Ricoeur, Paul, 29n4
romance: and political repair, 219

saintliness, 16, 22
Santner, Eric L., 30n6, 56n9, 66n5, 74n11, 106n19, 108n23
Scarry, Elaine, 28n3, 32n10, 109n25
scenes: life in, 66, 151, 229, 241
scenic break: Cordelia in, 51; Edgar in, 35, 123, 128-29, 155; Tom as, 52, 66, 128-29
scenic interconnections. *See* telepathy
Schlegel, August Wilhelm von, 17, 133n2, 161n7, 252
servants, 134-35, 138-39, 246
service, 134-35
Sidney, Philip: *Arcadia*, 11, 13
sight: limitations of, 52, 122, 168, 185, 237, 256
Skura, Meredith, 204n8
Smith, Bruce, 109n24
sources: of Edgar/Tom, 11-13
sovereignty: inheritance of, 245-46; origins of, 103-4, 105-6, 245; and state of exception, 29-30; in storm scenes, 45-6
space: not empty, 2-3. *See also* place
Spanish Tragedy, The (Kyd), 97
Spenser, Edmund. *See Faerie Queene, The* (Spenser)
Spivack, Bernard, 82n13
Spurgeon, Caroline, 89
Steward *See* Oswald (*Lear*)
Stewart, Stanley, 182n5
storm scenes (*Lear*), 45-49, 56-60, 85-88, 124, 127, 149, 199, 230-31
stranger, the, 25, 46n1, 59n16, 80, 98n4, 133, 167, 189n4
sublime, 117; Kantian, 196, 205; king's second body, 105-6, 245; negativity, 206; and theatrical techniques, 161, 237
substitution, 41, 54, 64, 232; as absolute responsibility for another, 126, 149, 237, 252
suffering, 1, 5, 14, 16-17, 22, 28-29, 32, 37-44, 50, 64, 75-76, 84, 90, 109-10, 124-26, 136-41, 147-49, 157, 186, 212-14, 221, 229-30, 244, 249, 256

survival: as curse, 38, 97, 131; as life under erasure, 64

Tate, Nahum, 17-18, 178-79n16
telepathy: between scenes, 135, 140, 160-61, 222-24, 230, 237-38, 247-48
Tempest, The, 52-53
theater: of cruelty, 63; limitations of common practice, 255-56; model of politics/morality, 52, 136-37, 223-24, 253-55; poetics of, 5; as reality, 186-87, 214-15, 236-37, 239
title page: of Quarto, 8-9
Tom, 9-10; ambiguated address, 72-74, 75; angel of death, 204; animating multitudes, 92-93, 105, 108, 113-14, 147, 256; appearance, 109, 112; body, 83-84, 85, 104-5, 107, 112, 203; cues, 70, 72, 84, 85; departure, 122, 151, 179, 204-6, 228, 232; doubled ontology, 54, 61-66, 74, 103, 191-92, 201, 217; Edgar's projection, 62-63; enigma, 9-10; exchanges with others, 228-29; existential impossibility, 64-65, 66, 95-96, 161; generated by Lear's prayer, 49-56, 216; ghostly, 15, 57, 77, 94-96, 124, 157, 186, 191-92, 200, 204, 248, 249; insisted upon, 154-55; isolation, 71-72, 76, 122, 146, 252; lack of puns, 98-99; leading Gloucester, 140-41, 155-56, 167-68, 168; life removed from objects, 142, 252; life unlived, 64-55, 66; magnetic historicity, 92-94, 99-100, 116, 248-49; morphing with Edgar, 124-26, 153-61; morphing with Gloucester, 141, 190-92, 200-201; morphing with Oswald, 210-11; multiple allegories, 54, 62-66, 78-82, 87, 92, 104-5, 109, 114; negative ontology, 101-2, 113, 129, 144-45, 148, 200; not heard, 67, 109, 114, 115-16; personifying theater, 63, 66, 215, 237, 254; places, 83-86; political possibility, 101-3, 104-8, 111, 246, 247, 249; possible savior, 206, 213; preparation for, 29-32, 49, 63; refrains, 71; resisting teleology, 102-3, 111-12, 203-4, 224; sacrifice, 108, 114, 232-33; scenic authority, 58; sin, 85-86, 100, 104; songs, 71, 75-77; sources, 13-16; spiritual possibilities of, 59-60, 63-4, 200-1, 203, 212-15, 237, 248-49; subject, 104-5, 107-8, 252; subjective annihilation, 126; suffering, 83-88, 92, 100; surviving as remnants, 203-4, 232; tuning the playworld, 59-60; uncanny temporality, 110-11; undead, 97-98, 212-13, 217, 232, 237, 247-48; ventriloquism, 85, 92, 93; voice as body, 108-9, 202; voices, 67-77, 87-89, 92, 107, 108-9; waiting to appear, 48-55. *See also* demonic possession; Edgar
Tom o' Bedlam, 13-16
Turner, Henry S., 59n15

unborn, 11, 212
undead *See* death

war: as permanent possibility, 101
Weil, Simone, 28-29n3; affliction, 147-48; attention as love, 150; decreation, 144; impersonality, 146; living with *Lear*, 144-45, 149; renunciation, 142-44
Whitehead, Alfred North, 58n14
Wittgenstein, Ludwig, 19
Womack, Peter, 18n15